Nicholas Oldisworth's Manuscript
(Bodleian MS. Don.c.24)

MEDIEVAL AND RENAISSANCE
TEXTS AND STUDIES
VOLUME 380

RENAISSANCE ENGLISH TEXT SOCIETY
SEVENTH SERIES
VOLUME XXXIV (FOR 2009)

Nicholas Oldisworth's Manuscript
(Bodleian MS. Don.c.24)

edited by
John Gouws

ACMRS
(Arizona Center for Medieval and Renaissance Studies)
in conjunction with
Renaissance English Text Society
Tempe, Arizona
2009

© Copyright 2009
Arizona Board of Regents for Arizona State University

Library of Congress Cataloging-in-Publication Data

Oldisworth, Nicholas, 1611?-1645
  Nicholas Oldisworth's manuscript (Bodleian MS. Don.c.24) / edited by John Gouws.
      p. cm. -- (Medieval and Renaissance texts and studies ; v. 380)
(Renaissance English Text Society ; 7th ser., v. 34)
  "Oldisworth's autograph fair copy of a collection entitled "A Recollection of Certaine Scattered Poems" (now Bodleian MS Don.c. 24) prepared in the early months of 1645, just before the author's death."
  ISBN 978-0-86698-428-7 (acid-free paper)
  1. Poetry, Medieval. 2. Literature, Medieval--Criticism, Textual. I. Gouws, John. II. Title.
  PR2326.O45N53 2009
  821'.4--dc22

2009045029

∞
This book is made to last.
It is set in ITC Berkeley Oldstyle,
smyth-sewn and printed on acid-free paper
to library specifications.
Printed in the United States of America

TABLE OF CONTENTS

Acknowledgments   xi

General Introduction   xv

Textual Introduction   xli

Bodleian MS Don. c. 24: Poems   1

    A Recollection of Certaine Scattered Poems [*Title page*]   3

    To his deare Wife, Marie Oldisworth [*Dedeicatory epistle*]   5

[1]	A Letter to Ben. Johnson. 1629	7
[2]	To his Friend beyond sea ("Friend: thinke not Time. . .")	12
[3]	On his seeing the Study of Master Michael Oldisworth	14
[4]	On Complements	16
[5]	To his Friend beyond sea ("And dost thou live?. . .)	17
[6]	To the right honorable, the lord Haies, earle of Carlile, &c	19
[7]	To the right honorable his Patron	20
[8]	On his Majesty's Recovery from the small pocks. 1632	21
[9]	On a Seale of gold and pearles sent. . .by Master Michael Oldisworth	25
[10]	In defence of a Girle, that went holding downe her head	27
[11]	The wordes of a Lover, speaking to the reflection of his Mistresses face in a Looking glasse	29
[12]	On Shottover	32
[13]	To a Separatist, that spoiled mens tombes, and built his house with tomb-stones	33
[14]	An Ode ("Husband, I would not have thee to conceive")	34
[15]	To the University of Cambridge. 1631	35
[16]	On a painted Houre-glasse	40
[17]	To Sir Edward Hungerford of Cosham	41
[18]	To the lady *Hungerford* of Cosham, December 28 1632	42
[19]	On Heraldry	44

[20]	To Mistris E.W.	45
[21]	The Nobleman's wooing	46
[22]	The Country-gentleman's Wooing	47
[23]	To his Cosin, Mistris Dorothie Litcott	49
[24]	On an uggly Wench	51
[25]	Sonnet, played by a Musician at my Entertaining of Master *Michael Oldisworth*, A	53
[26]	On my loosing my way	55
[27]	To a Lady, on her walking abroad	57
[28]	To the worshipfull, his honoured Cosin, Mistris *Susan Oldsiworth*: upon her Removall from *London* to *Thisselworth*	58
[29]	On Mistris Katharine Bacon	65
[30]	An epitaph on *Thomas Hulbert* Cloathyer of Cosham	66
[31]	To his Friend beyong sea ("Bacon, thou hardly wilt believe that Wee")	67
[32]	Hampton-court here speaketh	68
[33]	To his cosin *Michaël Oldisworth*, February 15 1631	69
[34]	On a Moore	72
[35]	An epitaph on little Thomas Bacon, who dyed sodainly	73
[36]	Another. [An epitaph on little Thomas Bacon, who dyed sodainly]	73
[37]	On treacherousnesse	74
[38]	STATES-WOMEN // A show taken out of *Aristophanes*	75
[39]	A Censure upon *Aristophanes* his States-women	76
[40]	On the death of a Cripple	80
[41]	On Sir B.R.	81
[42]	To the Witts of Oxford, Cambridge, and London	82
[43]	On the statue of Niobe well carved	84
[44]	To the worshipfull, Mistris Strange of Summerford, a Poëtesse	85
[45]	An Ode, of 12 kindes of Verses	86
[46]	On mortalls	87
[47]	To a yong Lady, that hadd the greene Sickness	88
[48]	An Ode ("Though both thy Tongue and Eies bidd mee refraine")	90
[49]	On Alexander Bainham Esquier, who was killed at the Siege of *Mastrich*. 1632	91
[50]	On a packet of Letters, drowned in their comming from his Friend beyond sea	92
[51]	His rewarding a Musician	93

[52]	An epitaph on a discontented man	94
[53]	An eglogue betweene a Carter and a sheaphard, made on Master *Michaël Oldisworth's* Comming into the country	95
[54]	To a Lady, that sung and played on the Lute	98
[55]	To his musicall Valentine Mistris Anne Henshaw	98
[56]	On the birth of James duke of Yorke	99
[57]	To his aunt, the lady Litcott of Molesey	101
[58]	On an envious man	102
[59]	An Ode ("What meane my Armes? what would they have?")	103
[60]	ITER AUSTRALE, 1632. Or, A journey southwards	104
[61]	On a Lover	109
[62]	Epitaph on Master Little of Abingdon, An	110
[63]	To one of my acquaintance	111
[64]	To Sir *Giles Fetiplace*, high Sheriffe of *Glocester-shire*. 1633	112
[65]	To B.R. a Dissembler	113
[66]	On a Race	115
[67]	To Mistris Thorold of Arborvill	116
[68]	Immoderate Love, An	117
[69]	For a discontented Scholar of Oxford, 1632, these following verses were written while the King was at Woodstock	118
[70]	On the picture of Beauty	119
[71]	On a Bagge of Perfume given him by a Friend	120
[72]	To an acquaintance	121
[73]	Lover's fancie, A	122
[74]	On Mistris Summer, who dyed in child-bedd	123
[75]	On the death of both Mistris Summer and her Childe	123
[76]	To a Lady, looking our of a window	125
[77]	On the death of Sir Rowland Cotton	126
[78]	On an Arbour made by Master Richard Bacon, on the sea-shoar opposite to the ile of Wight	127
[79]	To the builders or Repairers of Paul's Church in London	131
[80]	Paradoxe, A. To one whom hee both extremly loved, and extremly hated	132
[81]	Of Nobility	133
[82]	To his Friend beyond see ("Come, come: they Stay, mee thinks, is such a thing")	134
[83]	To Citizens	135

[84]	On the Commencement at Cambridge. 1632	136
[85]	To a gentle-woman that delighted too much in her garden	137
[86]	On London Waies. 1632	138
[87]	To his friend beyond sea ("Wee know not (dearest) in what part")	139
[88]	On the Christmas at Cosham in Wilt-shire	140
[89]	To Master M.B. the whilst his picture was drawing	141
[90]	On Master Swaine, who deceased upon good Friday	142
[91]	To his litle Brother Giles Oldisworth	143
[92]	For an Innes of courts man. To his Mistris	145
[93]	On Abraham Cowley the yong poët laureat	146
[94]	To Mistris Katharine Bacon	147
[95]	On the transparencie of Master Tooker's house at Strettam	149
[96]	A Satyre. On occasion of Master his departure out of England	150
[97]	For a Lover, standing by a Smith's shoppe: An Ode	152
[98]	To all his Acquaintance	153
[99]	For a Lover, whose Mistris concealed her selfe from him	154
[100]	To Master Michaël Oldisworth comming to Oxford, 1633. March 30	156
[101]	Amorouse Dreames	157
[102]	To an over-modest Ladie	158
[103]	To his Friend beyond sea, March 26. 1633	159
[104]	To the faire Mistris Burch, at his first sight of her	160
[105]	On his Majesty's going to Scotland. 1633	161
[106]	On his Majesty's being in Scotland	163
[107]	On his Majesty's coming from Scotland	165
[108]	For a Lover. To his absent Mistris	166
[109]	To a Curtezan	167
[110]	For a Gentleman. On the embracing of his Friend	168
[111]	For a Gentleman. To yong Master *Henry Gresley*	169
[112]	An Hymne to God	171
[113]	On the death of his deare friend Master Richard Bacon	172
[114]	On Sir *Thomas Overbury* and his poëme	173
[115]	At the Command of his reverend diocesan Godfry Goodman Bishop of Glocester. A translation of the *Te deum laudamus* after the tune of the 100 Psalme	174
[116]	A Divine Rapture	176
[117]	His Farewell to *Poëtrie*	177

[118]	*Poëtry's* Answer	178
[119]	His Reply to *Poëtrie*	179

Additional Poems from Folger MS. V.a.170   181

[AP1]	To the sacred Majestie of his dread soveraigne King Charles	183
[AP2]	On the picture of the Virgin feeding her babe	185
[AP3]	On a paire of handsome children	186
[AP4]	To his Enemie	187
[AP5]	An Ode ("Prethee away, Love: what a foole thou arte")	190
[AP6]	On an Ewe that was drowned	191
[AP7]	To a friend of Sir Thomas Overburyes	192

Commentary   193

Title Index   235

First Line Index   239

General Index   243

Acknowledgments

This edition has been many years in the making. I first came across Oldisworth while trawling through manuscript poetic miscellanies at the end of a period of research at the Folger Shakespeare Library. A group of poems in the MS. V.a.170 struck me as the work of a single person with a distinct poetic voice. Brief investigation revealed the name of the author and the fact that an autograph fair copy manuscript was held in the Bodleian Library in Oxford. Fortunately, I was flying home to South Africa via London, and between connections at Heathrow Airport I managed to take a coach to Oxford for a glimpse of MS. Don.c.24. The groundwork for the edition was done during a year as Visiting Fellow, and six months as a Visiting Scholar, at Wolfson College, Oxford. I am most grateful to the College for their generous hospitality and support, and especially to Jon Stallworthy and Julian Roberts, who sponsored my application and made my stay so rewarding. I have subsequently had two short-term Fellowships from each of the Folger Shakespeare Library in Washington, D.C., and the Huntington Library in San Marino, California. My old college, Lincoln, has over many years provided me with accommodation at the heart of Oxford, and just a few minutes' walk from the Bodleian Library. The last phase of my work would not have been possible without the generous and timely appointment as Professor Extraordinary at North-West University, Potchefstroom. Without their collective support this project would not have got very far. The research was also funded on an ongoing basis by the National Research Foundation (and its earlier incarnation, the Human Sciences Research Foundation). The financial assistance of the National Research Foundation (NRF) towards this research is hereby acknowledged. Opinions expressed and conclusions arrived at are those of the author and are not necessarily to be attributed to the NRF.

No research project of this kind can be conducted without the encouragement and support of librarians, archivists, and their support staff. I have been particularly fortunate in the helpfulness and patience of the staff of several institutions: the Folger Shakespeare, the Bodleian, the Huntington, the British, Christ Church, Corpus Christi and the Rosenbach Libraries; the Gloucester County Record Office and the Rhodes University Library. My work has also benefited from the comments of readers for articles published by the *Southern African Journal for Medieval and Renaissance Studies*, *Texas Studies in Literature and Language* and the *Oxford Dictionary of National Biography*, and I am grateful to the editors of these publications for permission to use material already published by them. I am particularly grateful to the Renaissance English Text Society editorial committee of the present edition (chaired by Arthur Marotti), and to Dr. Leslie MacCoull, the Associate Editor, and Bill Gentrup, the Assistant Director of ACMRS Publications, for their advice and comments. They have saved me from my own ignorance and from many infelicities, and had hoped to save me from even more. They are not responsible for the ignorance, follies, and lapses that remain.

Over the years, I have received encouragement and support for the project from many friends, mentors, and fellow scholars, some of whom are no longer with us. Among them are John Buxton, Jean Bromley, Attie de Lange, Elsie Duncan-Jones, Katherine Duncan-Jones, Paul Eggert, Martin Enock, Marc Falconer, Lionel Faull, Lin Gubb, Geoff Hadwick, Ruth Harnett, Jeremy Hughes, Victor Houliston, Jeremy Maule, Peter McDonald, Elihu Pearlman, Tim Raylor, Dorothy Schwartz, Peter Shillingsburg, Jon Stallworthy, Patricia, Lady Trend, Dyfri Williams and Laetitia Yeandle. I am particularly grateful to Richard Webster of Lincoln College, Oxford, a complete stranger (but no longer), who sought me out as this edition was going to press with information identifying Oldisworth's wife as Mary Chamberlayne. Richard, who is working on Oldisworth's sermons, has generously shared other information that has improved the introduction and commentary. In editing the work of a man whose poems are often the means by which he conducted his friendships, I am grateful that my own endeavours have been enabled by the friendships which have enriched and continue to sustain my life. My mother, Margaret Gouws, supported my work and died believing that I would not be able to part with Oldisworth. My wife, Anne, has had to endure absences and neglect, but I hope that the act of piety in rescuing the good-natured Nicholas Oldisworth from human oblivion might be some compensation. My daughter, Mary, and my son, Jonathan (Lollo), will I hope one day not hold against me the times I was inattentive and unwilling to play, and might even one day take some pride in my labours. I certainly hope their lives will be graced with fulfilling friendships.

The edition was prepared using Nota Bene software, which allowed me to do things that would otherwise have made life very difficult, if not impossible. For this alone, I would be grateful. But the personal support I have had over many years from the team at Nota Bene has demonstrated that technology, humanity and friendship are not incompatible.

The late, self-effacing John Buxton taught me that, amongst other things, one does not thank one's supervisor on the acknowledgements page of a thesis, and does not attach dedications to an edition. I would, however, like to dedicate the parts of this publication which are my own to his memory. Like Oldisworth, in whose paternal home in Coln Rogers he and his wife Margery

Acknowledgments xiii

went to restore their lives after the ravages of a most terrible war, John Buxton loved the English countryside and the tranquilities of domestic life informed by learning and friendship.

North-West University
Potchefstroom
July 2009

GENERAL INTRODUCTION

Some poets perish for not being understood; others are entombed by an all-too-comprehending critical practice. Just occasionally we are fortunate to stumble on a poet whom time and accident forgot, and then we are reminded of how moribund our own protocols of understanding have become. In the case of Nicholas Oldisworth there is an autograph fair copy of some 120 poems (Bodleian MS. Don.c.24) which remained in the family for at least fifty years after the author's death, disappeared for about two centuries, and then became a collector's trophy before disappearing, in the 1930s, into the vast anonymity of the mausoleian stacks of Sir Thomas Bodley's library.[1] The title-page of the manuscript reads:

> A Recollection of Certain Scattered Poems. Written long since by an Undergraduate, being one of the students of Christchurch in Oxford. And now in the yeare 1644 transcribed by the author, and dedicated to his wife. When I was a child, I spake as a child, I understood as a child, I thought as a child: but when I became a man, I put away childish things. 1 Cor. XIII. 11.[2]

This body of seventeenth-century poems has lain innocent and uncorrupted for three-and-a-half centuries, and now waits Lazarus-like for its resurrection and afterlife. Its return challenges our present credulities: the undeclared freight of critical practices which constitute our readings of poems is now a matter of controversy, but only in the case of those poems and authors whose history has already naturalized them within such practices, and the false consciousness of much recent theoretical posturing that has encouraged a witch-hunt by readers who, offended by what might be regarded as clandestine ideology, have arrogated to themselves the right to function as year-zero scrutineers of custom. In the case of poems and authors without a critical history, all such pretenses are rendered ineffectual, because we simply do not know how to read without presuppositions and established practices. More

---

[1] For the physical details of the manuscript and its provenance, see pp. xxxi–xlii below. Books and manuscripts in the Bodleian are not stored according to author, but according to shelf number.

[2] I have modernized the spelling.

xvi   *General Introduction*

importantly, the real, as opposed to the occluded, absence of factual informa-
tion about the poet compels us to acknowledge how important such informa-
tion about previous literary incarnations is for the location of our discursive
engagement with poems. In what follows I attempt to reconnoiter the site of
the poems' composition, in the hope that this will enable readers to discov-
er for themselves the attentiveness, intimacy, and charm of Nicholas Oldis-
worth's poems.

Nicholas Oldisworth (1611–1645)

The Oxford matriculation records describe Nicholas Oldisworth as the son of
Robert Oldisworth of Coln Rogers in Gloucestershire. This quiet village has
probably changed little since the seventeenth century.[3] Located on the trout-
fishing River Coln, it has escaped the attention of tourists to the better-known
village of Bibury a short distance downstream. The Saxon church was ancient
even in Oldisworth's day, and a little further inland is the even older Fosse
Way which leads into the Cotswolds, and so to Bourton-on-the-Hill, the home
of Oldisworth's grandfather.

The records make little mention of Oldisworth's mother, Merial, the daugh-
ter of Sir Nicholas Overbury and the sister of the ill-fated Sir Thomas.[4] Yet it is
the poet's maternal inheritance that features most strongly in his life. This is un-
derlined by the fact that he was born at Bourton-on-the-Hill and baptized in the
parish church on 14 July 1611.[5] In 1635 the living of the same church was later
presented to him by Sir Nicholas. (When he died, his successor as rector was his
younger brother, Giles.[6]) On 9 October 1637 he read to his grandfather a manu-
script compilation entitled "A Booke Touching Sir Thomas Overbury, who was
murthered by poyson in the Tower of London the 15th day of September, 1613.
being the 32nd yeare of his Age."[7] The disaster which struck the family at the
death of Sir Thomas must have been amongst the poet's earliest memories and
no doubt affected the conduct of his whole life.

---

[3] See Oldisworth's celebration of it in [28], 111–22.

[4] See *Alumni Oxonienses: The Members of the University of Oxford 1500–171*, 4 vol-
umes (London: Parker & Co, 1891–92). On the fate of Sir Thomas Overbury, see the
notes to [114] and **AP 7**.

[5] See the parish register, Gloucester County Record Office, PFC 54 in 1/1, p. 12.

[6] The Overbury's home overlooking the rolling landscape has been replaced by
another Manor house. The Parish Church of the village, which straddles the road up
a steep hill, remains, but like many Cotswold churches was remodeled in the nine-
teenth century, leaving no trace of the quiet men who ministered there.

[7] British Library Additional MS 15476.

General Introduction   xvii

He was educated at Westminster School under Lambert Osbaldeston (1594–1659) who, like so many of the headmasters of Westminster, was educated at the School and Christ Church, Oxford. Initially, Osbaldeston had been granted a joint patent as headmaster with John Wilson in late 1621. This was because Wilson's leanings towards Rome made him suspect. The initial appointment was probably made under the influence of John Williams, who became Dean of Westminster in 1620 and Lord Keeper and Bishop of Lincoln in the following year. In 1626 the patent of headmaster was renewed to Osbaldeston alone, once more with Williams's support. Osbaldeston's loyalty to Williams proved his undoing, when Archbishop Laud, an inveterate enemy of his brother prelate, turned his malice on the bishop's supporters. After various accusations against Osbaldeston failed, Laud finally in 1638 succeeded in bringing the headmaster to trial in the Star Chamber on a libel charge. There is serious doubt as to the soundness of the charges,[8] but Osbaldeston was sentenced to two fines of £5,000, to deprivation of his spiritual dignities, to imprisonment at the king's pleasure, and to having one ear nailed to the pillory in the Palace Yard and the other in Dean's Yard in the presence of his scholars. He destroyed his papers and went into hiding before this barbarous sentence could be carried out, and his place as headmaster was taken by Richard Busby.

Osbaldeston enjoyed the reputation of being a good and demanding schoolmaster, but it is clear that in the process he did much to encourage the high spirits of his pupils.[9] In a verse epistle to his cousin by marriage, Susan Oldisworth, the poet provides a lyrical account of his first day at Westminster:

> Foure yeares agoe, when I to schoole did packe
> Holding my Learning fast all on my backe,
> It pleasd king O[ls *altered to* sb]alston to lett us play
> Noe lesse, then for the date of one whole day
> O peaceful empire! Sure Augustus blisse
> Was but an idle prophecie of this.
> Tell mee, thou Sunne, who now didst shine more deare
> Then any other parcell of the Yeare,
> Tell me what solid Joy, what pure Delight,
> Two sweete, though yong Friends had then in thy sight
> There is a field which gamsters Tuttle name,

---

[8] See John Sargeant, *Annals of Westminster School* (London, 1898), 67–68.

[9] For a discussion of Westminster School, Osbaldeston and the practice of encouraging poetic composition among the students, see Raymond Anselment, "The Oxford Poets and Caroline Panegyric," *John Donne Journal* 3 (1984): 184–86; and Mary Hobbs, *Seventeenth-Century Verse Miscellany Manuscripts* (Aldershot: Scholar Press, 1992), 82–85,116–23.

A greene, playne, wide field. Here they early came
The morne presented [erasure] many a Chrystall gemme
Law [for Low] to their feete: but they neglected them. . . .

([28], 106 var., 1–14)

It is clear that his years there were both happy and profitable. The benign influence of the Headmaster should be seen not only in such an effusion of well-being, but also in his pupil's ability and willingness to express it in verse. Oldisworth was not the only one who responded to such encouragement. The youthful Abraham Cowley pays the following tribute:

TO THE RIGHT WORSHIPFUL,
my very loving Master, Master LAMBERT
OSBOLSTON, chiefe Schoole-
master of *Westminster-*
Schoole

Sir,
My childish Muse is in her Spring: and yet
Can onely shew some budding of her Wit.
One frowne upon her Worke, (Learn'd Sir) from you:
Like some unkinder storme shot from your brow,
Would turne her *Spring*, to withering *Autumne's* time,
And make her *Blossomes* perish, ere their Prime.
But if you Smile, if in your gracious Eye
Shee an auspicious *Alpha* can descrie.
How soone will they grow Fruit? How will they flourish
That had such beames their Infancie to nourish?
Which being sprung to ripenesse, expect then
The best, and first fruites, of her grateful Pen.

Your most dutifull Scholler,
Abraham Cowley[10]

Equally important are Osbaldeston's encouragement of his scholars after they left the school and their reciprocal willingness to acknowledge their indebtedness to him. Anthony Wood describes Osbaldeston as "a person very fortunate in breeding up many wits,"[11] and we realize that this was not simply a matter of chance or of passing interest. Oldisworth's gloss to the poem which

---

[10] Abraham Cowley, *The Collected Works*, ed. Thomas O. Calhoun, et al. (Newark: Delaware University Press, 1989), I, 49. I have reversed roman and italic type and not distinguished between small and large capitals.

[11] *Athenae Oxonienses*, 3rd ed., ed. Philip Bliss, 4 vols. (London, 1813–1820), III, 363.

General Introduction   xix

failed to be included in *Musarum Oxoniensium pro rege suo soteria* makes it
clear that four years after he left school his former headmaster ensured that
the poem reached the king.[12] If Oldisworth's testimony is seen to reflect as
much upon himself as on Osbaldeston, we need turn only to the wayward
Thomas Randolph who, a decade after leaving school, declares in a dedica-
tory poem to *The Jealous Lovers* (1632): "si bene quid scripsi, tibi debeo."[13]
Osbaldeston was probably also instrumental in eliciting Oldisworth's epigram
on the publication of Cowley's adolescent *Poetical Blossoms*.[14]

At Westminster Oldisworth began a friendship with Richard Bacon, the
son of Richard Bacon of St Dunstan's-in-the-West, Fleet Street, a dealer in
medicine.[15] In 1626 Bacon was one of the annual handful of Westminster
boys elected King's Scholars. He chose to enter Trinity College, Cambridge, as
opposed to Christ Church.[16] There is no record of his matriculation in Cam-
bridge, but it would appear that he took up the scholarship for about a year
in 1627 and 1628, after which he departed for the English College at Douay,
being admitted on 8 September 1629.[17] At Douay, where Bacon subsequently
taught rhetoric, he was joined by his brother Matthew in 1632.[18] In 1636 the
two brothers fled Douay to escape the plague, but Richard died soon after in
the Carthusian monastery at Nieuwpoort in Flanders.[19] Matthew went on to
qualify as a physician in Padua before practicing in Rome until his return to
England after the Restoration.

Once their schooling was completed Oldisworth and Bacon could not
have met often, but they appear to have kept in contact by letter. Oldisworth

---

[12] See [8] and pp. xxv–xxvi below for a discussion of the circumstances of the omission.

[13] Sig. 2¶1.

[14] See [93].

[15] See *The Douay College Diaries: Third, Fourth and Fifth (1598–1645)*, 2 vols., ed.
Edwin H. Burton and Thomas L. Williams (London, 1911), I, 277–78. Bacon is prob-
ably the companion mentioned in Oldisworth's account of his first day at the school.

[16] The record of his time in Cambridge is sketchy, but it is confirmed by Oldis-
worth's gloss to the first of his verse epistles to his friend: "These verses were writ-
ten 1629 to Master Richard Bacon, a hopefull Youth who was sometimes a scholar of
Westminster schoole, where hee was generally praised and beloved. At last hee dyed
in Travaile" (See [2] and notes).

[17] See *Douay Diaries*, I, 277–78, where it is recorded that Bacon had spent the
previous year at Cambridge. This is confirmed by Oldisworth's record, Bodleian MS
Don.c.24, fol. 18 ([15], 81 gloss) that Bacon played the role of Flavia in Thomas Vin-
cent's Latin play, *Paria*, performed before the King at Cambridge on 3 March 1628.
The play was published in 1648 (Wing H170); see Alan H. Nelson ed., *Records of Early
English Drama: Cambridge* (Toronto: University of Toronto Press, 1989), 912 and 959.

[18] See *Douay Diaries*, I, 305.

[19] See Matthew Bacon's autobiographical account in British Library Sloane MS
464, fols. 4–5.

xx   *General Introduction*

also wrote a series of poems, mostly verse epistles entitled "To his friend be-
yond sea," in which he regrets Bacon's absence and celebrates his beauty, in-
telligence, and virtue.[20] Not once does he mention his friend's religious af-
filiation or the reasons for his sojourn on the Continent. In 1632 Oldisworth
visited the Bacon family home, the manor house at Chilling Farm on the coast
between Warsash and Titchfield, near Southampton.[21] The house has long
been demolished.

Oldisworth went from Westminster to Christ Church as a King's Schol-
ar in July 1628 (according to College buttery records) or sometime between
Christmas 1628 and Lady Day 1629 (according to the matriculation records).[22]
Amongst the four other King's Scholars for that year was a fellow Gloucester-
shireman, the poet William Cartwright.

At Christ Church he would have known two Old Westminsters of an old-
er generation: Richard Corbett, who was Dean from 1620 till 1628 when he
became Bishop of Oxford (until 1632); and Brian Duppa, who was Dean from
1628 and Vice-Chancellor in 1632 and 1633. Corbett's reputation as a poet was
well established amongst his contemporaries. It is likely that Oldisworth met
Corbett in Oxford. Certainly the younger poet thought of him as some kind of
role model, and regretted that his elevation to the prelacy would bring an end
to his poetic career.[23] Duppa, though not a regular producer of poems, took
an active interest in poetry, and was responsible for the production in 1637
of *Jonsonius Virbius*, the collection of poems commemorating the death of Ben
Jonson. There is ample evidence of Oldisworth's contact with him. In Decem-
ber 1631 Duppa required him to make a verse translation of Aristophanes' *The
Ecclesiazusai*.[24] At the request of Duppa's wife he wrote a censure of Aristo-
phanes' derogatory view of women.[25]

According to the title-page of "A Recollection Of Certaine Scattered Po-
ems" the poems were written while Oldisworth was an undergraduate. This
is not entirely accurate. At least some of them date from after he took his first
degree, and one poem was revised in 1644.[26] Oldisworth's vagueness might
stem from the fact that as a Westminster King's Scholar he was automatically

---

[20] See [2] and notes.

[21] See [60], 93–138 and 153–74.

[22] Christ Church MS D.P.i.a.1, f.175. Oldisworth first appeared in the Buttery Book
(Christ Church MS (x).c.62) as "Owleworth" in the week beginning 11 July 1628.

[23] See [42], 37–44.

[24] See [38]. Regrettably Oldisworth provides only 25 lines of his translation. He
then adds in a gloss: "The rest this being but a translation I have not here transcribed".
Oldisworth's translation is reprinted in *The Oxford Book of Classical Verse in Transla-
tion*, ed. Adrian Poole and Jeremy Maule (Oxford, 1995).

[25] See [39].

[26] See [55].

General Introduction xxi

a Student of Christ Church, and so was free to prolong his stay in Oxford. He appears to have kept up his college connection even after he took up his duties at Bourton-on-the-Hill in 1635. Although he last signs the Sub-Dean's Book to register his absence from College in March 1635, his name appears in the extant Battels and Commons Books as late as October 1637, and was not officially left out until December 1641, when marriage had brought an end to his Studentship.[27]

He obtained his BA in 1632, being incorporated at Cambridge in the same year (an event he appears to mark by writing an epigram on Commencement at Cambridge in that year).[28] His MA followed in 1635.

On 2 August 1634 Oldisworth was presented with the living of Bourton-on-the-Hill by his grandfather, Sir Nicholas Overbury. We know little about Oldisworth's life in the next ten years. He copied eighteen sermons into a manuscript book and kept a careful record of when and where he delivered them—thus ensuring that he did not repeat his material too often.[29] The sermons are generally unostentatious, with only the occasional pedantic indulgence of learning to bewilder or impress a rural congregation. To judge from the content of the sermons, he was a dutiful pastor concerned with the inculcation of moderate doctrine and piety. Only in the very last sermons does a concern with the larger political events emerge: the fall of prominent men (amongst whom he probably numbered his ecclesiastical superior, Godfrey Goodman, Bishop of Gloucester) as presaging bad times, while such troubled times are to be regarded as visitations of divine justice. Bishop Goodman's crypto-Roman Catholicism held no attractions for Oldisworth, despite the fact that his dearest friend, Richard Bacon, was a recusant. The poems make very clear his attitude to Roman Catholic doctrine. For example, in the account of a journey made in 1632 he says of his hosts at Arborfield, near Reading:

Nay, and brave people also here wee finde,
Brave people both in Bodie, and in Minde.
Their old ones are most wise, most kind; their yong
Most beautifull, most nimble, and most strong:
Noe fault they have, but this; they doe belive
Bellarmin's doctrine. O how much wee grieve
To thinke that 'tis such worthy persons doome
To bee deluded (if noe worse) by Rome![30]

---

[27] See the Matriculation Book 1546–1635, Christ Church MS D.P.i.a.1, f.175.

[28] See [84].

[29] Bodleian MS Eng. Th.f.20. Oldisworth uses the same italic hand for his sermons as for the collection of his poems dedicated to his wife. He thus made no special effort to use a hand with which women are considered to have been more familiar.

[30] [60], 39–46.

xxii   *General Introduction*

But Oldisworth very discreetly does not identify his hosts, perhaps for the same reason that he never mentions that Richard Bacon and his family were Roman Catholics: the England of the first half of the seventeenth century was not as tolerant as subsequent generations would wish it to be.

Sometime in 1640 Oldisworth married—five years before the writing of his dedicatory letter to the poems.[31] (Once again the records of Coln Rogers are not extant. If they had been, we might now know the exact date of the marriage.) His wife was Mary Chamberlayne, the details of whose life are recorded on a monument in Tewkesbury Abbey:

> To the Happy Memory of
> MARY OLDISWORTH
> Daughter of Tho: Chamberlayne of
> Oddington Esqr: Wife to Nicholas Oldis=
> =worth Gent. Son of Robert Oldisworth
> of Fairford Esq. Mother of Mary the
> Wife of John Sherwood Gent. & also
> of Margarite Wife of Iohn Mann Gent.
> She lived a Virgin 29 Yeares, a Wife
> 5 & a Widow 39 and Died the 4th
> of August 1684 Aged 73.
> She was the pattern of Piety Charity
> Modesty Chastity Temperance &
> Frugality of pleasant Conversation
> Beloved by all & now Wanted by
> many All that was Mortal Lyes
> Interred near y̋ place expecting
> a Joyful Resurrection.[32]

All the children were born at Bourton-on-the-Hill: Mary, baptized on 6 January 1641; Francis, baptized on 11 June 1642 and buried on 28 November 1643; and Margaret, baptized on 8 February 1644. The mid 1640s were bad plague years. The parish records for 1644 and 1645 (completed by Giles Oldisworth) show that forty-one people died of the plague in Bourton-on-the-Hill. (Five other deaths are recorded, which is the norm for previous years.) Because of the plague, Oldisworth removed himself to Willington in Warwickshire (about eleven miles from Bourton-on-the-Hill and just outside Shipston-on-Stour). He

---

[31] In Don.c.24, fol.7, he mentions that in February 1645 he has been married five years. The marriage is not recorded at Bourton-on-the-Hill, and the records for Coln Rogers are not extant.

[32] See William Dyde, *The History and Antiquities of Tewkesbury* (Tewkesbury, 1790), 27. I am particularly grateful to Richard Webster for drawing my attention to this information, which had eluded me for many years.

General Introduction   xxiii

appears to have occupied himself by preparing what is now Bodleian MS. Don.
c. 24. The dedicatory epistle is dated 17 February 1644, but the year of transcrip-
tion is confirmed by Oldisworth's reference in a marginal gloss to the abortive
negotiations between royalist and parliamentary emissaries at Uxbridge be-
tween 30 January and 24 February 1645.[33] He died on 25 March 1645. The next
day he was buried in the chancel of the nearby church at Barcheston. This is re-
corded by his brother Giles in the Bourton-on-the-Hill parish register.[34]

Confirmation for this can be found in the Barcheston parish register.[35]
There is no trace of the site of the grave, the church having been refurbished in
the nineteenth century. Oldisworth's wife survived to a long widowhood, dying
in 1684 in the village of Batsford, about a mile from Bourton-on-the-Hill.[36] The
elder surviving daughter married a Londoner, and became Mistress Sherwood.
The youngest daughter, Margaret, who could hardly have known her father
(having been born in early 1644), married John Mann of Tewkesbury.[37] It was
she who inherited the manuscript from her mother, and turned it into a recipe
book. She recorded the gift in her own hand: "Margaret Man Her Book Given
Me By My Dear Mother". Below that she added a little more formally: "Master
Nicolas Oldisworth." The family made no attempt to publish the poems, and
in this they appear to be respecting the poet's wishes. The dedicatory epistle
is particularly revealing of Oldisworth's bewilderment at the turn of events in
the 1640s: his concerns were with his immediate and extended family, and he
sought to distance himself from the perplexities of power and politics.

Nicholas Oldisworth and the Christ Church Poetic Community

As a member of Christ Church from 1628, Nicholas Oldisworth was at the cen-
ter of the poetic community which dominated Caroline Oxford. The record of
his participation in the activities of that community is what one would expect:
a few poems in University commemorative volumes, others scattered through
various manuscript miscellanies, and a poem in one of the nostalgic verse
miscellanies with a royalist bias associated with Sir John Smith and James
Mennes.[38] Less characteristic is a series of forty-two unattributed poems in

---

[33] See line 43 and gloss.

[34] Gloucester Record Office, MS PFC 54 in 1/1, p. 83.

[35] Warwick County Record Office, MS DR 5/1.

[36] Gloucester Record Office, MS Admon: Mary Oldisworth 1684/319.

[37] Gloucester Record Office, MS Admon: Mary Oldisworth 1684/319.

[38] For Smith and Mennes, see p. xxxii below. The verse miscellanies *Musarum
Deliciae* (1655; 2nd ed. 1656); *Wit and Drollery* (1656; 2nd ed. 1661; 3rd ed. 1682); and
Wit Restor'd (1658) have traditionally be attributed to Smith and Mennes, but Timothy
Raylor, *Cavaliers, Clubs, and Literary Culture: Sir John Mennes, James Smith, and the Or-
der of the Fancy* (Newark: University of Delaware Press, 1994), finds "no evidence for
this assumption and much against it" (217).

one Oxford-related miscellany, Folger MS. V.a.170. Even more surprising is Bodleian MS. Don. c. 24, a collection of his early poems in an autograph fair-copy manuscript for presentation to his wife.

Seventeenth-century holograph fair-copy collections rarely survive, and there is nothing else like MS. Don.c.24 associated with Oxford and Christ Church poets, except perhaps for Cardell Goodman's "Beawty in Raggs" (Lambeth MS. 937 and MS. 1063).[39] Simply as a physical object the manuscript is valuable, since it provides us with a sense of what poets might have presented to the printing-house should they have been concerned to exercise control of their published work; more importantly, it gives us a very clear indication of the continuing and complex tradition of manuscript publication, which at times adopts some of the presentational features of printed texts. Because of Oldisworth's self-consciousness, this collection of about 120 poems detaches itself from the anonymity of the typical manuscript miscellany and engages with a coherent and recognizable personal and social history.

Caroline Oxford produced a great deal of English verse, much of it in forms which challenge reading practices that take no account of poetic communities and the social embeddedness of literary production. Although a small quantity was printed, the rest remained in manuscript, but rarely in the form of authorial working papers or fair copies. The poems made their way into manuscript miscellanies, collections which reflect the taste or the standing in the cultural-commodity hierarchy of the owner or owners of the volumes. As frequently as poems were attributed, often incorrectly, to prestigious writers such as Donne, Jonson, Carew, Strode, or Corbett, so many were transcribed anonymously. Very little is known about the personal and social activity which gave rise to these collections and their unknown owners, though the pioneering work of Peter Beal, Mary Hobbs, Harold Love, and Margaret Ezell on the process of circulation has revealed an important new field of study.[40]

---

[39] See Cardell Goodman *Beawty in Raggs or Divine Phancies putt into Broken Verse*, ed. R. J. Roberts (Reading: Whiteknights Press, 1958). William Strode's autograph collection, Corpus Christi MS 325, is not a dedicated presentation copy, while Bodleian MS Tanner 307, George Herbert's *The Temple*, which does attempt to mimic printed presentational forms, is not autographic. The Herbert manuscript has recently been edited by Mario A. Di Cesare: George Herbert, *The Temple: A Diplomatic Edition of the Bodleian Manuscript (Tanner 307)* (Binghampton: Medieval & Renaissance Texts & Studies, 1995).

[40] For recent influential explorations of the phenomenon see Mary Hobbs, *Early Seventeenth Century Verse Miscellany Manuscripts* (Aldershot: Scholar Press, 1992); Harold Love, *Scribal Publication in Seventeenth-Century England* (Oxford: Clarendon Press, 1993); and Arthur F. Marotti, *Manuscript, Print, and the English Renaissance Lyric* (Ithaca: Cornell University Press, 1995).

General Introduction XXV

Occasionally individuals like Martin Lluelyn (1616–1682) would publish small volumes of poems.[41] Posthumous collections by reputed figures such as Carew, Corbett, or Cartwright emerged from the press. Much later, the volumes associated with Sir John Mennes and James Smith would make available in print collections akin to the manuscript miscellanies. These are exceptional cases. Contributors to the manuscript miscellany stock were far more likely to have their work appear in print if they contributed to any one of the series of University commemorative volumes produced with particular frequency during the years of Charles I's personal rule. These volumes, which allowed writers to display their loyalty and their collegiate affiliation, constituted an innovation in the literary life of the University and are perhaps the best evidence we have of a very distinct poetic community at Christ Church.

The twenty-one volumes of commemorative verse published in Oxford between 1600 and 1633 contain only two poems in English. *Justa Funebria Ptolemaei Oxoniensis Thomae Bodleii Equitis Aurati Celebrata* (1613) has a single, eighteen-line poem by Peter Prideaux.[42] In the volume for Sir Henry Saville, *Ultima Linea Savilii* (1622), there is a ten-line epigram by Edward Wilson, fellow of Balliol. Convention required poems in the learned languages: Latin, Greek, and Hebrew. Earlier volumes occasionally also have poems in French. The first volume in Charles's reign, *Britanniae natalis* (1630), celebrating the birth of the future Charles II, followed this tradition, with 144 poems in Latin, three in Greek, and three in French, but in the volume celebrating the king's recovery from what was thought to be smallpox, *Musarum Oxoniensium pro rege suo soteria* (1633), there are four poems in English: one by Jasper Mayne in the first half of the book,[43] and a group of three by William Cartwright, Jeremial Terrent, and Thomas Lockey respectively towards the end.[44] In addition to the four published poems, there is one which did not make its way into the volume: Nicholas Oldisworth's "On his Majesty's Recovery from the small pocks. December 1632."[45]

A partial explanation for the publication of the four vernacular poems can be found in two further volumes published in the same year. Placed at the end of *Solis Britannia Perigaeum*, a collection of sixteen English poems (which includes contributions by Lockey, Mayne, Cartwright, and Oldisworth) is prefaced by one to the queen:

Our Mother tongue is Latine, yet since You
(With whom Your *CHARLES* ev'n absent scarce made two,)

---

[41] See *Men-miracles* (Oxford, 1646) [Wing (2nd ed.) L2625].
[42] Sig. H1.
[43] Sig. 2§4–2§4v.
[44] Sigs. G3–G4.
[45] See [8].

Did with our *Prince* our English Language wed,
And are his *QUEENE* now both in speech and bed;
Since You have interest in our joyes, to see
A Husband safe return'd, a Soveraigne wee;
Wee here translate some of our joyes, and sing
This part to You, the other to the *KING*.[46]

There is a similar introduction to the sixteen English poems (again with contributions by Lockey, Mayne, Cartwright, and Oldisworth) in *Vitis Carolinae Gemma Altera* (1633):

To the QUEENE.
Wee should forget (great *QUEEN*) to whom wee owe
Our future safety, should wee onely show
Outlandish Joyes, or write in such hard sort,
That you must apprehend us by report:
Since in a strange tongue wee should but increase
Our dumbnesse, and in Latin hold our peace;
And since, not understood, you well might doubt,
Whether you had a booke, or were without:
We have endeavour'd to approach your eye,
Though no Interpreter stood learned by
To tell our meanings, which you here may read
In the same Dialect in which you breed.[47]

Nevertheless, the relegation of the poems in English to a separate section at the end of the volume, and the presentation of them in italic type, suggest that they are supplementary to the volume, especially since the writers often produce poems in Latin as well.[48]

There may indeed be a wish to acknowledge the presence of Henrietta Maria, who could be presumed to know modern vernaculars but not the learned languages, and this would indicate that Royalist Oxford had begun to take into account the increased domesticity and intimacy of the royal couple.[49] Certainly there could be no better way of simultaneously affirming loyalty by naturalizing a foreign consort and disarming hostile criticism of the

---

[46] Sig. L1. I have reversed the use of roman and italic type.

[47] Sig. I1. I have reversed the use of roman and italic type.

[48] Latin poems by Cartwright and Lockey appear in *Pro rege*; three by Lockey and one each by Cartwright and Mayne in *Perigaeum*; one by Oldisworth and two by Cartwright in *Vitis Carolinae Gemma Altera*.

[49] See Kevin Sharpe, *The Personal Rule of Charles I* (New Haven: Yale University Press, 1992), p. 65.

General Introduction   xxvii

monarchy. These are the benefits and rationalizations of hindsight, though they are confirmed by similar developments at Cambridge.

During the Jacobean period Cambridge produced only one commemorative volume with English poems: *Epicedium Cantabrigiense* (1612), in memory of Prince Henry.[50] The first such Caroline volume appeared only in 1640. *Voces Votivae* clearly follows the Oxford lead. The section of eleven English poems is concluded with a justification:

> *A Conclusion to her Majestie.*
>
> *Dread Queen*, account it no disparagement,
> That we do pay this yeare an English Rent;
> As if some meaner stream did feed our quills.
> For when Your offspring, *Blessed Mother*, fills
> All languages, and takes up every song,
> 'Tis time at length to use our Mother-tongue.
>   Proceed, *Great Ladie*, till your fruitfulnesse
> Has puzzl'd various *Babel* to expresse
> Natures congratulations, till your wombe
> In breeding Conquerors all the world o'ercome.
> And let your numerous train of Starres (I mean
> Your glorious Race) exhale all *Hippocrene*.
> Yet if your Geniall bed exhaust our store
> Of words, we'll set some *Hebrew* roots for more,
> And try all dialeacts from the first Fall,
> Till we return unto th'originall
> Pure phrase of *Paradise*; *Your* Innocence,
> Suits best with language that is fetcht from thence.
> And when I see your Fruit, me thinks (*Great Queen*)
> Y'are like the *Tree of Life*, still fresh and green.
> For she that bears a *Prince*, immortall she
> Brings forth no lesse then Immortalitie.[51]

What still requires explanation is the set of poems (one of them unpublished) which created the precedent for subsequent volumes containing poems in English. All five writers were members of Christ Church, but more important, all had been educated at Westminster School. From Westminster many

---

[50] There are twelve English poems in all, gathered at the end of the volume, sigs. N4–P2ᵛ.

[51] *Voces votivæ ab academcis Cantabrigiensibus pro novissimo Caroli & Mariæ principe filio emissæ* (Cambridge, 1640) [STC 4495], sig. b4ᵛ. I have reversed the use of roman and italic type.

boys proceeded as King's Scholars to either Christ Church or Trinity College, Cambridge. According to the Elizabethan statutes, each of these colleges was required to elect four Scholars a year, but in practice only Christ Church did so on a regular basis. Westmonastrians preferred Oxford, for one very obvious reason. Whereas King's Scholars at Trinity were treated as undergraduates and had to earn their election as Fellows of the College, at Christ Church a King's Scholar was automatically one of the one hundred Students; in other words, he had the status of a fellow and under normal circumstances would retain it until he resigned or married. King's Scholars could therefore stay on at Christ Church for much longer than the three or four years it would take them to complete a first degree.

A Westminster boy arriving at Christ Church would not find himself amongst strangers. As well as his three or four contemporaries from the school, he would find schoolfellows from three or four previous elections and Westmonastrians from previous generations. In particular, between 1596 and 1650 he would discover that six successive Deans (Thomas Ravis, John King, William Goodwin, Richard Corbett, Brian Duppa, and Samuel Fell) had been to the school. (For the same period, not a single Master of Trinity had been at Westminster.) The new Student would also know a great deal about the College beforehand. All four headmasters from 1598 to 1695 were King's Scholars elected to Christ Church.

In 1628 Nicholas Oldisworth arrived at Christ Church in the company of William Cartwright. Already there he would have found Richard Corbett (the Dean, soon to be succeeded by Brian Duppa), William Strode, Zouch Townley (Ben Jonson's friend), George Morley, Gervase Warmestry, William Hemmings, Thomas Mottershed, Jeremiah Terrent, Jasper Mayne, Thomas Browne, John Donne (the younger), and Thomas Manne. Robert Randolph was to follow in 1629,[52] and Thomas Weaver and Richard West four years later. All of them had been shaped by the same educative and cultural ideals, and so poetic activity was not something external to who they were. For them, writing poems was not only an accomplishment they could occasionally lapse into, but also a way of constituting their identities. Collecting poems was not simply a fashionable hobby, but a means of acquiring and displaying the cultural capital which established their identities as learned wits. Oldisworth could move effortlessly into this milieu with its well-established traditions and practices, one which provided him with models such as Corbett, mentors such as Brian Duppa (the friend of John Donne and Henry King), and rivals for the attention of the community like William Cartwright. It is therefore not surprising to find amongst his writings a long journey-poem, *Iter Australe*, to

---

[52] His elder brother Thomas had proceeded from Westminster to Trinity College, Cambridge.

General Introduction xxix

match Corbett's famous *Iter Boreale*; or part of a verse translation of Aristophanes' *Ecclesiazusai* made for Brian Duppa.

The enabling conditions, I would suggest, for a poetic community are a locale, some form of structure or procedure which ensures the continuity of the community, and a number of dominant individuals, such Osbaldeston, Corbett, Strode, and Duppa. For the Christ Church poetic community, the most important figure is one who did not attend the University: Ben Jonson. His presence, for Oldisworth at least, is a source of inspiration and anxiety. By placing the lengthy "A Letter to Ben. Johnson. 1629" at the very beginning of "A Recollection of Certaine Scattered Poems," Oldisworth signals where his poetic allegiances lie.[53] Each verse paragraph begins with a hyperbolic demand for Jonson's death, clearly prefiguring post-Romantic anxieties about the disenabling influences of dominant predecessors. Because Oldisworth conflates the author with his work, he may also seen as anticipating, quite literally, belated theoretical debates about the Death of the Author.

The clearest evidence for the activities of the Christ Church poetic community is the existence of manuscript miscellanies with clear links to the college. Poems transmitted by manuscript have a very different history from those which appear in printed form. Print ensures relative stability of text and context, and so a kind of a personal indifference as to who does the reading. Any stranger can walk into a shop and buy a copy of a printed book. Being indifferently accessible to individual readers they are to that extent alienated from both authors and readers. Poems in manuscript miscellanies are radically unstable textually because they are subject to the individuality of the copyist: to that extent each manuscript is unique and characteristic of its compiler. By contrast, poems circulated in manuscript are contextually stable, since they generally pass from one known compiler to another, and there tends to be complicity in the act of transference: manuscript transmission requires knowable social networks. The more frequent and complex the transmission, the more sophisticated and complex the social network. The collections Beal and Hobbs associate with Christ Church tend to be those which

---

[53] See [1].

xxx   *General Introduction*

predominantly contain poems by members of the House.[54] In some cases we are fortunate to know who the compilers were.[55]

Poems may be copied either in groups or individually, from other collections or from loose papers, or from scribal copies or the author's fair or foul papers. Within a scribal community any one of these procedures, or a combination of them, may have been followed. Folger MS. V.a.170, for example, has a block of forty-two poems by Oldisworth.[56] Some of the poems are early versions of those found in Bodleian MS. Don. c. 24, while others are incomplete.[57] Six of the poems are not found in the autograph or in any other manuscript, and, given that at least two of them are incomprehensibly bad, it is probable that Oldisworth decided to discard them. (Before that happened the compiler of the Folger manuscript had access to Oldisworth's papers.) The earlier part of the miscellany is less consistently organized. There are poems by Shakespeare, Sir Henry Wotton, Donne, Jonson, Randolph, and Herrick, and a significant number by Thomas Carew. These are fairly standard fare in miscellanies of this kind. But the collection is dominated by groups of poems by William Strode, as one would expect from a miscellany with Christ Church connections. Equally noteworthy is the number of poems by other poets with Christ Church connections: Corbett, Duppa, Morley, John King, and Jasper Mayne.

Just as the poems of his fellow writers at Christ Church migrated from one miscellany to another, so individual Oldisworth poems found their way into collections beyond the confines of the House, and in so doing extended the connections of the poetic community. As one would expect, the most widely dispersed of Oldisworth's poems is the "Letter to Ben Jonson." Jonson sent a copy to his patron, the Earl of Newcastle, and a fair copy of it is to be found

---

[54] For example, British Library Stowe MS 962, Westminster Abbey Dean and Chapter MS 41, British Library Sloan MS 1792, and the privately owned manuscript edited by Mary Hobbs: *The Stoughton Manuscript: A Manuscript Miscellany of Poems by Henry King and his Circle, circa 1636* (Aldershot: Scolar Press, 1990). See Mary Hobbs, *Early Seventeenth Century Verse Miscellany Manuscripts* (Aldershot: Scolar Press, 1992), 9, 79, 94 and 116–20; Peter Beal, *Index of English Literary Manuscripts*, Vol. 2 (1625–1700), Part 2 (London: Mansell, 1992), 354–56, for example.

"The House" is the familiar name of Christ Church, derived from its Latin name "Aedes Christi".

[55] For example, British Library Harley MSS 6917/8 (Peter Calfe), British Library Additional MS 58215 (Thomas Manne), Westminster Abbey Dean and Chapter MS 41 (George Morely), and Corpus Christi College, Oxford MS 325 (William Strode).

[56] MS Folger V. a. 170, pp. 269–332.

[57] Many of the variant readings are of such a nature that they cannot be construed as arising from transmissional error. See, for example, the variants for [5], where "Chrystall" replaces the earlier "Venice", and "all agreed", "made an oath". The omission of the lines found in the Folger manuscript clearly improves the poem.

General Introduction   xxxi

in the Newcastle Manuscript, British Library MS. Harley 4955. The remaining six manuscripts all represent the early state of the text, but it is unclear whether they derive from the author's papers or from the Jonson copy. Bodleian MSS. Ashmole 47, Firth e. 4, Eng. poet. e. 97, and Folger MSS V. a. 170 and V. a. 322 all seem to have Oxford connections. The connection is not so clear in the case of Huntington HM 198 Pt I. There is also no obvious source for the text printed in *Wit Restor'd* (1658) [*Wing* M1719], 79–81. The volume is associated with Sir John Mennes and James Smith, and it might be that the poem found its way into the poetic community of which they were members: before moving to Lincoln College, James Smith had been at Christ Church.[58]

Another poem addressed and presented to a known recipient is the one on the king's recovery from smallpox.[59] All trace of the presentation copy or its descendants has been lost. Two of the manuscripts in which it is found, Folger MS. V. a. 170 and Rosenbach MS. 239/27, have clear Oxford and Christ Church connections. The third manuscript, Folger MS. V. a. 275, shows no obvious connections with the University or the College.

"To the Witts of Oxford, Cambridge, and London"[60] is the kind of poem one expects to find in miscellanies, since it challenges the younger generation to celebrate Gustavus Adolphus. Oldisworth aims at stimulating one of the principal activities of poetic communities: the emulous production of poems on the same subject. The many University volumes for royal occasions are an institutionalized form of this. Oldisworth also has a secondary purpose. In regretting the end of Corbett's poetic career, he is, for the same motives which underlie his "Letter to Ben Jonson," alerting the younger generation to the need for poetic innovation and independence. This perhaps explains why in 1630 he broaches a subject which appears to be politically sensitive. Unfortunately, Oldisworth appears to have mistimed or misjudged his challenge; there are only two copies of this poem in miscellanies, Folger MSS. V. a. 170 and V. a. 319, and no responses. By 1632 the Swedish king was dead on the field of Lutzen, and then it was safe for Oldisworth's less venturesome contemporaries to lament a man dead whom they would not commit themselves to praise living.[61]

A poetic community requires, I suggest, more than a set of enabling structural conditions and protocols. There should be some commonly held beliefs or ideology. The traditions of Westminster School and Christ Church provided all of these. In general, most members of both institutions could be said to

---

[58] He matriculated there on 7 March 1623, aged eighteen. He proceeded B.D., perhaps from Lincoln College, in 1633.

[59] See pp. xviii–xix and n.12 above.

[60] See pp. 82–83 and 211–12.

[61] See, for example, *The Swedish Intelligencer: The Third Part* (London, 1633) [STC 23525], sigs. 1¶–3¶4.

be Royalist, Anglican, and anti-Puritanical. Because of the influence of John Williams as Dean of Westminster, they would, however, not all be supporters of William Laud. It is perhaps more important to realize that Westmonastrians at Christ Church formed the nucleus of a sustained and coherent social group which constituted itself through poetic activity. The poems written and circulated were largely secular, occasional, and personal, and very often concerned with events and people associated with the University, and their purpose was to display the learning, wit, and urbanity of the writers and readers, often by "Flashes and fantastique Guere."[62] The sophistication aspired to could also be sexual, and it is therefore not surprising that certain poems by Donne and Carew feature prominently in the miscellanies. In short, everything aimed at establishing a self-understanding of the learned and high-mettled gentleman, loyal to his king and disdainful of hypocrites, Puritans, and Dissenters. Although this ideal is clearly related to that of the cavalier, the University context alone ensures that it is distinct.

An instance of a truly cavalier poetic community can be found in the group centered on Sir John Mennes (1599–1671) and James Smith (1604/5–1667), and so ably characterized by Timothy Raylor.[63] Mennes and Smith were younger sons with moderately-wealthy gentry connections in search of preferment at Court or in the professions. Both saw service on the Royalist side during the Civil War, and maintained their loyalties during the Interregnum. During the 1630s and '40s the manuscript circulation of their poems was strictly controlled, but, with the triumph of the republican cause, they did not resist the opportunities for public gestures of solidarity and insinuations of discontent afforded by publication in print. Hence the publication of the volumes containing a mixture of poems by themselves and others.[64]

The bulk of Oldisworth's poems are not associated directly with the University, and to that extent the poetic community which sustained him consisted of a network of non-metropolitan family and social connections among the rural gentry, in addition to the Christ Church circle. A number of poems are written at the behest of friends, family, or neighbors in rural Gloucestershire, in ways that set them apart from both the print-dominated culture of London and the Universities and the manuscript-circulating coteries associated with urban institutions such as schools, universities, the Court, and the Inns of Court. It is in this regional milieu that Oldisworth comes into his own.[65]

---

[62] See *OED* "Gear" s.v. 1: Apparel, attire, dress, vestments

[63] See his *Cavaliers, Clubs, and Literary Culture: Sir John Mennes, James Smith, and the Order of the Fancy* (Newark: University of Delaware Press, 1994).

[64] See Raylor, 202–5.

[65] Much work needs to be done on the non-metropolitan literary culture of Early Modern England. In my "Nicholas Oldisworth and the Complex, Multi-layered Cul-

General Introduction   xxxiii

The distinctiveness of Oldisworth's poems

Oldisworth is essentially a manuscript poet. Apart from those poems which
appeared in University volumes marking royal occasions (a fact proudly ac-
knowledged in the margins of the manuscript), the only poem of Oldisworth's
to appear in print was his "Letter to Ben Jonson," in *Wit Restor'd* (1658), as-
sociated with Sir John Mennes and James Smith. The poem does, however,
appear in several miscellanies, but generally the manuscript circulation of in-
dividual poems is not great. Only one other manuscript, Folger MS. V.a.170,
is known to contain a series of Oldisworth poems.[66] Within the sequence of
Oldisworth poems in the Folger manuscript there are six poems not found in
the Bodleian holograph.[67] If the copyist has rendered his source accurately,
these poems are not up to the standard of Oldisworth's other work, and there
were good grounds for not including them in his collection. In one or two oth-
er cases it is also clear that the copyist had access to earlier versions of those
poems which the author decided to retain in his holograph.

The range of Oldisworth's poems is quite varied. There are poems written
for royal occasions such as the king's recovery from smallpox in 1632; vari-
ous elegies in either the standard couplet form or in stanzas, with titles such
as "In defence of a Girle, that went holding downe her head," "The wordes of
a Lover, speaking to the reflection of his Mistresses face in a Looking-glasse"
(this "for Master Chandler of Coln Rogers when he was suitor to his future
wife"), "To a Separatist, that spoiled mens tombs, and built his house with the
tomb-stones," "On an uggly Wench", "Hampton-court here speaketh," "On
an Arbour made by Master Richard Bacon, on the sea-shoar opposite to the
ile of Wight," and "To a gentle-woman that delighted too much in her gar-
den"; witty epigrams on topics such as Shotover Hill, a painted hourglass, mis-
placed pride in a coat of arms, a moor (probably the nearest thing to a scur-
rilous poem in the collection), "treacherousnesse," builders or repairers of St
Paul's, and Abraham Cowley; complimentary epigrams on relations, friends,
and neighbors such as Sir Edward Hungerford of Corsham in Wiltshire, Old-
isworth's cousin Dorothy Litcott, Katharine Bacon, Michael Oldisworth, Mis-
tris Strange of Summerford a Poetesse, and on his little brother Giles Oldis-
worth; epitaphs, such as "An Epitaph on *Thomas Hulbert* Cloathyer of *Cosham*"
(at the request of Sir Edward Hungerford, who did not use it for the monument
he erected), two epitaphs on "litle Thomas Bacon, who died sodainly," and one
on Master Little of Abingdon; songs such as "A sonnet, played by a Musician at
my Entertaining of Master *Michael Oldisworth*"; straightforward lyric poems

---

tures of Seventeenth-Century Gloucestershire," *The Southern African Journal of Medi-
eval and Renaissance Studies* 14 (2004): 91–111, I draw attention to this need.

[66] See Peter Beal, *Index of English Literary Manuscripts*, II.2, 356–57.

[67] See the appendix of Additional Poems in this volume.

with titles such as "To a Lady, on her walking abroad," "To a Lady, looking out of a window," and "For a Lover, whose Mistris concealed her selfe from him"; and a journey poem, "Iter Australe," in imitation of Corbett's "Iter Boreale," though certainly not as accomplished.

Oldisworth did attempt to write the standard, rather brittle poems intended to project the self-image of a court or university wit. For the most part, these are his least attractive, rather embarrassingly sycophantic, poems. When he is unpretentious and at ease with his audience the poems have a real human interest, and present a sense of Oldisworth as a sweet-natured individual, who appears to have felt no need to imitate the poems which dominate the manuscript miscellanies. The only verbal echo I have found is of Donne's "The Flea," which he must have known in manuscript. He goes his own modest way, and he would most likely have applied his fellow Cotswold poet Clement Barksdale's words to himself from "The Defence. To Master Francis Powell of Christ Church":

> A careful friend told me my verses do
> Look like delinquents. *Frank*, I'll be judg'd by you.
> So long as my poor Muse makes no debate,
> Nor fancies aught that's dang'rous to the State;
> Though I'm not bold, yet I no censure fear,
> Neither of potent Commoner, nor Peer,
> For naming excellent Croft, or Knight or Dean,
> In this or that page of my verses mean.

In addition to the poems, the manuscript contains a rather enigmatic incomplete *roman a clèf* entitled *The Chronicle of Europe*. His brother Giles wrote a juvenile, disguised, family history entitled "Sketlius" (also in the Bodleian), so there is a family history of this kind of writing.

Oldisworth is therefore not simply another University poet. In compiling his collection he was not thinking in terms of a commonplace-book or gentleman's miscellany, but more in terms of the *silva* tradition of Jonson's *Epigrams* and *The Forest*.[68] Conventionally, the opening poems of such collections signal the compiler-poet's priorities. Thus, when Oldisworth begins the

---

[68] For a discussion of the *silva* tradition, see Alastair Fowler, "The Silva Tradition in Jonson's *The Forest*" in Maynard Mack and George deForest Lord, eds., *Poetic Traditions of the English Renaissance* (New Haven and London: Yale University Press, 1982), 163–80; and Frans de Bruyn, "Classical *Silva* and the Generic Development of Scientific Writing in Seventeenth-Century England", *New Literary History* 32 (2001): 347–73. The ordering of poems within collections is also discussed in Neil Fraistat, ed., *Poems in Their Place: The Intertextuality and Order of Poetic Collections* (Chapel Hill and London: University of North Carolina Press, 1986).

General Introduction XXXV

collection with a complimentary poem to Ben Jonson, signaling both his poetic loyalties and his own need for an independent poetic identity (the poems begins: "Die Johnson . . ."),[69] his refusal to satisfy expectation—by placing at the forefront of his work a poem for an aristocratic patron, or one in praise of the monarch—is itself significant. Jonson knew the poem and sent a copy to the Earl of Newcastle in 1631:

> I have obeyed your commands, and sent you a packet of mine own praises, which I should not have done if I had any stock of modesty in store. But obedience is better than sacrifice, and you commanded it. I am now like an old bankrupt in wit that am driven to pay debts on my friends' credits; and for want of satisfying letters to subscribe bills of exchange.[70]

(Jonson apparently did not find the slightly impudent, perhaps gauche, mixture of paradox and hyperbole offensive. The more time one spends with poems such as this, the more one comes to tolerate their endearing awkwardnesses.)

The second poem, which places Oldisworth's absent friend Richard Bacon in the foreground, further affirms Oldisworth's priorities. Richard Bacon is not named in the poem itself, but is identified by a marginal gloss, highlighting his obscurity and, given the emotional freight of the poem itself, the exclusivity of the relationship. Contemporary readers responded to the celebration of intimate friendship realized by the poem. Matthew, Richard Bacon's brother, who seems to have taken some of his deceased brother's papers with him to Padua when he went there to study medicine, transformed this poem into "A letter to Master Clement Harby at Rome." The main changes are the appropriate changes of "floods" (rivers) for "sea," and "At Padua and see thy friend" for the last line. Appropriations of this kind are what one would expect from the kind of poem, and the kind of audience, for which Oldisworth was writing. Poems are part of the social intercourse of private life constituted in part by manuscript circulation, not objects of aesthetic contemplation in either manuscript miscellanies or printed books. It is not often, however, that we find such clear evidence as to how the process worked.

The third poem is a lengthy epigram on the library of his cousin and patron, Michael Oldisworth, the secretary to both William and Philip Herbert, earls of Pembroke. In this poem Oldisworth not only establishes a sense of

---

[69] Bodleian MS Don.c.24, fol. 8–8ᵛ.

[70] *Ben Jonson*, ed. C.H. Herford and Percy Simpson, 11 vols. (Oxford: Oxford University Press, 1925–1952), I: 210. I have modernized the spelling and regularized the punctuation. The other poems were two by Lucius Carey, Viscount Falkland, and one by R. Goodwin.

xxxvi   *General Introduction*

his own worth and rank by paying tribute to his patron, but does so in terms of that eminently Jonsonian theme, the dignity of learning. The emphasis on personal values thus continues in "On his seeing the Study [library] of Master Michael Oldisworth"[71] and is extended in "On Complements," which derides the intrusiveness of courtly behavior into the secure obscurity of private life.[72] These are followed by another "To his Friend beyond sea," as a way perhaps of putting in perspective the following three, more conventional, status-establishing poems: "To the right honorable, the lord Haies, earle of Carlile, &c.," "To the right honorable his Patron [the earl of Carlisle]," and "On his Majesty's Recovery from the small pocks. December 1632." Despite its title, however, the last of these poems concentrates on the private domestic relationship of Charles and Henrietta Maria.

As with most collections influenced by the *silva* tradition, the opening and closing sections follow easily-discerned protocols. The interconnections between poems in the body of the collection are not obviously brought into the foreground, and this is in keeping with the "roughness" or miscellaneity aimed at with the genre. One should not therefore expect a sequential development in the sequence. There will, however, be incidental connections that function as a source of a sense of discovery and wonder within a seemingly random multiplicity (another feature of the *silva* tradition), and I have attempted to draw attention to some of them in the Commentary.

The last pages of the collection contain a sequence of poems that is, on the surface at least, in keeping with the epigraph on the title-page and with the poet's dignity as a clergyman. The poems appear to announce a renunciation of this world in favor of the next, by moving away from amatory and amicable concerns: "For a Lover. To his absent Mistris," "To a Curtezan," "For a Gentleman. On the embracing of his Friend," "For a gentleman. To yong Master *Henry Gresley*," "On the death of his deare friend Master Richard Bacon" (with no poem, simply a blank page), "On Sir *Thomas Overbury* and his poeme," "A translation of the *Te deum laudemus* after the tune of the 100 Psalme," "A divine Rapture," and, finally, a set of poems "His Farewell to *Poetrie*," "Poetry's Answer," and "His Reply to *Poetrie*." But an attentive reading of the final, self-reflective poems suggests that despite the complexly multivalent sequencing of the collection, the poems require a more sophisticated reading than adherence to the convention initially invites. The farewell to poetry is

---

[71] Oldisworth's cousin, Michael, (159[?]–1645?), graduated BA from Magdalen College, Oxford, where he was granted a fellowship. After proceeding MA in July 1614, he became secretary to William, Earl of Pembroke, the Lord Chamberlain. The Earl's influence led to his election to Parliament as the member for Old Sarum in January 1624. He was re-elected in 1625, 1626 and 1628.

[72] Oldisworth's privileging of private life might well stem from the family's reaction to the career of Sir Thomas Overbury.

General Introduction xxxvii

not the poet's renunciation of a worldly art, but the valediction to a sacred muse who is advised to withdraw from a shameful world. Poetry replies that before it withdraws it will celebrate the exemplary worth of a single figure (which the gloss identifies as Michael Oldisworth). In response, the poet advises Poetry to stay aloof

> As in a throne of Witt;
> And then to droppe down a Booke,
> On which who-ere shall looke,
> Shall wonder, and confesse Thou wert so hallowed
> Thou scornedst or to follow, or bee followed.

By a witty turn, Oldisworth uses the conventions to establish his own unconventional independence, which has been present in the collection from the very beginning, the tribute to Ben Jonson.[73]

The *silva* tradition is not the only framing device of the collection. There is also Oldisworth's dedicatory epistle to his wife, which some might consider the most interesting part of the manuscript. The letter presents us with a rather ordinary, affectionate person bewildered by the way public events have disrupted his domestic innocence. (The realization that Oldisworth was to die within five weeks of writing it adds a certain poignancy.) More importantly, the letter confirms the adult's conventional repudiation of the ways of his youth announced on the title-page while simultaneously and complexly affirming his nostalgia for that untroubled innocence. What enables him to sustain such seemingly incompatible stances is the maturity of the reciprocally assumed understanding and affection of his intended first reader, Mary Oldisworth. Particularly telling is Oldisworth's recognition of his wife's independent subjective life: "I doubt but Thou also, in those very dayes, hadst and didst enjoy thy faire virginlike contentments; though I then was not so happy, as to knowe either Them, or Thee." Belated readers generally do not attribute such attitudes to Early Modern males nor, given the canon of seventeenth-century English poetry, would they expect them either to inform, or be expressed in, the poems of the period.

Without regard for the enabling and constitutive context of their primary audience, his wife, Oldisworth's poems will not receive a proper reading. In "A Recollection of Certain Scattered Poems" Oldisworth unconventionally presupposes that his primary reader is a woman. He does write the standard love

---

[73] See John Gouws, "Religious Authority and Poetic Knowledge: The Alternative of Nicolas Oldisworth's Farewell to Poetry," *Southern African Journal of Medieval and Renaissance Studies* 17 (2007): 41–55, where I suggest that Oldisworth's religious perspective, along with other practices such as friendship, provides an independence from reductive and instrumental secular understandings of the human condition.

lyrics and flippant epigram such as [21] "The nobleman's Wooing," [22] "The country-gentleman's Wooing," [24] "On an uggly Wench," and [109] "To a Curtezan." Some poems even approach the erotic, such as [59] "An Ode," [73] "A lover's fancie," and [101] "Amorous Dreames." But of greater interest are the poems for which one would be hard pressed to find precedents. The University miscellanies abound in poems praising female beauty (poems generally of the one-size-fits-all, off-the-peg variety which could apply to anyone one chooses), but there are none where beauty is seen as an impediment to marriage, as for example, [94] ("To Mistris Katharine Bacon"), which is directed at a particular woman, Richard Bacon's unmarried sister. This departure from common practice is not an indulgence in conventional, giddy paradox, but perfectly serious, and attempts with sympathy and humor to address the anxieties of Katherine Bacon. Oldisworth repeatedly demonstrates his sensitivity to the personal circumstances of the women he addresses, as can be seen also in [10] "In defence of a Girle, that went holding downe her head" and [47] "To a yong Lady, that hadd the greene Sicknesse," a subject which generally gives rise to anonymous indecencies.

Oldisworth's empathic abilities are apparent also in the many surrogate or vicarious poems: [20] "To Mistris E.W."; [64] "To Sir *Giles Fetiplace*, high sheriffe of *Glocester-shire*, 1632"; [74] "On Mistris Summer, who dyed in child-bedd"; [75] "On the death on both Mistris Summer and her Childe"; [92] "For an Innes of courts man. To his Mistris"; [99] "For a Lover, whose Mistris concealed her selfe from him"; [108] "For a Lover. To his absent Mistris"; [110] "For a Gentleman. On the embracing of his Friend"; and [111], "For a gentleman. To yong Master *Henry Gresley*." These poems presuppose that poetry is a mode of social conduct rather than an aesthetic product or artifact. Though he does not create a commodity, the coterie poet is able to provide routines or protocols for others. In order to accomplish this, he needs to find the rhetoric appropriate to circumstances and self-understandings other than his own. Poems written on behalf of others are different in kind from what may be called more conventional ventriloquist poems such as [14] "An Ode," a religious poem reminiscent of George Herbert, in which the poet speaks with a female persona, or [32] "Hampton-court here speaketh," an even more conventional prosopopeia, in which the poet takes on the persona of a building, Hampton Court. In the case of these latter poems, the poet works within a figurative rhetorical strategy; in surrogate poems his strategy is dictated not by a figure but by the circumstances of the person on behalf of whom the poem is written. In his collection Oldisworth provides the information which allows us to identify and adapt our reading of these vicarious poems. Without the information the poems would lack the adhesion to actual social conduct which renders them imaginatively viable. There are doubtless a great many seventeenth century poems in miscellanies and printed collections which, for the lack of the enabling circumstantial social information, fail to pick up

General Introduction   xxxix

their bones and walk for belated readers. Oldisworth's collection alerts us to this possibility.

Oldisworth often writes without disguises. This is particularly true of the series of poems to his absent friend, Richard Bacon: [2], [5], [31], [50], [70], [78], [82], [87], [96], [103], and [113]. The poems are for the most part verse epistles, as one would expect from a poet following close on the heels of Donne and Jonson, but there are also lyrics and even a version of the country house poem, [78], though in the context of the collection they are all meditations on loss, nowhere more so than in the culminating poem in the series, with its poignant eloquence of a blank page. Oldisworth's candor is refreshing, and challenging to a generation of readers unused to the strategies and hyperbolic language of eroticism in poems of friendship. It requires us to revisit Shakespeare's sonnets and poems such as Donne's "To Sir Henry Wotton" ("Sir, more than kisses, letters mingle souls") and William Strode's "To a Friend" ("Like to the hand which hath been used to play"). Written in an age that valorized the traditions of *amicitia* inherited from the ancient world, these poems, and those by Oldisworth, are a remarkable testimony to the enduring, though easily misunderstood, traditions: individual poems extend and even transform the poetic practices of literary friendship. Certainly, in the case of the collection as a whole, the dedicatory epistle to his wife in which Oldisworth subscribes himself as his wife's "true friend," extends and renders complex the common perception of the protocols of friendship.[74]

In breaking with ancient tradition by acknowledging his wife as a friend, Oldisworth is subscribing to practices of private life emerging in Early Modern England. A great many of the poems are about domestic and personal matters, or are the means of conducting private or intimate relationships, whether amatory, amicable, or spiritual (often with a shared vocabulary). Even public poems, such as those for royal occasions, invariably resort to gestures and tones of domestic conduct. Thus, Henrietta Maria's anxieties for her husband's welfare and health are applauded: "Queene Marie expressed marvailous true affection to the king, in the time of his sicknesse, though his disease was

---

[74] Henry King, another Westminster School and Christ Church poet, also refers to his wife, who died in 1623, as a friend in his much-copied "An Exequy To his Matchlesse and never to be forgotten Friend"; see *The Poems of Henry King*, ed. Margaret Crum (Oxford: Clarendon Press, 1965), 68–71 and 197–98. The notion of marriage as a form of friendship seems to have gained ground in the early decades of the seventeenth century; see Jeremy Taylor, *Holy Living* ed. P. G. Stanwood (Oxford: Clarendon Press, 1989), 156, where he describes marriage as "the noblest of friendships." For further discussion of this topic, see John Gouws, "Nicholas Oldisworth, Richard Bacon, and the Practices of Caroline Friendship", *Texas Studies in Literature and Language*, 47 (2005): 366–401.

xl   *General Introduction*

infectious."[75] Jane (Killingtree) Duppa becomes part of the context of a trans-
lation from the Greek; and the *Te Deum* is translated at the behest of Godfrey
Goodman, Bishop of Gloucester. The poems are not only about the domestici-
ties and intimacies of private life, or become the means for conducting the life
of an intimate sphere, but the very process of writing, reading, and circulation
also helps to constitute and reaffirm the commitment to private life. In other
words, the poems are not intended for the indiscriminate scrutiny of print,
and it would be a mistake to think of Oldisworth as a poet who failed to get
into print. Rather, like other poets in poetic communities, he chose the res-
ervations of manuscript circulation as an affirmation of a way of life. This is
how the poems should be read.

Oldisworth's poems are interesting for their own sake, but the manu-
script by which they have come down to us, Bodleian MS. Don. c. 24, also
provides us with evidence for something we might only have guessed at be-
fore. The historically specific titles and marginal comments about people and
occasions give a fascinating insight into social literary practices, in ways that
open up the reading of many of the seemingly unlocated poems of the period.
There is now clear evidence, for instance, that a poem written "for" someone
might be a poem written on his or her behalf, rather than a poem written with
that person as primary audience. With this kind of evidence, what might be
in their own right interesting poems — because they are located within their
enabling milieu — become remarkable ones.

---

[75] "On his Majesty's Recovery from the small pocks. December 1632", [8], 31 gloss.

Textual Introduction

Manuscript sources

Bodleian MS. Don.c.24

Folio. [1–192 + iv + "193" + v + "194" + "195"] = 204 folios
323 x 210 mm.

The leaves are gathered as follows: 1–4, 5–6, 7–14, 15–22, 23–30, 31–38, 39–
44, 45, 52, 53–60, 61–68, 69–76, 77–84, 85–92, 93–100, 101–108, 109–116,
117–124, 125–132, 133–138, 139, 146, 147–154, 155–162, 163–168, 169–176,
177–184, 185–192.

Folios 1 and 1ᵛ *blank stub*; 2 *stub*, "Nicolas Oldisworth"; 2ᵛ *blank stub*; 3 "At Mʳ
Barker's Sale" "Margaret Man Her Book [Margaret Man Her Book Given Me By
My Dear Mother *all deleted*] Given Me By My Dear Mother." [*In pencil, in later
hand*: Phillipps MS 18123] "Mʳ Nicolas Oldisworth"; 3ᵛ *blank*; 4 *blank*; 4ᵛ *in
pencil*: "627," "Oldisworth's Poems, of Wooton under Edge Gloucestershire"; 5
*blank, though from here on, the book is ruled with left and right margins through-
out*; 5ᵛ "By Nicolas Oldisworth"; 6 [*in double ruled frame*] |A Recollection Of
Cer- | -taine Scattered | Poëms | [space] Written long since by an Vnder- |
-graduate, being one of the | students of Christchurch | in Oxford. | [space]
And now in the yeare 1644 trans- | -scribed by the author, and | dedicated to
his Wife. | [space] [rule *scored out*] | [space] When I was a child, I spake as |
a child, I understood as a | child, I thought as | a child: but when | I became
a | man, I putt | away chil- | -dish | things. | 1. Cor. xiii. 11 [rule *scored out*]; 6ᵛ
blank; fols. 7–77ᵛ; 78–92ᵛ The Chronicle of Europe in five Books [*incomplete*];
93 and 93ᵛ *blank*; 94–117 *recipes of Margaret Mann*; 117ᵛ *blank* (folio 98ᵛ, in-
verted, "These are for M<istress> Margery"). Oldisworth supplied pagination
(in parentheses) in the top outer corner of each page. The text is written in
Oldisworth's own large italic hand. The manuscript is bound in brown calf
over boards. There are remains of green ties on the outside of the front and
inside of the back cover.

Note: We do not know who inherited the MS. from Margaret Mann. It appears
as lot 627 in Thomas Thorpe's catalog for 1834, Part iv, n.276 99 (343–47). It

xlii   *Textual Introduction*

was sold for £5/14/6. The purchaser might have been Edmund Henry Barker of Thetford. A note on fol. 3 of MS. Don. c. 24 indicates that the manuscript was bought at Barker's sale. There is no indication of this in *A Catalogue of the extensive, useful, and singularly curious library of a well-known scholar* for the the the sales of 23 February and 1 June 1836, though the catalog of the second day's sale refers to many uncataloged items. The purchaser was probably Philip Bliss, at whose sale on 21 August 1585 it was sold as lot 165 for £10. The purchaser, one Thompson, was probably acting for Sir Thomas Phillipps. The manuscript appears as number 18123 in the Phillipps catalog (*The Phillipps Manuscripts: Catalogus Librorum in Bibliotheca D. Thomæ Phillipps, Bt, Impressum Typis Medio-Montanis 1837–1871* [London: The Holland Press, 1968]). In the dispersal of the Phillipps library it was sold on the sale of 19 June 1893 as lot 591 for seven guineas to one Dixon (see A. N. L. Munby's annotation to Bodleian 2591.b.1/3), and was resold on 24 April 1911 as lot 851 for £38 to Bertram Dobell. Subsequently, it was offered for sale in Colbeck, Radford & Co. catalogue no. 24 of June 1932 (item 142) for £125. It was bought by the Friends of the Bodleian for £90, and presented to the Library. The recipes copied by Margaret Mann into the manuscript should at some point be made available in the resources offered by the Perdita Project based at a Nottingham Trent University website. The manuscript is described in Mary Clapinson and T.D. Rogers, *Summary Catalogue of Post-Medieval Western Manuscripts in the Bodleian Library, Oxford*, 3 vols. (Oxford: Clarendon Press, 1991), 1:116, and by John Gouws, "Nicholas Oldisworth and MS. Don.c.24," *Bodleian Library Record* 15 (1995): 158–65.

Folger MS. V.a.170 *(formerly MS. 646.4)*

Octavo. [vi] + 37 + [i] + 226 + [x] = 280 folios
190 x 142 mm.

Folios 1–6 *missing*; 7–43 (pp. 13–86) *miscellaneous poems*; 44 (pp. 87–88) *missing*; 45–125^v (pp. 89–250) *miscellaneous poems*; 126–134^v (pp. 251–268) *blank*; 135–166^v (pp. 269–332 *poems of Nicholas Oldisworth*; 167 (p. 333) *incomplete poem in different hand*; 167^v–200^v (pp. 334–400) *blank*; 201–3 (pp. 401–5) "A Song: | Alas poor scholer"; 203^v–205 (pp. 406–9) "Poems upon Anne Green"; 205^v–270 (pp. 510–40) *blank*; 271–271^v (pp. 541–42), *stub*; 272–272^v (pp. 543–44) *torn leaf, being the remains of an index of poems*; [273–80], *stubs*. The manuscript has been ruled with margins throughout (including the stubs). Pagination is supplied in the top right hand of each recto. The manuscript is written in several hands. The section containing poems by Oldisworth is written in a single, large, italic hand. Given the presence of poems by William Strode, George Corbet, Brian Duppa, Ben Jonson, Jasper Mayne, George Morley, and John King, in addition to the substantial number of poems by Oldis-

Textual Introduction xliii

worth, this collection is likely to have been compiled by someone with Christ Church connections. The manuscript is bound in brown calf over boards.

Note. The manuscript was purchased from Bertram Dobell by Henry Clay Folger in 1915. It was described by Seymour de Ricci and W. J. Wilson, *Census of Medieval and Renaissance Manuscripts in the United States and Canada* (New York: H. W. Wilson, 1935), 1.332, and later by Peter Beal, *Index of English Literary Manuscripts*, vol. 2 (1625–1700), part 2 (London: Mansell, 1992), 356.

Other MSS

Bodleian Library, Oxford
    Ashmole 47
    Firth e. 4
    English poetical e. 97
British Library
    Harley 4955
    Harley 6918
    Sloane 396
Folger Shakespeare Library, Washington, D.C.
    V. a. 322
    V. a. 275
    V. a. 319
Rosenbach Museum and Library, Philadelphia
    Phillipps MS. 239/27 [Phillips MS. 9536]
    Rosenbach MS. 1083/17 [Phillipps MS. 8270]
Herny E. Huntington Library, San Marino, California
    HM 198 Part 1

Printed editions

Solis Britannici Perigæum. Sive Itinerantis Caroli Auspicatissima Periodus. Oxford, 1633 [STC 19033].
Vitis Carolinæ Gemma Altera sive Auspicatissima Ducis Eboracensis Genethliaca Decantata ad Vadaisidis. Oxford, 1633 [STC 19035].
Wit Restor'd. London, 1658. [Wing M1719].

The Present Text

My aim has been to produce, as far as possible, not a diplomatic transcript but a readable text of the poems based on Oldisworth's autograph presentation copy in Bodleian MS. Don. c. 24, and on Folger MS. V. a. 170, for those

xliv   *Textual Introduction*

poems not found in the holograph manuscript; and to provide in the critical apparatus for the autograph poems variant readings and passages found in the Folger and other manuscripts, and for the poems found only in the Folger manuscript a record of my editorial interventions.

Although it is not possible to replicate manuscript in print form, I have attempted to represent the spelling and layout of the originals as accurately as possible. In the interest of readability I have expanded all contractions and suspensions and brought the use of long "s," "i," "j," "u," and "v" into line with modern practice. Oldisworth has two ways of indicating emphasis. The first consists of slightly larger characters, with more space between the letters than usual. This I have rendered by italics. The second, usually reserved for proper nouns, consists of block capital and block small-capital letters, all densely inked. This I have rendered simply as capital and small-capital letters, since the use of bold type would be too intrusive. I have supplied line numbering for all poems longer than five lines, but in the interest of keeping the text as clear as possible I have not enclosed the line numbers in square brackets. I have not attempted to follow the lineation of Oldisworth's prose marginal glosses. Since I have chosen to produce neither a diplomatic transcript nor a facing-page transcription, I have not reproduced features which depend on whether the original is found on the recto or verso of a leaf. Thus glosses, which in Oldisworth's manuscript are always at the outer edge of the leaf (to the right of the poem on a recto, and to the left on a verso), have all been placed on the right. I have treated the seventeenth-century convention for representing quotation with inverted commas in the outer margin in the same way, placing all the quotation marks to the left of the text.

The poems in the original are not numbered, but for ease of reference I have supplied numbers in bold between square brackets. Oldisworth's pagination in Don. c. 24—in parenthesis in the top outer corner of each page—has not been followed because it is not consistent. Instead, I have supplied the foliation of the Bodleian Library in square brackets in the left-hand margin. Folger MS. V. a. 170 is paginated, and I have followed this.

The textual apparatus has been compiled in conformity with the principles set out above. The lemma from the source, rendered in italics, is closed with a square bracket, and the variant reading is then given, with the siglum for the manuscript or printed source from which it derives. In cases where variant readings are shared, the sigla of representatives are separated by commas. Should there be more than one variant reading, these are separated by a semicolon. When the state of the manuscript, or the position and nature of a variant is reported (for example, *gloss* or *end note*), the lemma is closed with a colon; variant readings are then given as usual. Variant readings have been treated in the same way as the reading text. Unless punctuation is the point at issue, it has not been registered in the lemma; final punctuation of variant read-

Textual Introduction   xlv

ings has also not been registered, though it has been assumed that the reader would supply the necessary changes.

Some notational forms in the textual apparatus require explanation. I have used parallel slashes, / /, to indicate that the enclosed material has been interlined. Square brackets, [ ], have been used to limit the scope of editorial comments rendered in italics where necessary. Where manuscript characters are unreadable because of damage or deletion, I have indicated this by enclosing a period mark per character, up to a maximum of three, between angle brackets, thus <. . .>.

BODLEIAN MS DON. C. 24: POEMS

A Recollection of Cer-
-taine Scattered
Poëms

Written long since by an Vnder-
-graduate, being one of the
students of Christchurch
in Oxford.

And now in the yeare 1644 trans-
-scribed by the author, and
dedicated to his Wife.

When I was a child, I spake as
a child, I understood as a
child, I thought as
a child: but when
I became a
man, I putt
away chil-
-dish
things.
1 . Cor. XIII. 11

[folio 7]

To his deare Wife, Mar-
-rie Oldisworth.

Sweet Mall
Wee two have now beene marryed five   5
yeares: and hitherto (praised bee God)
wee have wanted nothing, but Peace.
For my part, I thanke God for those
good dayes, which I have seene in my
youth: wherin I had Leisure to please   10
my owne fancie, and to write such Toyes,
as here doe follow. And I doubt not
but Thou also, in those very dayes,
hadst and didst enjoy thy faire virginlike
contentments; though I then was not   15
so happy, as to know either Them, or Thee.
Time was (Mall) when tabrets and pipes
were more respected, then drummes and
trumpets: which drummes and trumpets
were seldome heard in England, but at   20
a Masque, or at a Play. Time was, when
I could ride from Borton to London, both
without Companie, and without Danger,
and carry my Pockets full of Monie.
But now where is that Monie? My gold-   25
scales (thou knowest) lie uselesse and unemployed:
nor doe I see my Soveraigne's face in silver
at home much oftener, then I see his face
in flesh and blood in Oxford. Yet have I
spent as much, in Contributions and Free-   30
quarters, as would not onely have sett
mee out of debt, but have begunne compe-
tent Portions for thy two little daughters.
I pray god send us Patience: for, although
wee are likely to stand in Need of many   35
things, yet are wee likely to stand most
in Neede of Patience. So entreating thee
to bee of good Cheare, and not to trouble
or disquiet thy minde with the Feare

and expectation of those Evils, which per-   40
chance may never come; I rest

From Willington   Thy true Friend   This was written
1644. Febr: 17   Nicolas Oldisworth   in the time
                                                             of the Treaty
                                                             at Uxbridge
                                                             betweene the
                                                             king's side and
                                                             the Parliament's

BODLEIAN MS DON. C. 24: POEMS   7

[folio 8]

[1]

A Letter to Ben. Johnson. 1629.

Die Johnson: crosse not our Religion so,
As to bee thought immortall. Lett us know
Thou art a Man. Thy workes make us mistake
Thy person; and thy great Creations make
Us idol thee, and 'cause wee see thee doe
Eternall things, thinke Thee eternall too.
   Restore us to our Faith, and die. Thy doome
Will doe as much good, as the Fall of Rome,
'Twill crush an Heresie: wee n'er must hope
For truth, till two bee gone, Thou and the Pope: 10
And though wee are in danger, by thy Fall,

BA = Bodleian MS. Ashmole 47, fols. 107–8^v.
BF = Bodleian MS. Firth e. 4, pp. 104–5.
BE = Bodleian MS. Eng. poet. e. 97, pp. 147–48.
F$_2$ = Folger MS. V. a. 322, pp. 76–78.
H = Huntington MS. HM 198 Part 1, pp. 121–23.
N = British Library MS. Harley 4955, fols. 185–86 (The Newcastle Manuscript).
1658 = *Wit Restor'd*, ed. Sir John Mennes and James Smith (London, 1658), pp. 79–81.

Title: *A . . . Johnson*] To Master B. Jonson F$_2$; To Master Benn Johnson **H**.
           1629] *om.* **BA, BF, BE, F$_2$, H, 1658.**
1   *Die . . . crosse*] Did Johnson crosse, **BA.**
2   *to . . . immortall*] not to thinke thee Mortall **BE.**
3   *a Man*] no god **BA, BF, BE, F$_2$, H, N, 1658.**
4   *Creations*] creation **BA.**
6   *thinke*] thinkes **BA**
7   *doome*] Dom[<.> *scored out*]e **H.**
8   *Will*] 'Twill **BF.**
           doe] do us **BA.**
9   *an*] a[n *added later*] **N.**
10   *two*] thou **1658.**
           till . . . gone] tell tow begone **H.**
11   *wee*] I **BF.**
           are . . . by] may bee certayne in **BA, BF, BF, F$_2$, N, 1658**; may be most sure on **H.**

To loose our Witts, our Judgements (brains and all)
Wee are content thou shouldst besott us thus.
Better bee fooles, then superstitious.
    Die: to what Ende should wee thee now adore?
There is not Scholarship to reach to more.
Our Language is refin'd: Professours doubt
Their Greeke and Hebrew shall bee both putt out;
And wee, that Latine studyed have so long,
Shall now dispute, and write, in Johnson's tongue.   20
Nay, courtiers yeeld: and every beauteous wench
Had rather speake thy English, then her French.
And for our Mater! Nature stands agast,
Wondring to see her strength thus best at last;
Invention stoppes her course, and bidds the World
Looke for noe more: shee hath already hurld

---

12   *our . . . Judgements*] both witt and judgment **BA**, **1658**; our witt, our Judgement **BF**,
          H, **N**; our witt, Judgment: Yea **BE**.
13   *Wee . . . thus*] Though [Thou **1658**] sacke nor love nor time recover us **BA**, **BF**, **BE**,
          F$_2$, **H**, **N**, **1658**.
15   *to*] For to **F$_2$**, **H**.
        Ende] *om.* **BE**.
        should] shall **BA**.
        thee] *om.* **F$_2$**, **H**.
16   *not*] no **BF**.
        reach to] live to **BA**, **BE**, **F$_2$**, **H**, **N**, **1658**; live [*blank space*] **BF**.
17   *Our*] or **BA**.
18   *Their*] Our **BF**.
        shall . . . both] both shalbe **H**; both shall live **1658**.
        both putt] rooted **BF**.
19   *wee*] they **F$_2$**, **H**.
        that] who **BF**.
21   *courtiers*] courteours **F$_2$**.
        every] eke the *in later hand* **BF**.
22   *her*] thy **BF**.
23–32 *And . . . higher*] *om.* **BE**.
23   *And*] But **BA**, **BF**, **F$_2$**, **H**, **N**, **1658**.
        our] thy **BA**, **1658**.
        Nature] fancy **BA**, **F$_2$**, **H**, **N**, **1658**; fancies **BF**.
        stands] stand **BF**.
24   *Wondring*] Wondering **BA**.
        thus . . . at] to beat **BA**.

BODLEIAN MS DON. C. 24: POEMS   9

Her treasure all on one. Thou hast out-done
So much our Wish and Expectation,
That were it not for Thee, wee scarce had known
Fancie it selfe could ere so farre have gone.   30
Give lit'rature (a While) Leave to admire
How shee gott so high: shee can gett noe higher.

    Die: seemes it not enough, thy Writing's date
Is endlesse, but thine owne prolonged Fate
Must equall it? For shame, engrosse not Age,
But now, thy fifth Act's ended, leave the stage,
And lett us clappe. Wee know, the Stars, which doe
Give others one Life, give a Laureat two:
But thou, if thus thy Bodie long survives,
Hast two Eternities, and not two Lives.   40

    Die, for thine owne sake. Seest thou not, thy Praise
Is shortned meerly by this length of dayes?
Men may talke this, and that: to part the strife,

---

27   *on*] in **F**$_2$, **H**.

28   *Wish*] witt **BA**, **1658**.

29–32 *That . . . higher*] *om.* **BF**.

30   *Fancie . . . selfe*] Nature herselfe **BA**, **F**$_2$, **H**, **1658**; Nature it selfe **N**.

31   *lit'rature*] Poetry **F**$_2$, **N**, **H**.

31–2   *Give . . . higher*] *om.* **BA**, **1658**.

32   *can*] could **F**$_2$.

33   *Writing's*] verse's **BA**, **BF**, **BE**, **F**$_2$, **H**, **N**, **1658**.

34   *thine*] thy **BA**, **BF**.

36   *thy*] the **BA**, **BF**, **F**$_2$, **H**, **1658**.
       fifth] fift **BA**, **BE**, **BF**, **F**$_2$.
       Act's] act **BA**, **1658**.

37   *which*] that **BA**, **F**$_2$, **H**, **1658**.

38   *one Life*] two lives **BF**.
       give] gives **H**.
       two] too **BA**.

39   *thus*] thow **H**.

41   *thou*] tho **BA**.

42   *shortned meerly*] shortned only **BA**, **BE**, **F**, **F**$_2$, **H**, **N**, **1658**; only shortned **BF**.
                       this] thy **BE**.

43   *Men*] Man **BA**.
       talke] take **BF**.
       and] or **BA**.
       that: to] that to **F**$_2$.

If I may judge, thou hast noe fault, but Life.

Cold

[folio 8ᵛ]

Cold authors please best. Mee thinks, thy warm Breath
Casts a thick Mist before thy Worth: which, Death
Would quickly dissipate. If thou wouldst have
Thy baies to flourish, plant them on thy Grave.
Gold now is drosse, and Oracles are stuffe
With us: for why? thou art not low enough,   50
Wee still looke under thee: stoope, and submitt
Thy glorie to the Meanesse of our Witt.
The Rhodian colossus, ere it fell,
Could not bee scann'd nor measur'd halfe so well.
Art's length, Art's depth, Art's heighth can n'er be found,   55

---

44   *If . . . judge*] thy torment is **BA**; My tenant is **BF, BE, F, N**; My tene[n *del.*]t is **F₂**; my
        tenett is **H**; thy tenet is **1658**.
45   *Cold*] Old **1658**.
        please best] still speed **BA**; speed best **BF, BE, N, H**; speede[s *del.*] best **F₂**; do speed
        best **1658**.
        Mee..warm] thy wormye **BA**.
46   *casts*] cast **H**.
        Casts . . . Mist] Doth cast a miste **BE**.
        before] betwixt **1658**.
        Worth] workes **F₂, H**.
47   *wouldst*] wilt **BA, BF, BE, F₂, N**; will **H**.
48   *plant*] paint **BA**.
        thy] the **BA, BF**.
49   *now is*] is now **F₂, H**.
51–54   *Wee . . . well*] om. **BF**.
52   *Meanesse*] meanest **BA, 1658**.
54   *nor measur'd*] or levell'd **BE**; or measur'd **F₂**; or measured **H**.
        well.] well.
        Lie [by **BA**; Be **F₂, H**] level to our view, so shall wee [wee shall **BE**] see
        Our third and richest Universitye [**BA, BE, F₂, N, H, 1658**].
55   *Art's length . . . found*] The arts dimensions never can be found **BF**.
        length] height **BA**; lenght **F₂**.
        depth] length **BA**; heighth **1658**.
        heighth] depth **BA, 1658**; height **BE, F₂, H**.
        can] will **BE**.
        found] /found/ **F₂**.

BODLEIAN MS DON. C. 24: POEMS   11

Till thou art prostrate layd upon the ground.
Learning noe farther than thy Life extends:
With thee beganne all Art, with Thee it endes.

---

56   *Till*] tell **H**.
        art] lye **BF**.
        layd] streight **BA, BF**; stretch'd **BE, F₂, H, N, 1658**.
57   *Learning*] Lookeinge **BF**.
        farther] further **BF, F₂**.
58   *beganne*] begunne **BF**.
        Art] Arts **BF, 1658**.
        endes] ends [*attributed to* Nic Oldisworth **BE**; N. Oldisworth **F₂**, Nich: Oldisworth
        N]

[folio 9]

[2]

To his Friend beyond sea.

Friend: thinke not Time, or Winde, or Place,
Or Sea can hinder our Embrace.
Our purer Spirits still doe meete,
And through the aire, each other greete.
  Time, Place, Sea, Winde   5
  Are all combin'd
To make our absent Joyes more sweete.

Time onely knowes how to improve,
Not to blott out, or spoile, our Love;
Wee have noe Time, but what doth runne   10
Govern'd by Thee, more then the Sunne.
  Unlesse it bee
  In thoughts on Thee,
Wee never thinke, the day is donne.

Place doth not sunder, nor divide   15
Our hearts, but makes them stretch more wide.
Our passions, which before did lie
In prison, now abroad doe flie.
  The breadth of Place
  Gives Fancie space,   20
And setts our soules at liberty.

These verses were written 1629 to Master Richard Bacon, a hopefull Youth who was sometimes a scholar of Westminster schoole, where hee was generally praised and beloved. At last hee dyed in Travaile.

Sloane 396 = British Library Sloane MS. 396, fol. 4–4ᵛ.

TITLE: A letter to Master Clement Harby: att Rome **Sloane 396**
2 *Sea*] floud **Sloane 396**.
3 *purer . . . doe*] nobler partes, our souls still **Sloane 396**.
4 *through*] in **Sloane 396**.
13 *on*] of **Sloane 396**.
19 *breadth*] breath **Sloane 396**.
   Place] space **Sloane 396**.
20 *space*] place **Sloane 396**.

BODLEIAN MS DON. C. 24: POEMS

And all the Winde twixt us and Thee
Is but a puffing Agonie
Of sighs and Blasts which doe expire
From the vast depth of our Desire.   25
  And this is Winde
  Of such a kinde,
As onely blowes, not cooles the Fire.

Instead of Seas, our Land doth swimme
In brinish Teares upp to the brimme;   30
Teares, which nor rage, storme, nor complaine,
But waite Thee in a calmer Straine:
  That when thou please,
  Thou mayst with Ease
Take water, and come back againe.   35

---

24 *sighs*] sights **Sloane 396**.
25 *vast*] *om.* **Sloane 396**.
26 *And . . . Wind*] *repeated over page* **Sloane 396**.
29 *Seas*] floods **Sloane 396**.
31 *nor*] or **Sloane 396**.
35 *Take . . . back*] At Padua see thy freind **Sloane 396**.

[folio 9ᵛ]

[3]

On his seeing the Study
of Master Michaël Oldisworth.

Never, till now, I thought that unreadd Bookes
Could teach men Knowledge: but the onely Lookes
Of this place dart such Learning through mine eies,
That on a sodaine I am growne more wise.
Here dwells true Beauty; I had rather see   5
The lovely face of this faire Librarie,
Than all the White-hall ladies at a Play,
By their bright aspects turning Night to Day.
Lett handsome Women hate mee, if I finde
Ought in them, but what (in an higher kinde)   10
Adornes these paper'd shelves; doe men delight
In colours? see, not onley Redd and White,
But any other Hue: doe men stand on
Due symmetrie, and just proportion?
Angles and lines are drawne so rightly here,   15
As all the authors of Mathematiques were;
For my part, I can Want of nothing spie,
But onely of the courtship how to lie,
Dead friends indeed tell truth. You seldome have
Two hearts, or two Tongues, found in one man's grave.   20
     Those upper Volumes are the mouthes of God,
Holy and sharpe DÎvÎnes, whose very Nodde
Makes all the Devils tremble: these below
Are *Nature's* proude clerks, and pretend to know
What-ere is understood, felt, heard, or seene,   25
When (good-folkes!) they scarce know why Grasse is green.
On this side stand *Historians*, and on that
Stand *poëts*; both are liars, that is flatt,
Yet poëts are the better: for, they wrappe
Truth under tales; wheras Historians lappe   30
Tales under truth. Those there are wrangling fooles,
Drown'd in their owne Doubts, who have taught the schools
To contradict the Schooles, and made the Lawes
Oppose themselves in every second clause.
Take heed; here lurkes the plodding *Politick*,   35

Michael Oldisworth Esquier was once a fellow of Magdalen college in Oxford. afterward secretary to William earle of Penbroke, and last of all secretary to Philip earle of Penbroke and Montgomerie.

Naturall philosophers.

Controversie-writers.

BODLEIAN MS DON. C. 24: POEMS

Who loves to lett men blood, and is as quick
At killing, as hee next him, the *Physician*;
With whom the *Globist* and *Arithmetician*,
The *engineer*, and more (whose names alone
Puzzle some Readers) joyntly take their throne.   40
                                         But

[folio 10]

But how have I those two great Councelors mist,
The noble *Oratour* and *Moralist*,
Those two, which queene THEOLOGĩE so honor,
That they at ev'ry turne doe waite upon Her?
Yee spurres of Honesty, and twinnes of Fame,   45
Proceed as ye beginne: yee serve a Dame
Who your corrupt and grosse parts will refine,
And make you, like her selfe, pure and divine.
   Of all the Wonders in this Paradise
None pleaseth mee so much, as that Device   50
To keepe so many Workes of diverse tongues
In ranke and order: noe Affronts, noe Wrongs
Are offer'd, but as Brother does helpe Brother,
So these Bookes helpe and hold upp one another.
O that the Libraries in every Colledge   ·   55
Would hence learne to grow civill: on my knowledge
They are so wild and madd, that men are faine
To binde each Writer with a severall Chaine.

> Rhetorick
> and moral
> Philosophie
> are servants to
> Divinity.

[folio 10ᵛ]

[4]

On Complements.

And why to mee doe You stand bare,
Who so farre my superiour are?
Why doe you cringe, and duck? You knowe,   These verses
These duties I to You doe owe: were given to a
                                              Courtyer, 1630.
'Tis to usurpe, 'tis to doe Wrong,   5
To say, these acts to You belong.
But now the World is growne so base,
Wee cannot keepe our meanest Place;
Rich men become so niggardly,
They robbe the Poore of Poverty: 10
And great ones grudge that Wee possesse
Ev'n so much, as our Litlenesse.

BODLEIAN MS DON. C. 24: POEMS   17

[folio 11]

[5]

To his Friend beyond sea.

And dost thou live? Wee stand amaz'd, to reade
So rare a Flour transplanted is not dead.
If merchants wonder how a chrystall Glasse
From shore to shore uncrackt and safe can passe,
Or how a garden-streame so cleare can runne,   5
When it hath left the Fount, where it begunne,
What miracle art Thou, whose choiser frame
Through diverse parts of Europe holds the same?
Haile unexpected Worth: wee did not looke
For such true Life in a translated Booke.   10
    Nor like the Newes of any private fate,
But as some Blessing had befalne the State,
Wee noise thy Health; and joy to heare it told
Outlandish mines will nourish English gold.
    Doubtlesse the Earth, the Water, aire, and Fire   15
Have joyntly all agreed to keepe entire
Thy litle world. The earth will sooner finde
A grave to lodge her selfe, then prove unkinde
To bury Thee; The water, ere there want
Fresh droppes, to cherish such an hopefull Plant,   20
Will drowne the very sea: the angry Fire

F = Folger MS. V.a.170, pp. 286–87

Title: *To*] An answer / to F.
2   *transplanted*] transported F.
3   *chrystall*] *Venice* F.
12   *But as some*] [But as some *catchword*] But some F.
15   *aire*] [a *altered to* Ai]re F.
16   *all agreed*] made an oath F.
21   *sea*] seas F.
21   *Fire*] F[ir *over erasure*]e F.

Will burne the Fire; the dying Aire, expire.
Before so rich a Jewell shall bee lost,
Nature will putt her whole Free-hold to cost.

---

24   *cost*]   cost.

       Welcome now all mishapps. Enjoying thee
       Wee are content to loose both Calis and Ree.
       What is the price of thousand Subjectes lives
       Take one for: the Prince of youth survives.
       Wee are content to threaten, fight, and yeild,
       To give the Duch the sea, the French the field
       To take wrongs, and make leggs. wee are content
       At whome to undergoe this banishment
       Of missing thee Wee care not though our Soule
       Bee absent from us if we knowe tis whole. **F.**

BODLEIAN MS DON. C. 24: POEMS   19

[folio 11ᵛ]

[6]

To the right honorable, the
lord Haies, earle of Carlile, &c.

So joyes a rising Saint, when Angels tell
His soule, that shee is likely to doe well,
As I joy at the tidings of this Favour
Your honour shews my muse; You please to save Her,
When shee deserves nought else, but Hell and Death: 5
O lett it hold proportion, that my Breath
Bee alwaies spent in singing holy laies
To Your unmatcht and everlasting Praise.

F = Folger MS. V.a.170, p. 319

Title: *the lord Haies*] James F.
3   *I*] wee F.
4   *my*] our F.
6   *my*] our F.

[folio 11ᵛ]

[7]

To the right honorable his Patron.

My rebell Eares, I wondred what they meant,
　　They came and told mee, they would hear noe more;
To cutt them off mine Arme was fully bent:
　　What could they say, my mercie to implore?
Forsooth they were so full of Carlile's fame,　　　　　5
They would not harbour other Sounds for shame.

Mine eies, perceiving how mine Eares did scape,
　　Forbare to carry Errands to my Braine;
To teare them out, my Nailes did fiercely scrape:
　　What said mine Eies, to winne my grace againe?　　10
Forsooth when they had seene the heav'nly Lights
Of *Doncaster*, they scorn'd all earthly sights.

My soule tooke snuffe, that shee was thus bereft
　　Of two chiefe Senses, and away she went;
I overtooke Her, ere shee quite had left　　　　　15
　　My body, and demanded what shee meant.
She answer'd not, but fledd, and stay'd at Dover,
Till *Haies*, the great embassador went over.

Rob'd of my soule, I was about to kill
　　My selfe; yet with my selfe I spake a word:　　20
What is this *Doncaster*, *Haies*, and *Carlile*?
　　Forsooth hee is your meritorious Lord.
Then tooke I heed how I my selfe did wrong:
For, my selfe did to You, not mee, belong.

F = Folger MS. V.a.170, p. 328, *No variants.*

BODLEIAN MS DON. C. 24: POEMS   21

[folio 12]

[8]

On his Majesty's Recovery from
the small pocks. December 1632

Count me (vice-chanc'llour *Duppa*) or a traitour,   These verses
Or else a babe. Loe, I alone doe loyter,   were presented
                                                            to the king
And when my fellowes write, and print, and sing,   by Master
I so much say not, as God save the king.   Osbolston
    But (Sir) if you will know the Reason why   5   school-master
                                                            and prebend of
I am thus slack; the King's recoverie   Westminster.
Seemes to mee but a fable, and a trick,
    I doe not thinke, the King was ever sick.
Those markes, you talkt of, in his royall face,
Were signes of Health. You pitty'd his good case;   10
You wept 'cause hee was well, and were afrayd
Lest hee might to his Safety bee betrayd.
Which way could Hee, who Ryott shuns, and Ease,
Have fewell in him fitt for a disease?
They must be such men, as his subjects bee,   15
That gett the pocks, and not such men as Hee.

F = Folger MS. V.a.170, pp. 303–5.
FT = Folger MS. V.a .275 [George Turner Commonplace Book], pp. 87–88]*
R₁ = Rosenbach MS. 239/27 [Phillipps MS 9536], pp. 209–10
* Folger MS. V.a.275, which was used for the initial collation, has been misplaced. Colla-
tions have been re-checked against Film Fo. 4376.8.

Title: *Recovery*] late Recovery F, FT, R_1.
        December 1632] *om.* F, R_1.
1   *(vice-chanc'llour Duppa)*] *om.* FT
        gloss: *om.* F, FT, R_1.
3   *print*] praie FT.
4   *not*] *om.* F.
8   FT *does not indent.*
10   *signes*] markes F, FT, R_1.
        case] cease F.
11   *and were*] *om.* F.
13   *Which . . . shuns*] How could hee, who shunnes Ryott, lust F, FT.
16   *gett*] cach FT.

His heav'nly Bodie is so chast, so pure,
So like the spheares, that noe Corruption sure
Could pierce into it. Tell mee, who ere sawe
The sunne distemper'd? who ere found a flaw   20
In any Star's or Planet's constitution?
Who knewe the Moone ere send for a physician?
I feare, our Liege was wrong'd. I fear, his Stains
And spots, rose meerly from his people's braines.
If his dread Flesh could ere infected bee,   25
Why was it not infected then, when Hee
Travell'd through France and Spain? In those hott climes
Another would have caught both Plagues and Crimes,
But hee, like Gold which in the fire is tryed,
Came brighter from them, and more purifyed.   30
This makes his Queene so bold, and so secure:
Shee visits him, shee huggs him. She is sure,
Noe budd, which sprouts forth on her husband's Skinne,
Can ever guilty bee of such a sinne,
As ruine her yong Beauty. Shee dares kisse   35
The worst thing that grows there, what-ere it is.
O such a Ladie does excell a Crowne,

Queene Marie expressed marvailous true affection to the king, in the time of his sicknesse, though his disease was infectious.

---

17   *so pure*] and pure FT.
18   *spheares*] sp/h/eares F.
21   *any*] the F, FT.
     or] or the F; or in the FT.
23   *our*] [< . . . > *del.*] our FT.
24   *rose*] were R₁.
     braines] braine F.
25   *infected*] infeted F.
26   *infected*] infeted F.
27   *France . . . Spain*] Spaine and Fraunce FT.
     climes] Clyme FT.
29   *hee*] so FT.
     in] on FT.
30   *them*] thence FT.
31   **gloss** *om.* F, FT, R₁.
33   *Noe budd*] nothing FT.
     which] which [sp< . . . > *del.*] FT.
     on] of FT.
34   *Can ever*] Will ever [be of *del.*] F; Will ever R₁.
35   *As . . . kisse*] for with her young bewty shee dares kisse FT.
37   *does*] doth FT.

BODLEIAN MS DON. C. 24: POEMS 23

And putts great Britain, France, and Ireland down:
O such a Ladie sweeten's her Lord's Raigne,
Which else would bee a taske too full of paine. 40
                       'Tis

[folio 12ᵛ]

'Tis not his Scepter, which makes *Charles* a king,
'Tis not his throne, nor any such like thing:
'Tis first his princely Minde, and next his Wife
Who loves Him dearer, then shee loves her life.
    Well: if wee grant, the King was sick, yet Wee 45
Are certaine, he was from all perils free;
Death came not neare him. Hee indeed was fitt
For heav'n, but was not going thither yet.
God might have tooke him from us, I confesse;
And our Misdeedes doe still deserve noe lesse: 50
Yet in his Mercie, hee will onely wound us
With warre, or Famine, and not thus confound us.

---

38   *putts*] pulls **F.**
       Ireland] England **R**$_1$.
41   *'Tis*] it is **FT.**
43   *his*] him **FT.**
43   *Minde*] bloode **FT.**
44   *who*] which **FT, R**$_1$.
       dearer] better **FT.**
45   **FT** *does not indent.*
46   *he . . . perils*] from all perils hee was **FT.**
47   *Death . . . him*] Hee came not neare death **F, FT.**
50   *do*] *om.* **FT.**
       deserve] deserves **FT.**
52   *or*] and **F.**
       not] *om.* **F.**

Alas! what would become of every one,
If *Charles*, our wise and gentle Prince, were gone?
  Or had hee been as ill, as ill could bee,   55
Had hee been plainly dead; yet still should Wee
Hope that hee might bee rais'd again by Prayer.
Rather then loose Him, wee would n'er despaire
To worke a Miracle. True; Wonders cease,
But wonders, in such high affaires, as these, 60
Noe wonders are. When three Realms stand in danger
God were noe god, if god could prove a stranger.

---

54   *Charles*] he **F, FT, R**₁.

      gone]   gone

           [but god preseves him /I trust/ now and *all deleted*] ever will
           good god preserve him and keepe him from all ill
           and for thy mercye place him in Sion hill.
               In Regis Caroli reuale scentiam
           Comsoror Elizabet dilectum obijsse putaret
           fratrem, visa sibi est, bis viduata viro
           com soror Elizabet, delectum viuire sciret
           fratrem, visa sibi est, rursus habere virum
               Finis   **FT**

56   *should*] would **R**₁.

55–62 *Or . . . stranger*] *om.* **FT**.

[folio 13]

[9]

On a Seale of gold and pearles
sent him, for a token, by Master Mi-
chael Oldisworth.

Sir, had you sent mee Gold alone,
Or any single precious stone,
Although I could not love you better,
Yet I should more have beene your debtor;
Or had you sent mee, in a piece   5
Of horne, so well-cutt Armes as these
(Where three quick Lions shew such power
As they had newly left the Tower)
You were so farre from Injurie
That you had much ennobled mee: 10
But joyning all these Gifts in one,
Your bounty hath mee halfe undonne;
The scholars will not lett mee looke
Once in a twelve-month on a Booke,
All my whole Worke from Morne to night   15
Is to unboxe this wondrous Sight.
I have noe time to eate, or sleepe,
(Nay, I have scarcely time to weepe
For losse of Time) whilst I reveale
The miracles of this rich Seale.   20
What duke (sayes one) what Prince, what King,
Was hee, could spare so great a thing?
Sure, sure noe private man would spend
So much on an inferiour Friend;
Who sent it you? the king of France?   25
Or Spaine? or Sweeden? Or may chance
The pope to turne you traitor meant,
And for a Bribe this Jewell sent.
    Noe: there's an English Squire, whose Purse
(Large, as his Soule is) did disburse   30
The price of this; hee makes a toy
Such things as these, to give a Boy.
His open Handes (like Cupid's wings
When welcome Hee gladd tidings brings)

Claspe round my Heart and make it more   35
His owne, which was his owne before.
And know, though Pearles and Gold yee spie,
Vnless yee see them with my Eie,
Yee blindly skippe, and misse a Gemme,

                                        Which

[folio 13ᵛ]

Which setts a glosse on all of them;   40
A gemme, which came not from the East,
But onely from the Lover's breast.
    Long may hee live: and when his date
Of years is almost out, may fate
In name of Pity grant mee this,   45
To take from mine, and adde to his.

[folio 14]

[10]

In defence of a Girle, that
went holding downe her head.

Yee fooles, which meerly judge by outward Show,
Why bidd you Her looke upwards? Wise men knowe
Those folkes thrive most, who shew their faces least,
And plants without ambition prosper best:
The towring Cedar, and the haughty pine   5
Prove vaine, and barren; whilst the crumpled Vine
Yeelds such sweet juice, the gods mistake and thinke
'Tis nectar, 'tis their owne celestiall Drinke.
What grows (I pray) on Masts, or poles? give mee
Trees bending in the back; I love to see   10
Boughs crouch and kisse the Earth, as they made suit
To her, that shee would multiply their fruit.
Then doe Corn-masters chiefly like their Cropp,
When it stands nodding, and holds down its toppe.
The brasen founder is not thought-of well,   15
Vnlesse in dangling wise hee hangs his Bell.
And of two buckets, when there Water needes,
The falling one is alwaies hee, that speedes.
'Tis an ill Note of light Wares, if the Scale
Rises, and mounts aloft: you seldome shall   20
Finde any persons walke upright, and straite,
But youths, whose empty Brains are of noe weight;
Your wise old men, whose heads are full of skill,
Under their burden sinke, and grovle still.
  Submitt your selves, stiff necks: grow not too bold, 25
But humbly stoope, if you would Heav'n behold;
How quickly blinded are those Eies, which dare
Against the blazing Sunne directly stare?
Huntsmen praise none but that same kind of Hound,
Whose prostrat Nostrils skirre along the ground: 30
And maidens, skill'd in flowrs, delight to pluck
Noe sweetes so much, as those which bow and duck.
The streaming of a Banner pleaseth most,
When it flies low, and well-nigh licks the Dust:
Nor does it mis-become the Indian Figge   35

To droppe his head, and make his topmost twigge
Againe to take new roote; sure we might doe
Farre better, if Wee us'd the same trick too,
And quietly dispos'd our selves to gaze
Not on the giddy Skie, but on the Grasse.   40

                                        Believe

[folio 14ᵛ]

Believe it, Nature never did intend
That men, like spires, should still point-upp an ende;
Who can bee so ingratefull to the Earth
As (knowing Her to bee our place of birth)
To slight her, and encline another way?   45
Alas, good Mother! shee nor night, nor day,
Hides her face from us; and what pity 'twere
If wee, her sons, should hide our face from Her?

[folio 15]

[11]

The wordes of a Lover, speaking to the reflection of his Mistresses face in a Looking-glasse.

Stand still, bright Shadow; pompous Type, stand still:
One litle Jogge both Thee and mee may kill;
If thou enjoy thy Life, thou canst not live,
To move, is straight to die. those Sleights, which give
A grace to others, robb Thee of thy soule: 5
Prove not more lovely, lest thou prove more foule.
Guilty thou art of thine owne Death, if thou
Keep not that posture still, which thou keepst now;
And though thou shedd noe blood, yet dost thou sinne
In blotting of an image so divine.   10
O save thy life: or if thou needes wilt trie
What pretty kind of gambol 'tis to die,
Lett mee bee blam'd ('tis pity thou, so faire,
By any Staine thy purenesse shouldst impaire)
Lett mee thy Beauty drowne, and in a Storme   15
Of mingled Sighs and Tears, shipwrack thy forme:
How easy thou art to bee made away!
By breathing on thy shape I can thee slay;

These verses were made for Master Chandler of Colnrogers: when hee was suitor to her, who now is his wife.

F = Folger MS. V. a. 170, pp. 298–99

Title *Om.*] The Wordes of a Lover, speaking to F.
1   **gloss**: *om.* F.
4   *straight*] *om.* F.
       sleights] deft Sliyghts F.
5   *A grace*] Beautie F.
7   *Death*]: do[o *over* .]me F.
11   *life*] selfe F.
14   *thy*] her F.
       shouldst] should F.
15   *thy . . . drowne*] drowne thy Aspect F.
16   *sighs*] sights F.
18   *By*] With F.

Thou art more brittle than the very place
Wheron thou standst, thou art more frail than Glasse.   20
Such is Fate's spight, that what wee fancie most
Is still in greatest hazard to bee lost.
Ere thou goe out of print, ô Cupid's booke,
Teach and instruct mee how my Love doth look,
Shew mee her Smiles, her Frowns, her close Diguise,   25
Her tempting, languishing, imperious Eies;
Shew mee her purple Cheek, and ivory Brow,
Shew mee those things, which onely Thou dost know:
My mistris is reveal'd to Thee alone;
Noe colours can describe Her, but her owne.   30
Happy am I that (though her glorious Light
Dazzles mee) yet I can enjoy Thy sight;
I am content behind her back to stand
And humbly view Her at the second hand:
So mortals, when they dare not bee so bold   35
The sunne in his full splendour to behold,
Use water, and see clearer when they shun him,
Than when they plainly fixe their Eies upon him.
    Sodaine, and cruell! art thou fledd already?
Who could have thought, thy sweetnes was so heady?   40
Though shee (my Mistris) stormes, and like the Ocean
Roares when wee pray, and slights our best devotion,

[folio 15ᵛ]

Yet shouldst Thou bee more calme; Thou art a Child,
A child new-borne, whose part is to bee mild:
Thou canst nor goe, nor stand; thou hast noe tongue   45

---

20   *art*] [st *erased*]art F.
        than: <tha>n; the F.
27   *ivory*] candied F.
38   *Eies upon*] opticks on F.
39   *fledd*] gone F.
41   *(my . . . and*] bee rough, and forward F.
42   *Roares . . . devotion*]
            Which mocks our vowes, and with her giddy motion
            Floutes our fantastiquenesse, and loudly roares
            To jeare the Beadsman, which her ayde implores F.
45   *nor goe*] not goe F.

BODLEIAN MS DON. C. 24: POEMS   31

Either to offer, or returne, a Wrong.
But ô yee Gallants all bee warnd by mee
Flie womens Plotts: an handsom Dame (you see)
Though voyd of Sense, my Ruine would contrive,
And kill mee, though her selfe were scarce alive.   50
  Farewell, thou Hypocrite; thy specious Glosse
Shall never winne mee to bewaile thy losse:
Thou wert but a brave Nothing; or at most
Thou wert but a quick Shade, a living Ghost.

---

49   *Though*] thou F.
       voyd] v[y *altered to* o]yd F.
54   *but*] b F.
       Shade] spright F.

[folio 16]

[12]

On Shottover

If Oxford bee the kingdome's Eie,
This forrest then, which grows so high
Above the Universitie,
The kingdome's Eie-browe needs must bee.

[folio 16ᵛ]

[13]

To a Separatist, that spoiled mens tombes, and built his house with the tomb-stones.

But all this While I feare a spice of Pride:
Is not our Zelot stately, to provide
(So long before his death) this Tombe of tombes,
This house, which hath as many Graves, as Roomes?
   Speak true, in earnest speak; what was thy Plott   5
To raise newe *Golgothas*? thou needest not
Thy rebell Flesh with others Ghosts deterre;
Thy selfe art but a painted Sepulcher:
Or if thy Spirit for such strictnesse calls,
Goe mortifie thy members, not thy Walls.   10
Else, when the finall Morning shall appeare
That all the dead must wake, what uncouth Feare
Shall make thee start, and flie thou knowst not whither,
To see thy House and Thee arise together?
For so, when one shall want his knotty Chine,   15
Another cries, This ankle here is mine,
Thy walles will downe; and they with one accord
Will all disclose thy Thefts before the Lord:
Not how thou didst thy tedious Sermons steale
(When thou by often Snaffling didst conceale   20
Their author's style) but how thou stolest Men,
So that they scarce could find themselves agen.
   A base Exploit! enough to make us doubt
That men, if not the Piggs, will roote us out,
Though deeply layd; enough to make us turne   25
Our Christian buryall to a Pagan urne.

[folio 17]

[14]

An Ode

Husband, I would not have thee to conceive
    That thou art
    Next my Heart;
Thou art both yong and faire; yet by thy Leave
  There is a certaine Hee   5
  Who farre surpasses thee.

Thine eies indeed shew lively; but his are
    Thrice as bright
    As the Light:
And if to them I should the Sunne compare,   10
  The sunne it selfe were made
  Noe better then a Shade.

Thy tongue in some fewe Cases speaks with power,
    But his Word
    Is a Lord,   15
Which setts upp Beggars, and pulls Monarchs lower:
  Hee with his smallest Breath
  Can give or Life, or death.

Thine is an empty and a hollow Kisse;
    His embrace   20
    Fills with grace,
And yeelds a solid Joy, a constant Blisse:
  O that I forthwith might
  My selfe to Him unite.

Why ragest thou? Thou knowst, thy selfe saydst still   25
    Thou didst love
    Him, above
Thy wife; and yet I never tooke it ill.
  If thou wilt know, 'tis Hee
  That made both thee and mee.   30

BODLEIAN MS DON. C. 24: POEMS   35

[folio 17ᵛ]

[15]

To the University of
Cambridge. 1631.

Wee know thee not, nor have wee ever seene
Thy royall Palaces (thou mighty Queene)
But hearing Oxford laud thy reverend name,
Wee were acquainted with Thee in thy fame:
They say, thy Majesty is such another   5
As *Marie* was, a Virgin, though a Mother,
They say, Antiquitie doth not impaire
Thy constant Beauty, thou art old and faire,
They say, thou canst not die; of all thy Breede
There is noe heire that hopes thee to succeed,   10
But these are petty Miracles; they say
Thou hast rich Braines to spare and give away,
This strikes us home, so choise a thing is Witt
The heav'ns themselves will rarely part with it.
    Just three years since, thy *Trinity* brought forth 15   Master Richard
A babe, whose very Name did promise Worth   Bacon was of
(Bacon) a name which Viscounts wish to have   Trinity colledge
Sett first amongst the titles on their Grave;   in Cambridge.
Why dost thou muse, as though thou couldst forgett

F = Folger MS. V.a.170, pp. 293–97.

Title: 1631] *om.* F.
4   *fame*]   fame.
         And though our bodies may not yet behold
         Thy glorie face, to face: our Mindes are bold
         To honour thee by faith; and thinke it more
         Devotion to beleeve, then to adore. F.
7   *say*] /say/ F.
10   *succeed*] [exseede *del.*] succeede F.
13   *home*] [w *erased*] home F.
14   *heav'n*] godds F.
15   *three*] foure F.
         gloss: *om.* F.

Thy darling *Bacon*? *Bacon*, who doth yet   20
Refresh thy loynes, and makes thee proud that wee
Will thus acknowledge Him to spring from thee:
Hee was noe common Youth, that wears a gowne
To gadd about the streets and view the Towne,
That eates five Meals a day, and seldome looks   25
On any other but the Butler's bookes,
That sells his Penne and inke, that never writes
Except for Cloaths or Mony hee endites,
That studies chiefly how to coyne Excuses,
And heares noe Language but his owne Abuses;   30
Hee was a pattern to the meaner sort
How to dispose their Labour, Rest, and Sport,
And so farre onely every one did seeme
To follow Vertue, as they followed Him.
    Paying to Death the nightly Dues of sleepe,   35
Hee thought it honest Felonie, to keepe
Some minutes back; and so by stealth hee gott
More houres of life, than Nature did allott:
Marke him yee tissue Dames, and Ladds of plush
At whose late Sloth the Mornings use to blush,   40
Mark him, and hide your faces; hee was one
Which for his fine Composure stoopt to none,
                                                                              And

[folio 18]

And yet hee rose so early, that if You
Make two daies one day, hee made one day two.
    Knowing his duty to his heav'nly Lord   45
Hee humbly heark'ned to his sacred word,
And answer'd him againe with bended knees;
Not that hee dreamt, by such Designes as these,
To purchase Blisse, or scape the jawes of Hell:

---

26   *Butler's*] Buttry F.
28   *Except*] Unlesse F.
34   *they*] hee F.
37   *back*] backe [backe *del.*] F.
39   *yee*] you F.
        Dames] *om.* F.
42   *fine*] quaint F.
49   *the*] *om.* F.

BODLEIAN MS DON. C. 24: POEMS

Had there beene noe Reward for doing well,   50
Noe punishment for sinning, *Bacon* still
Would hold the same; his Conscience was his Will.
    Hee readd the Workes of *Plato*, and the rest
Not caring for the last men, but the best,
Authors are like greate Families, whose blood   55
As it is new, or old, is badd, or good.
His nimble Judgement could with Ease digest
Those lines, with which weake Stomachs were opprest,
And, by an Art to few yong writers knowne,
Convert another's mater to his owne,   60
So farre that Alchymists would oft admire
To see how Hee could, with his inbredd Fire,
Translate base Metalls, and distill a glasse
Of *Virgil's* gold from *Ennius* rusty brasse.
Yet as a Spider weaves the finest lawne   65
When meerly from her selfe the thred is drawn,
So hee wrought best alone; compar'd to Him
Bookes were but foolish, and all Lights were dimme.
Hee took great Heed still, not to sitt long at it,
Too much doth not instruct the Soule, but flatt it;   70
Nor would his innate Sweetnesse lett him stay
From visiting his Friend: hee must away
To see his absent selfe, and take a part
Of what-ere grew in his divided Heart;
Tell us, ô tell us, yee that had the grace   75
So pure an Angel daily to embrace,
Tell us the Heav'nlynesse of those Delights,

---

58   *with*] om. F.
59   *to*] two F.
62   *inbredd*] native F.
68   *Bookes . . . dimme*]
            Martiall was foolish, and the Sunne burnt dimme,
            The councells false, the Fathers all unsound.
            His owne authoritie was surest ground F.
69   *great . . . sitt*] heede alwayes how he sate F.
70   *Too*] Two F.
71   *innate*] inbredd F.
        stay] s[<. . .>*altered to* ta]y F.
72   *Friend*] friendes F.
75   *Tell . . . you*] Tell ô tell you F.

Wherwith hee fedd your Hearings, and your Sights.
Yee need not tell us how the Court loves Plaies,
Or how the King brookes Masques, ere since the days   80
When Lady *Bacon* acted, when each limbe
Spake, like a perfect Oratour, like Him;
The whole Land (if your Universitie
Bee not amisse esteem'd the kingdome's Eie)
The whole Land saw, and wond'red: this one boy   85
Was both, your stage's Envie, and its Joy.

    Cardes, shooting, tennis, bowling, dice, and Wine
Nor did hee much pursue, nor much decline;

                                  His

Yong Master Bacon acted a Lady's part before the king, with great applause.

[folio 18ᵛ]

His most Delight was in the games of France,
To ride with skill, to fence, to sing and dance: 90
In all hee pass't, and singly did each one
As if hee had beene borne for that alone;
Speak (Cambridge) has thou heard of any such
Amongst the bravest Spanish, French, or Dutch?
Noe: could once Leyden, Paris, or thy other   95
Sisters beyond sea, shew but such another,
They would upbrayd the World, as though the gemme
And phenix of Mankinde belongd to them.
How happy then art Thou, who art so full
Of treasure, that, while greedy Strangers pull   100

77–78   *Tell . . . Sights*]
        Tell us how Nectar tasted, how the Spheares
        Imprinted saintlike Musicke in your [? y *erased*] eares
        Or how Apollo lookt, when hee beganne
        To leave his godhead and become a man **F**.
80   *the . . . brookes*] Charles favors **F**.
81   **gloss**: *om*. **F**.
82   *perfect*] perfete **F**.
83   *your*] you **F**.
85–86   *this . . . Joy*]   And yor stage
        For one boys sake from age shall raigne to age **F**.
90   *with skill*] to swimme **F**.
        to fence] [*and altered to* to] fence **F**.
93   *Speak . . . such*] Speake, speake (dread princesse) Didst thou ere find such **F**.
100   *while*] whilst **F**.

BODLEIAN MS DON. C. 24: POEMS

This jewell from thy breast, thou mournst noe more
Then great *Carlile* (when legat hee goes ore)
Mourns for a talent, which hee spends, to grace
His king and country, in a forraigne place.
Wee gratulate thy Store, and wish thee still   105
Such starrs to scatter and bestow at will;
Yet rather then outlandish Foes shall gaine
By thy Expense of Light, if ere againe
Thou dropst a Planet, tell Rome 'tis bespoken,
And send it hither, preethe, for a Token: 110
Thy dearest Oxford, though shee hath to spare
Of her owne Lampes, with Thee will gladly share.

        In answer to these Verses, Master Vincent,
a noted Divine of Trinity college, who
had beene Bacon's tutour, wrote mee an
epistle, or Latine letter; wherin speaking
of his said pupill, hee used these wordes:
"fuit quidem in illo juvene summa quaedam
"animi lubentia, cum externo corporis decore
"conjuncta, quâ omnium oculos atque affectus
"ad se facile pelliciebat; fuit ingenium
"versatile et acutum, doctrina non vulgaris, &c

---

103   *Mourns*] Mo/u/rnes F.
End note: *om.* F.

[folio 19]

[16]

On a painted Houre-glasse.

The sand here never runs, nor thwarts your Will;
But here (as you would have it) Time stands still.

BODLEIAN MS DON. C. 24: POEMS   41

[folio 19^v]

[17]

To Sir Edward Hungerford
of Cosham

When I behold how numberlesse, how holy,
How wise, how constant, how submisse and lowly
They are, who serve you, Sir: mee thinks, your Traine
Is the Church militant. Yet straight againe
When I behold their Happynesse, and blisse,
Mee thinks, your Traine the Church triumphant is.

For these Verses
I was largely
rewarded with
gold.

F = Folger MS. V.a.170, p. 281

Title: *of Cosham*] *om*. F.
1   **gloss**: *om*. F.

[folio 20]

[18]

To the lady *Hungerford* of Cos
-ham, December 28 1632.

O strange! Till I came hither
I knew not (Madam) whither
   This whole last Yeare was gone:
But now its Quarters I
All foure in You can spie,   5
   In you, and you alone.

Its tributary Spring
Flowrs white and redd doeth bring
   To your Cheekes, to your Browe:
The lilly and the Rose,   10
Should they compare with those,
   Would blush, and pale would growe.

Its winter thinkes it good
To coole and purge your blood
   Hence 'tis, you are so chast: 15
And on your dainty Handes
In flakes of Snow it standes,
   Whence faire and white they last.

Its autumne brave things breedes
From out of those choise Seedes,   20
Which in You doe abound:
You are so deeply blest,
You bring forth Fruites, the best
   That can on earth bee found.

F = Folger MS. V.a.170, pp. 280–81

Title: *of Cosham*] at Cosham F.
8   *doeth*] does F.
16–17 *And . . . standes*]   And farther, it spreads Snowe
                            On all your partes belowe F.

BODLEIAN MS DON. C. 24: POEMS

I had almost forgot   25
Its summer; which keepes hott
    Your charity, and Love:
Which though it blossome here,
Yet is it rooted there,
    Where dwells all Joy, above.   30

Thus (Madam) to our Losse
The old Yeare you engrosse:
    But if you prove so kinde
As now to lett mee goe,
Within fewe dayes, I know,   35
    I shall a newe Yeare finde.

---

28   *blossome*] blossomes F.

[folio 20ᵛ]

[19]

On Heraldry

A viscount, proude of his late-purchas'd Coate,
Compar'd it with a Lord's of ancient note:
Mine are the better Armes (sayes hee) 'Tis true,
Answer'd the Lord, for why? yours are more newe.
Says hee, Your coat is plaine, and not so stor'd   5
With trimmings, as is mine: to which the Lord,
Had I beene present, when my Coate was made,
As you, when yours, a finer I had hadd.
Saies hee, yours? what ist worth? The lord replies,
'Tis worth just nothing, I can sett noe price,   10
Noe man will buy my Coate, it is so old:
But yours for thirty pounds the Herald sold.
My armes (saies hee) are perfect and complete:
Noe (quoth the Lord) you are not well-arm'd yet:
For, since a Coat like *Archy's* coat, you beare,   15
You should a Cappe of the same making weare.

[folio 21]

[20]

To Mistris E.W.

So proud, and yet so sluttish? Fie for shame:
And yet I cannot count you much too blame.
Partly for my sake, partly for your owne
You doe well, not to bee too nearly knowne.
It were the way for both of us to die,   5
If either of us should approach too nigh;
For, should I once but touch you, I might wonder
Did not your rotten Flesh straight fall assunder:
And should you once but breath on mee, I think
Forthwith I should be poison'd with your Stink.   10
Goe then, bee haughty still: for why? I know
'Tis for pure Neede, not State, that you are so.

These verses
were made for
Mistris K.B. who
was at enmity
with Mistris
E.W.

[folio 21ᵛ]

[21]

The nobleman's Wooing.

Welcome, thou totall summe of earthly Blisse:
    Wealth's mint-house, Pleasure's garden, Honour's throne.
What-ere wee mortals wish for, loe! here 'tis.
    Welcome, ô welcome all good things in one.
Thou dost the Universe of Joyes containe.   5
More happynesse is but the same againe.

What need wee look for brightnesse in the Skies?
    Or in the Musick of the sphears rejoyce?
Behold, two thousand Sunnes in thy cleare Eies:
    Nor is there Harmonie, but in thy Voice.   10
Would men delight their Touch, their Tast, their Smell?
They cannot doe it els-where halfe so well.

Plenty of Gold lies mingled with thy Haire.
    From thy sweet Drops of sweat, pearls trickle down.
Thy cheekes and Browe engrosse what-ere is faire.   15
    Thy height of Majesty is in thy Crowne.
And by the Rules of thy authentick braine
Dukes, kings, and Emperours may square their Raign.

Yet nor thy golden Haire, not heav'nly face,
    Nor pearly Sweat, nor any outward part,   20
Is that same thing, which I would faine embrace.
    I care for nothing of Thee, but thy Heart.
So I fast Hold may take within thy breast,
I am content to lett goe all the rest.

---

15 *Browe*: Browe[s *erased*]

[folio 22]

[22]

The country-gentleman's Wooing

My dearest, if thou wilt agree
To come for ay, and live with mee,
True ease and Quiet thou shalt finde
Both in thy body, and thy minde.
 Greene plaines, cleare Springs, and shady Groves   5
Shall yeeld thee what thy yong Sense loves,
Nor will wee lack or Mounts or Bowers,
Or birdes, beasts, fishes, fruits, or flowers.
The wanton Eccho shall rejoyce
To answer thy harmonious voice;   10
And to the Honour of the Spring
Sweete layes the Nightingale shall sing.
Our linnen shall bee fresh. Our foode
Shall common bee, and yet bee good:
Nor are the dearest Meates the best,   15
'Tis mirth, not Cost, which makes a Feast.
At my house is not shedd a teare,
Or blown a Sigh, through all the Yeare.
Our neighbours frankly shall come in,
To break newe Jeasts, and drinke old Wine.   20
For foule daies, Cardes and dice; for faire
The foxe, the partridge, or the Hare.
The scaly tenants of the Brooke
Noe sooner on thy face shall looke,
But they will leap upp, and take pride   25
To die, and dangle by thy side.
 Come, preethee, come: come, lett us sitt
With close, though chast Embracements knitt.
'Tis merry Griefe, and joyfull Anguish,
In such unspotted armes to languish.   30
If any thing thou chance to spie
Of mine, which doth delight thy Eie,
Make bold; and thinke, those goods which thine are,
Not to bee so much thine, as mine are.
 Ahah! and doe I see thee here?   35
Now chear upp, sweete. What can we feare,

When our chiefe Study is to play,
And all our Life is holy-day?
Noe thought shall now molest my Heart,
But this, that Wee must one day part.   40
And then too I resolve to have
If not thy Death, at least thy Grave;
That meeting wee may, after this,
Joyne soules againe in eldlesse Blisse.

[folio 22ᵛ]

[23]

To his Cosin, Mistris Dorothie Litcott.

Sweetest, if you believe your Glasse, and mee,
Mongst all the English nymphs you cannot see
One fairer then your selfe. Your radiant Eies
Shine so, that they doe oft prevent the skies,
And save the Sun a labour; by their Light   5
Making it midd-day in the midst of night.
Your haire, if you amongst some Skaines of gold
Should place it with a merchant to bee sold,
The buyer doubtlesse would not onely chuse
This rare sort, and those common kindes refuse,   10
But hee would sett an higher price, and bidd
More coyne for this, as for the finer threed.
Marke how the Roses frett, and blush for shame,
That you should robb them of their publick fame,
Whilst purer Clarett through your cheeks is spredd   15
Then their most fresh, most sweet, most gorgeous Redd;
Mee thinks, I heare them scold, and aske the gods
What reason Nature hadd, to make such oddes
Betweene the crimson in a Virgin's face
And in their Leaves: and more, to back their case   20
They urge that they straight fade, when You are yong
And likely to enjoy your Beauty long.
The lillies are the wisest flowrs, that bee;
For, they hang down their heads, and will not see
The whitenesse of your skinne, for fear lest they   25
For envie might grow pale, and pine away.
    Trust mee (bright Creature) though the rest of You
Is not expos'd to any mortal's View,
But lies hidd, and lockt upp; yet this I may
Without suspicion of a Flatterer say,   30
Your soule is richly sheath'd: she could not have
An outside of more value, though shee gave
Her selfe, her precious selfe, to purchase it:
O that court-Ladies had but so much Witt
As musing on your Lustre, to deplore   35
Their want of feature, and bee proud noe more.
    Alas, why must wee alwais misse the Sight

Mistris Dorothie
Litcott, eldest
daughter to Sir
John Litcott of
Molesey, is now
marryed to the
onely sonne of
the rich Sir John
Offly.

Of your cleane Soule? such a good pattern might
Reforme our Lives, and make the World beginne
To think how base 'tis still to sleepe in Sinne.   40
                                        Well,

[folio 23]

Well, yet in spight of Fate, wee can descrie
Some litle glimpse of your minde, through your Eie,
The chrystall of whose casement is so cleare,
That through it diverse Vertues doe appeare,
But those so new, and of so high a kinde,   45
That wee for them noe Names invented finde.
Much goodnesse too wee can in You perceive
By that Perfume, which in the Aire you leave,
When you breath fasting: one Kisse (oh, one Kisse)
Is worth an ocean of celestiall blisse.   50
And if I sayd that your whole Body were
Transparent, and translucent, like a Spheare,
Through which the Stars are seene, I said but true;
Or if that silken Flesh, which covers you,
I should compare to some perspicuous Veile,   55
My illustration would not wholly faile.
Not wholly faile? take water, Ice, and Glasse,
Your through-light Body shall all three surpasse;
Your body is so nothing grosse, or foule,
It seemes noe Body, but a second Soule.   60

BODLEIAN MS DON. C. 24: POEMS

[folio 23ᵛ]

[24]

On an uggly Wench.

Know you mine hostesse? shee's the Queen of slutts,
And rules the stinking route of female gutts.
The tallow, which night-walking Birders lappe
In raggs, resembles Her, when shee doth wrappe
Her fatt sides in foule linnen; and the Heat   5
Which melts that Candle, lookes just like her sweat.
Cutt-off the stumpe of a black Horse's taile,
Dipp it in slimy Mudd and rotten Oyle,
Then the short Hair about the raw Flesh spreade,
And there's the type of her bald greazy Head.   10
By noe description you can better know
The length and heighth of her distorted Brow,
Then by conceiving how it bears that shape
Which her mouth bears when shee vouchsafes to gape.
Yet one thing wee praise in her: if shee heares   15
Ill, or amisse, 'tis noe fault of her Eares,
For they are wide enough, and full as bigge
As you can find in any well-grown Pigge.
Nor does her Snoute lack measure: some have thought
Her nostrils were by some newe tradesman wrought,   20
They looke so like the Sheath of those redd tweezers,
Which hold a comb, a bodkin, glasse, and cizers.
Her litle Eies lie hidd, and darkened bee
Within her braines, as they were loath to see
Their owner's ghastlynesse. Who-ever seekes   25
To view the vallies of her hollow Cheekes,
Must not doe all at once: but first beginne
To climbe the promontorie of her Chinne,
Then standing on the isthmus of her tongue,
Which hangs from out her chaps (it is so long)   30
Hee must runne upp her Lippes, and thence descrie
Those pitts and quarries of deformitie.
But woe to him, who dares approach so neare her;
Doggs shunne her noisome Breath, and Beggars fear Her
Worse than the pestilence: she seldome lights   35
On any Orchard, but the fruit she blights;
And in the Morn, when shee her Breakfast takes,

Her breath doth turne it to a very Jakes.
    If the great Knobbs on camels backs amaze us,
Or the two partes of that cleft hill *Parnassus*,   40
What doe her Shoulders? to which those two partes
                         Are

[folio 24]

Are but as wennes, and those knobbs but as wartes.
Wee thank her, that shee hides her botchy Thighes,
And that vast paunch where all her garbidge lies,
'Tis well done of her, alwaies to conceale them;   45
For, should shee once (in some wild mood) reveal them,
The strongest and most healthy stander by
Through queazynesse would straight fall sick, and die.

BODLEIAN MS DON. C. 24: POEMS 53

[folio 24v]

[25]

A sonnet, played by a Musician
at my Entertaining of Master *Michael Oldisworth.*

Come Vertue, Honour, Wealth and Pleasure
   Helpe mee to entertaine my friend;
For, I and Nature, all our treasure
   Upon him, are agreed to spend:
     There, where noe Kindnesse can bee lost   5
     Wee erre, if wee spare any Cost.

Come active Wisdome, and array
   His minde with such translucent grace,
That his internall Beauty may
   Surpasse the splendour of his face;   10
     Then, when the Bodie is not foule,
     'Tis easy to refine the Soule.

Yee trumpets of Renowne and Fame,
   Come, keepe his ayery part from death,
Perfume the Windes, and spread his name   15
   Where ever any Mouth drawes breath;
     If none were farther known, than hee
     Sure goodnesse would more frequent bee.

F = Folger MS. V.a.170, pp. 308–10

Title:	*played . . . Oldisworth*] *om.* F.
2	*to*] *om.* F.
4	*Upon*] on F.
5	*noe Kindnesse*] nothing F.
9	*internall*] inward F.
11	*Then*] *om.* F
15	*name*] fame F.
17	*farther*] *om.* F.
	than] but such as F.
18	*Sure*] *om.* F.

Straight, in an unexpected fleete
    Lett the chiefe metals of the West   20
With the chiefe Easterne jewels meete,
    And both consent to make him blest;
    The quintessence of Sea and Land
    May joy to bee at his Command.

Fresh colours, and harmonious Soundes,   25
    Ravish his Hearing, and his Sight;
Sweete Tasts and Smells, observe noe boundes
    In pleasing him with choise Delight:
    By the best partes of humane blisse
    Lett him halfe know what Heaven is.   30

Why stand yee still, yee precious things?
    'Tis true, yee have a lawfull plea,
Who-ere to Him such Presents brings
    But carries Water to the Sea:
    'Tis idle Bounty to adde more   35
    To them that have enough before.

---

19   *Straight*] *om.* F.
20   *chiefe*] *om.* F.
21   *chiefe*] *om.* F.
22   *both consent*] conspire F.
26   *Ravish*] Feed F.
28   *pleasing*] flattring F.
29   *partes*] *om.* F.
30   *halfe know*] guesse F.
33   *Who-ere*] Who F.
34   *But*] *om.* F.
35   *idle*] needlesse F.
36   *To . . . have*] Where there was F.

[folio 25]

[26]

On my loosing my way

Have you seene fairies dance the Ring? or clowns
Besiege a May-pole in your country-townes?
Have you seene Badgers fetch a circling race,
Or giddy Seas the wanton Iles embrace?
So doe I wheele; and compassing the ground   5
Of three miles long, I make nine hundred round.
Some think, the Earth is call'd a Center thence,
'Cause 'tis the point of my circumference;
Some think, the fable of the wandring Jewe
In mee is not unlikely to prove true.   10
My courser, as fantastique as the Winde,
Observes noe boundes; and where hee cannot find
A path, he makes one: like the Lampes above,
Which hertofore durst never gadd nor rove,
But rode still on, and kept the *milken way*,   15
Wheras of late the greatest part doe stray.
   Noe wonder, if the Sheapards (viewing mee)
Beginne to erre in their Astronomie,
And thinking None but Planets can be hurld
So oft, as I am, round about the world,   20
Encrease the number of the Orbes of heaven,
And say, the reeling Sphears are more than seven.
Rather I marvaile at the pride of *Drake*
Who dreamt Noe mortall ere would undertake
To follow him or clipp so vast a ball.   25
My selfe dare fitt a girdle to this All,
Single I dare doe, what hee did with power;
Hee ventur'd once, I venture every houre.
Could I but have his Comming home, and enter

F = Folger MS. V.a.170, pp. 319–20

Title: *my loosing my*] his loosing his F.
23   *Drake*] Darke F.
26   *selfe*] life F.

My port with him, as well as I can venture,   30
Did I not (like the Sun) transgresse my line,
I would scorne *Drake*; but now, though I decline
And rise againe, though upp and downe I bend
I draw noe nearer to my journey's ende:
    I runne a bootlesse Maze; and whirling so   35
I stand-still faster than most men doe goe.

---

32   *would . . . Drake*] should schorne Darke F.

[folio 25ᵛ]

[27]

To a Lady, on her
walking abroad.

Faire Madam: since the World begunne,
    Till you did shew the grace
    Of your celestial face,
More n'er was seene than one bare Sunne.
But now, when You abroad shine cleare,   5
    And by your two bright Eies
    Adde splendour to the skies,
Behold, three sunnes at once appeare.

[folio 26]

[28]

To the worshipfull, his honoured Cosin, Mistris *Susan Oldisworth*: upon her Removall from *London* to *Thisselworth*.

Cosin, whilst You were one of London-people,
To whom *Paul* stands bare, and holds off his steeple,
Whilst you kept Court at that luxurious Lane,
Where most, besides Saint *Martin*, are profane;   St Martin's lane,
My country Penne would alwaies shun the City,   5   neare Charing-
For feare to make the Aldermen too witty: crosse
But now, since you beginne to take your Rest,
And (like the Sunne) to settle in the West,
Since you have taught the Lords to carry forth
London, and beare it downe to *Thisselworth*,   10   Thissel-worth,
My feather'd Quill shall flie at your Command,   which other-
And tire his wings, to lett you understand   wise is written
How much I joy to hear you grown so wise,   Isleworth,
As thus to chandge *Hell* for a *Paradise*.   stands west
                                                         from London,
   O that some God would grant me but a Chaire   15   and not farre
Fixt in the lower region of the aire,   from Brainford.
To sitt a While, and see those Soules tormented
Which have not done like You, turn'd and repented.
Damn'd to their narrow Stoves, they live so hott,
They melt and stew, like collops in a pott;   20
Eight or nine Housholds sojourn on the stall

F = Folger MS. V.a.170, pp. 269–77

Title: To . . . *Thisselworth*] To his honoured Cosen | Mistris Oldisworth F.
1   *London-people*] that huge people F.
3   *luxurious*] triumphant F.
4   **gloss**: *om.* F.
10   **gloss**: *om.* F.
13   *I joy*] hee joyes F.
14   *chandge*] cha[d *altered to* n]ge F.
17   *those*] the F.
20   *collops*] fatt Geese F.

BODLEIAN MS DON. C. 24: POEMS   59

Of one Shoppe, whence they oft would catch a Fall,
Did not the knaves, which cobble shooes below,
Support the sinking boards, and save the Blow.
There is scarce left space for a Dogg at doore,   25
Their porches are so throng'd with swarms of poor:
Their bedds creep into benches: and there they
Doe lie all night, where they have sate all day.
Seldome they stir forth, but they take some Harm:
They have not room to move a legge or arme;   30
Their subtile Coach-men have an yearly pension
Of gawdy cloaths, for that profound invention
To drive foure Horses through a needle's eie,
Which whoso does not, never gan goe by.
    For nought, but for to sweat, their Doctors send   35
Sick folks to church. The preacher, to ascend
Into his pulpitt, is constraind to tread
On this man's shoulder, and the next man's head;
When hee is safe, hee need pray for the rest
That none of such A crowd to death bee prest.   40
Mankinde standes here (noe fewer then Mankinde)
                                      So

[folio 26ᵛ]

So thick together, that you sometimes finde
(O strange!) men falling not, although they sowne,
Men walking, though they never touch the ground.
When sacred *Holsworth* with his Eloquence   45   Doctor Richard
                                                                        Holsworth a
                                                                        famous preacher
                                                                        in London.

---

23   *shooes*] shoo[e *over* w]s F.
29   *Seldome . . . Harm*] They quarrell oft, but nere take any harme F.
30   *move . . . or*] fight, or move an F.
34   *Which . . . by*] And squize a Chariot supernaturally F.
35   *Doctors*] Doctour F.
39   *When . . . hee*] Now (he is safe) hee F.
41   *standes*] is F.
42   *you sometimes*] sometimes you F.
43   **gloss**: *om.* F.
44   *Men*] O strange! men F.
        never . . . the] touch not F.

Captives their soules, and charms their docil sense,
They all are joyn'd so closely, every one
May to his fellowes say, Bone of my bone;
The whole Throng seemeth but one man-and-wife:
There you, by stifling, soone may lose your Life.   50
Oh, who can count that Town a Dwelling fitt,
Where ev'n the churches Murther doe committ?
 You know the vast and metropolitan Gutt,   London
Which cookes doe name *Tom Thumb*: in that are putt   described.
Blood, grots, hearbs, salt, and Droppings of the nose,   55
And all most rudely mixt, and thrust most close;
Such is this monstrous Heape of villages,
Where you shall find Nobility, and Riches,
Vertue, Witt, Basenesse, drawn together in,
And pent-upp with a Wall of pudding-skinne.   60
Yee happy Birdes, who in this pinching age
Enjoy so large a Prison, as a Cage,
Rejoyce and sing: what Londoners call free   Free men of the
Is bondage, compar'd to your Libertie.   City.
 Yet out they gett sometimes, to suck-in Death,   65

46–52 *Captives . . . committt*]
    Rowzes your soule, and wakes your heavy sence
    When each worde, when each Gesture saves a life;
    Marke if some Husbands cleave not to theyr wife;
    Some children to their Dad, so close that one:
    May sweare, Flesh of his Flesh, Bone of his bone. 5
    Marke if there leane not many hundreds more
    Against the windowes, listning without doore,
    Then diverse Clearkes, farre richer, and more garish
    At any solemne Wake, have in their parish. F.
53 *know the*] see that F.
  gloss: *om.* F.
54 *Which . . . that*] (Maydes christen it Tome Thumbe) wherin F.
56 *most rudely*] so justly F.
  most] so F.
  close;]   close,
  That none can stirre, or wagge out of his border,
  But even in confusion there is order?F.
60 *pent-upp*] blockt-up F.
63 *what . . . call*] That which the Towne calls F.
  gloss: *om.* F.

BODLEIAN MS DON. C. 24: POEMS

Halfe-smoak, half Plague, instead of wholsom breath,
And smell such Stinks, as rose-upp from the mudd
When heav'n had washt the Earth's face with a Flood;
This breedes that dulnesse in their rotten braines,
To complement still in the self-same Straynes,   70
This makes the formall shaking of their breech
Bee ever the best part in all their Speech.
They are with Frownes outlookt by those they meet,
And tost, like foot-bals, through the clownish Street;
They all were swordes, and on their guard they stand,   75
As each man were within his enemy's Land:
Noe mirth, unlesse you pray them suppe, or dine,
Two litle Smiles will cost three Quarts of wine,
They sell their very Jeasts, and make you pay
For laughing at the folly of a Play;   80
Once I remember, going through the Court,
Whilst reeling *Mulsack* made the Pages sport,   Mulsack the
His boy in earnest askt mee halfe a crowne   chimney-
For seeing of his Master tumble downe.   sweeper of
    Quite founder'd and bejaded on the stones,   85   White-hall.
                                           They

[folio 27]

They take boat, to refresh their weary bones,
Where they bind Salves on their soar feet, to draw
The rankled blood, which festers and growes rawe.

---

66   *instead . . . wholsom*] halfe dust instead of F.
68   *heav'n*] God F.
73   *with*] by F.
74   *foot-bals*] Footeba[l *over* a]ls F.
75   *were*] weare F.
         swordes] tooles F.
76   *As . . . Land*] As if each man came from a severall land F.
78   *wine*] wines F.
82   **gloss**: *om.* F.
84   *tumble*] tumbling F.
87   *they bind*] binding F.
         soar] so[ar *over erasure*]e F.
88   *rawe*]   rawe
         They heare these kindes of Jeares from those that passe
         Yee cast your shooes, yee neede bee turnd to grasse F.

Landing, they faine would sleep: but whooping Boyes,
Cartes, cries and hammers keepe such Bedlam-noise,   90
Ghosts are disturbd, and deafe Eares under ground
Before their houre expect the last Trumpe's sound:
Take heed, my heires (I charge you) when I die,
Take heed lest I in Reach of Bow-bell lie,
Rather enclose mee in a chest of lead   95
And throw mee in the sea when I am dead,
That *Drake* and I may hugg and burst with laughter
To hear the Land roare louder then the Water.
   Fie on this haughty Dunghill; where five bricks
Together patcht, and strength'ned with three sticks,   100
Is term'd *an House*: where Brewers, bakers, butlers,
Smiths, tapsters, sadlers, haberdashers, cutlers
(And worse Trades) all conspire to helpe the Devill
To one another, for their mutual Evill.
Away to *Thistleworth*, the place of pleasure,   105
Where joyntly Art and Nature shew their treasure.

---

91   *Eares*] yeares **F.**
93   *heed*] /heed/ **F.**
106 *shew their*] shewes thi/e/r **F.**
     treasure]   treasure
     Foure yeares agoe, when I to schoole did packe
     Holding my Learning fast all on my backe,
     It pleasd king O[ls *altered to* sb]alston to lett us play
     Noe lesse, then for the date of one whole day
     O peaceful empire! Sure Augustus blisse   5
     Was but an idle prophecie of this.
     Tell mee, thou Sunne, who now didst shine more deare
     Then any other parcell of the Yeare,
     Tell me what solid Joy, what pure Delight,
     Two sweete, though yong Friends had then in thy sight 10
     There is a field which gamsters Tuttle name,
     A greene, playne, wide field. Here they early came
     The morne presented [*erasure*] many a Chrystall gemme
     Law [*for* Low] to their feete: but they neglected them,
     Which made the lovesicke goddesse chandge her hue   15
     And mourne in trickling droppes of liquid deawe,
     Thames, as with their aspect shee had beene rapt
     Leapt upp with jocund waves, and eftsoones clapt
     Here cleane washt handes. The nymphes, which wayte upon /her/,
     Made humble Bends to them and did them honour,   20

BODLEIAN MS DON. C. 24: POEMS

Bearing their wooden trayne. Yet they refusd
To kisse them, though they were thus kindly usde.
Oft did an eager virgin seeme to profer
Her watring lippes, and salutation ofer
Oft did a Syren jogge; when cruell they   25
Withdrewe their beauties, and made hast away.
The hoping River ceast not to implore,
Till seeing them steppe out, to goe on shore,
Shee melted into teares, and rashly drowned
Her selfe for sorrow in her owne Profound.   30
Trees of all sortes, on both sides of the way
Bowd downe their neckes to them, and nodding lay
The aspin feared his stiffnesse could not make
Enough obeysance: and that causd him quake.
The blowing Hawthorne pale for envye grewe,   35
As hee beheld them deckt with whiter hue
The lawrell and the Palme could scarce forbeare
To droppe some royall sprigges, which they might weare
On their crownd heades, whilst they sate downe to feast
Not on the choysest Cates, but one the best.   40
Cosen, you know, Behinde your present House
There growes an antique Grove, whose frizzled boughes
Invite the Nightingales to sitt, and sing.
Next which, the silver of a bubbling Spring
Refines the neighbour Bankes, and breedes such Floures   45
As youthfull wooers straw in coy Dames bowers.
Here lightly feeding on an Hony-combe,
They raisd such Talke as made the Birde stand dumbe.
Each accent equalled Musick, whilst theyr Armes
Chastly combined encreast those powerfull charmes.   50
Here had they still layne, they had still layne here
Had not the hunting of a ni[m *over erasure*]ble Deere
Tempted them home. By chance a straggling Hound
With gallant chiding made the wood resound,
And warnd them where to finde such princely sporte   55
As might not misbecome Charles and his Courte.
They followed it; and by good fate did erre
So right, that they came just to Westminster.
You silly goddes, Mars, Bacchus, and the rest.
Who proudly dreame that none but you are blest   60
Speake true, Did you ere dwell neare famous Surrey
If ere yee did, (I say) the more fooles were yee
To leave such fine Seates, and lett mo/r/tall elves
Have better Heavens, then yee have your selves. **F.**

Come, view the Gardens, orchards, parks, and fields,
The palaces, in which each Chamber yeeldes
A litle towne: one roome affords more lustre
Than all the London ruines in a cluster.   110
    Yet (Cosin) if you meane to see indeed
The true and reall Country; you had neede
Come to Colnrogers; where a meadow Brooke   Coln-rogers,
Runnes glasse, in which the dapper Willows looke   a village in
                                                                                           Glocester-shire,
Whilst they adorn their locks: the Earth above   115   where these
Is neither Cliff, nor Close, nor Heath, nor Grove,   verses were
Or rather 'tis all foure; and so it bendes   written.
That eying the proportion of both endes,
You think on some great Bow, to which the Brooke
Is fitted, like a string, from nooke to nooke,   120
Or on some Eie-brow, at one end made bare,
Whose naked grasse seemes Skin, whose trees seeme Hair.

---

111   *meane . . . see*] please to know **F.**
113   *Come*] Downe **F.**
116   *Cliff*] clift **F.**
121   *on . . . end*] else on some greate Eyebrowe, halfe made **F.**
122   *Hair.*]   hayre.
         Rafe, Dick, and Harry bring logges to the fire,
         Jone skimmes the milke the Groome provides attire
         For his selfe and his mule, of the same Cloath.
         One peece of winnow-sheete will serve for both
         Sha[p *altered* r]pe windes shall get you stomache to your meate.5
         I pray you doe not spare. The more you eate
         The more you shall bee welcome. Our friend here
         Is dearer to us farre, then is your Cheare. **F.**

[folio 27ᵛ]

[29]

On Mistris Katharine Bacon.

Now will wee never wonder, though wee meete
So many uggly Wenches in each streete;
    Loe, here is one
    Who hath alone
Robb'd all her fellowes of what-ere is sweete.   5

[folio 28]

[30]

An epitaph on *Thomas Hulbert* Cloathyer of Cosham.

Stand still, who-ere thou art, and lett thine Eies
First reade, then weepe: Here Thomas Hulbert lies,
One, whom the best of men did respect and love,
As this same monument may partly prove.
Nature endow'd him with such matchlesse partes,   5
Hee noe way needed to bee taught the Artes,
And though hee hadd a Trade, and dealt in Cloath,
Hee was a Scholar and a Courtyer both,
A father strict, yet tender ore his Childe,
A loving neighbour, and a Master milde,   10
Who never did the needy Poore contemne,
And god enricht him by the handes of them:
Nor did he Care in his owne Houshold ende;
But did to Towne, and Country too, extend.
In serving God, in honouring the King,   15
In wayting on his Sh'riff, in every thing,
So well hee spent this mortal life's short span,
Hee seem'd a Wonder, rather then a Man.

Hulbert's monument was sett upp by Sir Edward Hungerford, knight of the Bath.

> These verses I wrote at the Request of
> Sir *Edward Hungerford*, who pre-
> scribed the matter of them to mee,
> intending to sett upp this Epitaph
> at his owne Cost, because *Thomas
> Hulbert* had diligently waited on him,
> when hee was high Sheriffe of *Wiltshire*.

[folio 28ᵛ]

[31]

To his Friend beyond sea.

Bacon, thou hardly wilt believe that Wee
Which are so zealous in commending thee,
Should scarce endure to heare thy publick Praise:
Yet so it is. When any stranger sayes,
Thou hast the active bodie of thy Father   5
And thy faire Mother's face; wee had farre rather
That hee would swear how thou wert uggly grown,
Or how thy Teeth and Haire were not thine owne.
Why art thou handsome. Beauty is the pride
Not of a Gentleman, but of a Bride.   10
    Truly wee hope that though thou wentst from hence
Sweet, prety, and delightfull to the sense,
Time will impaire thee so, that wee may finde
Noe gifts at thy Returne, but in thy Minde.
Not that wee wish thee any kinde of ill   15
(Wee for thy Welfare pray, wee blesse thee still)
But that wee have noe other way to prove
The constancie and purenesse of our Love.
What thanks deserve wee, if wee doat on feature?
A thing, which ravishes each silly creature.   20
Wee dive into thy Soule, and there finde out
Jewels and Mines not dreamt-of by the Route.
    Doe, doe: continue fine. This shall bee all
Thy recompense, that where wee us'd to call
Thee our deare Brother, now another While   25
Our comely Sister thee wee will enstile.

[folio 29]

[32]

Hampton-court here speaketh:

Not that I am a King's house, or that I
Am new; or that I am broad, long, and high,
Or that I am so rich within, or that
I am so faire without, keepe I this state:
My glorie is, that the conspicuous World   5
Is on both sides, before, behind mee hurl'd;
Woods, rivers, Cities, beasts, birds, corne and Grasse
Are all presented to my Eies of glasse.
The Sun, when hee the whole Skie hath runne ore,
Hath farther gone, than I, but not seene more;   10
You scarcely would believe that splendent Hee
With all his pompe begins to envie mee:
Oft have wee stood, face shining against face,
To trie which could eclipse the other's grace.
    What would you view? Earth, water, Heav'n, and Fire,   15
Lie open to you, as you would desire:
Noe kinde of Want my Praises should impaire,
Could you but hence see two things; Hell, and Aire.

*Hampton-court
hath excellent
Prospects.*

BODLEIAN MS DON. C. 24: POEMS   69

[folio 29ᵛ]

[33]

To his cosin *Michaël Oldis-*
-worth, February 15 1631.

It was the time that every Bird and Beast
(Except owles, batts, and Drunkards) tooke their rest,
When I dreamt, I was dead. Mee thought, I felt
My handes leave Feeling, and forthwith I smelt
My nose hate Smells; nay, I did see in sooth   5
Mine eies close upp: then speaking to my Mouth
(Which then left off to speak) I heard mine Eare
Grow deafe, and threaten never more to heare;
"Thou thing accurst, thou Mouth, that oft deprives
"The hungry scholars-Wayters of their Lives   10
"(While eating upp thy Commons, all and some,
"Thou leav'st noe scrappes for those that after come)
"How haps it, thou art so unthankfull growne,
"That when our Benefactour comes to towne
"Thou art thus dumb, and stupid? Hast thou spent   15
"Thy spirits with the Feare and dread of Lent?
"Or are thy Teeth gagg'd with the bones of fish?
"Or dost thou water at a Shroving-dish?
"For shame, divulge our Patron's noblenesse,

F = Folger MS. V.a.170, pp. 310–12

Title: *his . . . 1631*] the right worshipfull his honoured Cosin Machael Oldisworth F.
5   *nay . . . sooth*] and presently I sawe F.
6   *eies*] /eyes/ F.
           Mouth] Jawe F.
9   *thing*] limbe F.
           Mouth] Jawe F.
11   *While*] Whilst F.
12   *scrappes*] Ortes F.
13   *so*] thus F.
14   *That*] As F.
15   *Thou art thus*] To stand so F.
18   *dost . . . at*] does thy minde runne on F.

"Or at least, tell us why thou holdst thy Peace;   20
"And thinke that, as 'tis secret Blasphemie
"To hide the Gifts cast to us from on high,
"So to stand mute, when Worthies are in place,
"Is close Detraction, and profound Disgrace.
    My mouth (alas!) lay speechless; then me thought   25
I call'd the women, which fresh linnen brought
To shrowd my corps: but here befell a Jeast,
Our colledge Woman, scolding with the rest
About my Shirt, whose Right it was to have it,
Would yet not take it, though to Her I gave it.   30
For, being loath to heare them brawl and jangle,
"I rose, and pray'd them, Good folks doe not wrangle,
"You will not lett mee sleepe; if my foule shirt
"Bee all you stand upon, it seemes noe Hurt
"That it bee judg'd hers, who hath oftest layne   35
"With gownes for pleasure, or with Cloaks for gaine.
                                                        They

[folio 30]

They all agreed to lett my Shirt alone;
So, by good chance, I have my Shirt still on.
    Then shoulder'd forth, mee thought, I saw my Hearse
Bedeckt with many a learned Students verse,   40

---

20 *tell*] till **F.**
            Peace]   peace;
            Silence at other seasons we like well.
            But when we goe to church, ring out the bell **F.**
24   *Disgrace*]   disgrace.
            Wee know. Thou scornst the pedling Lawyers tricke
            Who though hee hath Fees plenty, still doth seese
            To get more coyne, or else his throught is hoarse.
            The edge of Money cutts the fluent course
            Of poets wellspunne voyce. Tis seldome found. 5
            That pitchers crambd with gold in consort sound. **F**
25   *mouth*] jawe **F.**
26   *linnen*] linnens **F.**
27   *shrowd*] swath **F.**
30   *yet*] om. **F.**
38   *shoulder'd*] should red **F.**
39   *learned Students*] Students willing **F.**

BODLEIAN MS DON. C. 24: POEMS   71

Which I would faine have readd, to see how they
Would flatter mee, now I was gone away,
Mens witts and vertues, bee they great or small,
Are still most prais'd, when they are none at all;
But ere those dainty Lines peruse I could   45
The knave Cleark sang *Amen*, and threw down mould
On my sadd corps: then, then me thought I lost
My bookes, my friends, and (that which vext mee most)
Mee thought, I lost You. Poor wretch! must I die
Die, not for Him? nor in his Companie?   50
Was it for this, my Parents brought mee forth
To prove ungratefull? lett n'er man of worth
Againe love Scholar, or delight to see
The modell of a breathing Librarie.
    Thus wept I, when me thought, a glorious Child   55
Came flying to my Soule, and sweetly smil'd,
"Thou droppe (sayd hee) of *Overbury's* blood,
"Whose ayme is still, not to bee great, but good,
"Enjoy thy Teares: these winter Tempests bring
"The blest Encrease of an eternall Spring.   60
Rapt with Assurance of celestiall Blisse,
I knew, I did but dreame; such News as this
Is too good: then me thought, I strove to wake,
I strove, not for mine owne, but for your sake;
Nor live I to my selfe, my chiefest Ende   65
Is to declare the goodnesse of my Friend.
    Shew mee how in my grave I may laud You,
I shall be gladd to have this Dreame prove true.

---

46   *mould*] /mould/ F.
47   *friends*] bodie F.
        that] om. F.
53   *Againe*] Against F.
58   *ayme*] bent F.
61   *celestiall*] spiritu/a/ll F.
63   *thought*] tho/u/ght F.
        wake] [<.> del.]/w/ake F.
64   *I . . . sake*] om. F.
66   *my*] the F.

[folio 30ᵛ]

[34]

On a Moore.

Wonder not, if a black wench I desire:
What apter things, than Coales, to kindle Fire?

BODLEIAN MS DON. C. 24: POEMS   73

[folio 31]

[35]

An epitaph on litle Thomas Bacon,
who dyed sodainly.

Loe, laughing as I was at Play,
I left my game, and went away:
Then (reader) weepe not over mee,
But rather laugh for companie.

[36]

Another.

If ever any Angels die,
An angel doubtlesse here doth lie;
In whom proude Nature shew'd the Earth
Too fine a piece for humane birth:
And therfore Heav'n, noe more to make   5
The like of Him, his Platforme brake.

F = Folger MS. V.a.170, p. 306

---

[35]
Title: *litle . . . sodainly*] T.B. F.
1   *Loe*] *om.* F.
3   *Then (reader)*] Reader F.

---

[36]
2   *An . . . doubtlesse*] Doubtlesse and Angell F.
5   *Heav'n*] God F.
6   *of Him*] againe F.

[folio 31ᵛ]

[37]

On treacherousnesse.

What meant our English grandsires to contrive
The death of Wolves, and keep Themselves alive?
To kill Beasts, and save Men? to make away
Tame creatures, and lett savage Monsters stay?
Old doating wizards! could they not foresee   5
What would ensue, if none were left, but Wee?
Each would devoure his fellow, and betray
His mate, without a third to part the Fray;
Husband would swallow wife, friend eat upp friend,
And want some gentle Dragon, some good fiend   10
To save their Lives: sister would ruine Brother,
Sonne way-lay father, daughter poyson mother,
And wish in vaine, that any honest Devill
Would teach Mankind how to become more civill.

F = Folger MS. V.a.170, p. 291
F₃ = Folger MS. V.a.170, p. 317

Title: *Treacherousnesse*] a Dissembler F₃.
3   *make*] drive F₃.
6   *were*] /were/ F.
8   *a*] the F.
10   *fiend*] friend F.
11   *save . . . Lives*] quench the buirnt F₃.
14   *civill*] eivill F₃.

BODLEIAN MS DON. C. 24: POEMS   75

[folio 32]

[38]

STATES-WOMEN // A show
taken out of *Aristophanes*.

Enter *Praxagora*, speak-
ing to her Candle.

O glorious Eie, thou miracle of Sight
 That in the dark canst see, and viewst the Earth
When it is wrapt in pitch; thou Day by Night,
 Thou artificiall Sun: whose wondrous birth
And fortune both are from a Woman's hand,   5
 Assist our Meeting with thy choysest flames;
Dart out such raies, as those when thou dost stand
 By lovers bedds, and seest the youthfull Dames
Melting with heat, and from their fires dost learne
In a refined sympathie to burne.   10
Thou art noe Traytour, that wee neede distrust
 Thy slippery Faith; thy beams are wont to aide,
Not to disclose: wee ever found thee just
 And true to our Designes; when any Maide
Steals to the Cellar for a cuppe of wine,   15
 Or undermines a Pie, thou holdst thy tongue.
Or if a Lady will bee smoothly fine
 And shave her selfe, thou n'er wilt doe her Wrong:
The criticks of our sinnes, if thy will know
They may goe looke; thy Light will nothing show. 20
Trusty and well-beloved, wee admitt
 Thee to our Councell ——————— But now I
thinke on it, why doe none of them come? wee
must bee at the Towne-hall by Breake of
day; or else wee may chance to have the Men
there before us. &c. &c. &c.
   &c. &c.
    &c.
    All goe out.

This I
translated out of
the Greek poet
Aristophanes,
in December
1631, by the
appointment of
Doctor Duppa,
our Deane of
Christchurch.

The rest of this
being but a
translation, I
have not here
transcribed.

[39]

A Censure upon *Aristopha-*
-nes his States-women.

The show is done: and now the Throngs debate,
Are men, or Women, fitt'st to rule the State?
  To trie this Cause, they choose out three to sitt,
A male, a Female, an Hermophradit:
The female shee beginnes. If FORTUNE bee   5
The onely thing that rules, why may not Wee
Pretend a title to the Crowne, as well
As men? I hope, an Ewe may beare the Bell
The sheapard standing by; and Does may leade
                                        The

*This Censure
I added, at
the Request of
Mistris Duppa,
our deane's wife.*

[folio 32ᵛ]

The bucks, when both the Bucks and Does doe dread   10
The keeper's staffe: who cares, which bears the sway
Pewter or Brasse, when both doe Gold obey?
  Or if there bee noe Fortune, yet lett NATURE,
Which hath adorn'd us with the better feature,
Attaine her scope and ende: why is the Rose   15
The chiefe of flowrs, but because it showes
Fresher, and fayrer? Why doe wee delight
In precious Stones? why? 'cause they please our Sight?
Take beauty from the Cedar, and the Pine
Shall vie with it for height; for fruit, the Vine: 20
Or if by Strength wee ought to judge of trees,
The oak shall toppe them both. In some degrees
The moone and stars doe both surpasse the Sunne,
Yet brightness winnes the day, when all is done.
  But for it seemes too bold a Woman's taske   25
To praise her Face, wee dare putt on our Maske,
And plead with you. *Virginitie*, which is
The most divine of any humane Blisse,
Is all our owne; males seldome are betrayd,
But yet 'tis grosse to call a Man *a Mayd*.   30
Our slippes (you know) are easy to reveale,
You have us alwaies under hand and seale;
But though wee made a narrow Search of You,
Wee might finde some false, wee could prove none true,

BODLEIAN MS DON. C. 24: POEMS

While litle motes defile a crystall glasse   35
Great blotts in wooden bowles unseen may passe.
Did *Vesta*, when shee meant, her Priests should live
For ever chast, to shorn-haire Orders give?
Or did *Diana*, for her Maides of honour,
Choose beards, or empty Breasts, to wait upon Her?   40
Noe, they well knew that Men and Chastitie
Are still at oddes, and never can agree,
Which makes you all so greedy to untie
The honour'd knott of our *Virginitie*:
But wee are pure; and who can better wield   45
A scepter, then a creature undefil'd?
Or what should place a mortal neare the gods,
If not what putts twixt us and them noe oddes?
    But you perchance require an active Spirit,
Which stands not on its Simplenesse, but Merit;   50
Nor doe wee leave you there: wee are the same
With you in Soule, and every thing, but Name.
                                                                              Who

folio 33

Who knowes not how the *Amazons* did beate
The neighbour Countries round? or how the Feate
Of one *Europa* wonne twelve severall Landes?   55
Or how by vertue of a Woman's handes
Carthage was founded? *Carthage*, that did tame
Mankinde, and putt the world of Rome to shame.
Who knowes not how our Wisedome is your shield,
Your onely Shield at home, and in the field?   60
Were you not fedd by Us, by us preserv'd,
Within a short time, you would all bee starv'd.
Your selves confesse, Not onely lower bodies
But great *Jove* is beholded to a Goddesse,
Great Jove would perish, did not *Pallas* sitt   65
Over his head, to furnish him with Witt:
And why doe You, when you have done with bookes,
Beginne to study us, and reade our Lookes,
But 'cause you find in Us some higher Art,
Than what male-authors can to you impart?   70
Wee are borne wise: the Sibylls n'er felt rodd,
And yet they wrote the Oracles of God:
Wee are so wise, wee need not goe to schoole,

A man, that is noe scholar, you call Foole;
And PRUDENCE is a common Woman's name,   75
As if that Wee and Wisedome were the same,
For shame, submitt. Submitt, and Us obey
Or if you envie Us, lett Wisedome sway.
     I wonder with what face you can denie
That, in plaine termes, which else you doe implie,   80
A courtyer, to his Love when hee makes Vowes,
Entitles her his MISTRESSE (not his Spouse)
And souldyers, when abroad they lose their lives,
Say 'tis not for themselves, but for their Wives:
Well-fare Antiquitie, your fore-fathers knewe   85
Our sexe's Worth, and gave us still our due,
If any thing of Note they hapt to finde
They did ascribe it to the female kinde
(Each muse, each Vertue, and each Grace divine
Was of noe gender, but the feminine)   90
And so the earthly and celestiall powers,
The faculties, and soules of men, were ours;
But wee doe bring You forth, and You requite
Our labour thus, to barre us of our Right,
Wee give you all yee have, yet You complaine   95
That women want Abilities to raigne.
I know not what wee want, unlesse it bee
Some of your Vices, from which Wee are free;
I grant, wee cannot quaffe, nor swear, nor roare,
Nor duell, nor oppresse, nor robbe, nor whore: 100
                                        If

[folio 33ᵛ]

If this bee a Defect, wee are content
Wee will not governe, for our Punishment;
But if, in all that Fate or Art affords,
Wee yeeld to You in nothing, but in Wordes,
Though (I confesse) wee are not so well-tongu'd,   105
I hope, the Kingdome well not see us wrongd.

     The male replies. Wee know, You are well-tongu'd
Nor will the Queendome ever see you wrongd.
You have the priviliege of those that love us,
You take your Ease, you spend, you sitt above us,   110
But to deliver upp our persons to you

Were not to make you greater, but undoe you:
You are not good for Warre, nor for the artes,
Weake are your Braines, and weaker are your Hearts;
You are so fraile and silly, wee scarce know   115
If you at all have any Soules, or noe.
Were it but so, that Heav'n had made your powers
As strong, and apt for service, as are ours,
There were some Hope that, in the Change of things,
Women might sometimes bee both Lords and Kings;   120
But now the Distaffe, and the Wheele become
You better, than a Scepter, and a Drumme:
Women man never rule, nor Children neither,
Women and Children well may goe together.

The moderatour sayes: To ende the Strife,   125
Wee grant, the Husband is HEAD ore his Wife,
And so the Male doth putt the Female downe,
None but the Head is fitt to wear a Crown;
But when this Play was made, yee know, the State
Of *Athens* was, like ours, effeminate,   130
And so the Female winnes: for why? 'tis meete
If once the Head declines, to raise the Feete;
Thus wee conclude, that then, and onely then,
When men turne Women, women may turne Men.

> The ende of
> the Censure.

[folio 34]

[40]

On the death of a Cripple.

Who would not now bee of his leggs bereaven?
Loe! lamest men make greatest Speed to heaven.

[folio 34ᵛ]

[41]

On Sir B.R.

Asoone as I was dead, the World beganne
To write Artes of THE COMPLETE GENTLEMAN
There needed noe such Worke, whilst I did live,
My bare Example did the best Rules give.
   Then think, you see noe new book: think, you see
   Onely the Copie of translated mee.

A dead man, is a
man translated.

5

[folio 35]

[42]

To the Witts of Oxford,
Cambridge, and London.

England, I cast thee off: thou shalt not bee
My country any longer. Doe but see
How stupid thou art grown; the *Sweeden* king
Each houre imperiall Trophies home doth bring,
And thou standst dumbe: dumbe, not with admiration,   5
But with the bare want of a Commendation.
Dares then thy Friend the old Religion raise?
And dar'st not thou so much as write his Praise?
Dares hee spend Blood, and dar'st not thou spend Inke?
Dares hee adventure what thou dar'st not thinke?   10
Base! base! thrice base! Lett mee flie any where,
Rather than tarry to endure Shame here.
What ho! why Poëts? are yee drunk for ever?
Dead, dead-drunke world without end? shall wee never
Enjoy your Resurrection? either wake   15
(For shame) or in your Sleepe some Verses make.
When landlords tell their Tenants, what huge townes
Adolphus daily winnes, the wondering Clownes
Aske if there bee noe Ballad to bee hadd
Which tunes this storie; they are not so madd   20
As to believe it, till it bee in print:
And busy Children, hearing how by dint
Of sword, the tyrant Emperour is beaten,
Question their fathers, if the King of *Sweeden*
Bee in the Bible or the Psalter nam'd.   25

These verses were written about the yeare 1630.

F = Folger MS. V.a.170, pp. 307–8
F₄ = Folger MS. V.a.319, fol.59–59ᵛ

3	**gloss:** *om.* F, F₄.
8	*thou*] /thou/ F.
9	*spend*] sheede F, shedd F₄.
	Blood] bloods F.
14	*Dead, dead-drunke*] Dead are yee F, F₄.
21	*till it*] till /it/ F.

BODLEIAN MS DON. C. 24: POEMS   83

'Tis strange that any Prince should bee so fam'd
Without the Aide of authors. I commend
Honest *Natt Butter*: hee abroad doth send
Such newes in weekly Prose, as shew at least
That hee can lie, who-ere can doe the rest.   30
    Shake-upp your mouldy soules; Devise a Worke
Which may convert the *Jew*, and make the *Turke*
Defie his *Alcoran*, and scorne to looke
On any other, but an English booke.
The very *Germanes* lay it in our dish   35
How wee lack fancie; I am loath to wish,
Yet I must wish, that reverend Corbett were
Noe bishoppe: hee such Pyramids would reare,
As should out-last all Time, and feele noe Fire
But that, wherwith the whole World must expire.   40
                                        It

[folio 35ᵛ]

It were an happy Turne for us, if Hee
Both to our Lives and Witts would rector bee,
Both to our Hearts and Braines: but 'tis a thing
Rarely perform'd, at once to preach and sing.

---

28   *Honest . . . Butter*] Nathaniel Butter F, F₄.

31   F₄ *does not indent*

32   *convert*] reforme F, F₄.

35   *in*] *om.* F₄.

37   *that reverend*] illustrious F, F₄.

41   *an*] a F₄.

       us] [< . . . > *del.*] us F.

42   *and*] and [Rector *del.*] F₄.

44   *sing*] singee [*attribution to* N.W.] F₄.

[folio 36]

[43]

On the statue of Niobé
well carved.

Poëts, 'tis false: yee say that *Niobé*
Was long since dead and gone; when all men see
That shee yet lives, and lookes as shee would have
Another Husband sooner than a Grave.
Or if wee grant that Shee to stone was turn'd   5
Yet is that false, which in your bookes wee learn'd:
You say, it was *Latona*, when wee knowe
It was the Carver, who did change her so.

BODLEIAN MS DON. C. 24: POEMS 85

[folio 36ᵛ]

[44]

To the worshipfull, Mistris Strange
of Summerford, a Poëtesse.

My censure, and my Verdict, which you crave
On all your Poëms (Cosin) here you have.
Two faults I find, and but two faults in troth,
They are too sacred, and too witty both.
So witty they are, that I sometimes feare   5
They border on prophane Conceipts too neare.
That are so sacred, that I think sometimes
They doubtlesse are some Sermons, and noe Rymes.
Such verses sure, as yours, the Angels sing
When they extoll the everlasting King.   10
One while for Hymnes and psalmes I them mistook,
Yet by and by, when I did better looke,
Jeasts, epigrams, and fancies I them deemed.
So grave together, and so light they seemed.
More then a Poët you are in each line: 15
In each line you are more than a Divine.
If I might have my Wish, a Woman should
Bee that, which never any man yet could:
If I might have my Wish, great *Charles* should take you
And both a Bishop and a Laureat make you.   20
'Twere but what You deserve, though 'twere a Wonder
Above to see Baies, and a Rotchet under.

F = Folger MS. V.a.170, pp. 290–91

Title: *To . . . Poëtesse*] To Mistris Strange F.
         of . . . Poëtesse] *om.* F.
2   *Poëms*] Po[. . .] F.
7   *That*] They F.
9   *yours*] these F.
11   *Hymnes*] Hym[nes *over* < . . . >] F.
19   *I*] *om.* F.

[folio 37]

[45]

An Ode, of 12 kindes of Verses.

Now
Thou

My deare
Art here,

Thy strange Light   5
So my Sight,

Sharpens, that I
Can all things spie;

But (alas for Woe!)
When thou hence shalt goe,   10

Mine eies so wett will bee,
That I shall nothing see.

Stay then, ô stay, prove more kind
Than to strike thy Lover blind;

My Cupid is not so unwise,   15
That hee deserves to lose his Eies.

For thine own sake, if not for mine, stay,
Lest, what honours thee, thou cast away;

Trust mee, though thou art faire, yet few or none
As I doe, will admire thee being gone: 20

In most men there is an odd humour, to neglect
Other folks Worth, and Praise, which is Worth's effect.
What pity 'twere, to drowne that Sense, of all the rest,
Through whose Means thou and I might both bee joyntly blest?

[folio 37ᵛ]

[46]

On mortals.

How often, in our selves, wee see reflections
Both of our Deaths, and of our Resurrections?
At night wee all depart, and each man dies.
At morne wee leave our Graves againe, and rise.

[folio 38]

[47]

To a yong Lady, that
hadd the greene Sicknesse.

Nay, Madam, you may very well bee seene;
Hide not your face: what though your Cheeks shew green,
They shew the better; greene is such an hue
As pleaseth (I think) every one, but You.
How foule and monstrous would the Earth appeare,   5
If grasse were redd, were white, and not greene were?
Why should that colour, which our mother's face
So well becomes, so deeply yours disgrace?
Suppose that You were sett in *Nature's* stead,
What would you doe? how would you have things bredd?   10
Would you make Plants grow motly, or the Corne
With rosy fingers imitate the Morne?
Oh! it were dainty Sport, to see a Leeke
Ruddy and blushing, like some guilty cheeke.
 Yet you are not so greene, but that in You   15
Much other Beauty shines: your veines are blue,
Your lippes are damask, and your handes are white,
Grey are your Eies, your gold-like Haire is bright.
Or though you were as greene, as garden-peas,
Our optick sense you would the better please,   20
And seeme the fairer; else men are not wise,
If they dislike what most preserves their Eies:
Aske physick-doctors which is the best way
To keepe our Sights entire, and they will say
Looke on greene gemmes, green cloaths, and when you use 25
Glasse spectacles, the green Glasse alwaies chuse.
Greene is a fertile colour, and doth suite
With such Maides, as are likely to beare Fruit;
Take the most part, they are but wither'd Plants
Which goe in other hues: and sure there wants   30
Much sappe and wholsom Moisture there, where Ladies

F = Folger MS. V.a.170, pp. 329–30

---

11   *motly*] mothy F.

BODLEIAN MS DON. C. 24: POEMS

Shew sleeke and gawdy, like dead painted babies.
    But you frett chiefly 'cause a Sicknesse 'tis;
As though there were noe worse Disease, than this:
Think on the Pocks, the Plague; think on some ach,   35
Or on a naughty Husband; think on Age.
Yours is a Queene's disease, and fitt for such
As live in idleness; the toilsome *Dutch*
N'er feele it; and the *Switzers* sooner have

A

[folio 38ᵛ]

A king amongst them, than a Griefe so brave.   40
Enjoy your Cheekes; and laugh to think how silly
They are, who triumph that the Rose and Lilly
Joyne in their muzzels: tell them how their WHɪTE
Betrayes their Feare, and backwardnesse to fight;
Their REDD betrayes their bloody minde, and showes   45
They faine would kill, though they dare strike noe blowes.

---

31   *Ladies*] /Ladies/ F.
37   *Queene's*] [deas *del.*] Queens F.

[folio 39]

[48]

An Ode.

Though both thy Tongue and Eies bidd mee refraine,
    And drive mee from thy Musick, from thy Sight,
    One is so sweet, the other are so bright,
Thy tongue and Eies both bidd me come againe:
Thus, as my Case now stands, the truth to speake,   5
        Thine eies and Tongue
        Are both too strong,
And yet thine Eies and Tongue are both too weake.

BODLEIAN MS DON. C. 24: POEMS

[folio 39ᵛ]

[49]

On Alexander Bainham Esquier,
who was killed at the Siege
of *Mastrich*. 1632.

Hee could have pickt noe fitter time to die,
Hee, who did alwaies love good Companie;
Now *Sweeden's* king, the *Palsgrave* now is gone,
'Tis more than meet, brave *Bainham* should make one:
For, I am sure, if Valour may it carry,   5
Behind the stoutest of them hee'l not tarry.
Trusting to nothing but his Braines and Handes,
Hee slighted Wealth, and threw away his landes;
This is indeed true Valour: lett mee see
The best Prince of them all doe so as Hee.   10
Poore hungry Swordmen! they exhort their bandes
To fight for what hee scorn'd, to fight for Landes;
And, till they once are glutted with a Grave,
They never thinke that they enough Earth have.
Hee knew well, Dirt was made to trample on;   15
Hee kickt-off all his Mannors, hee left none:
To have, and to possesse, is ploughmens fate,
'Tis *Bainham's* praise, to want a great Estate.
   Nor did his Valour in his Riches ende,
But to his Wife and Children did extend;   20
Though she were vertuous, though They hopefull were,
(Though his owne Flesh) hee scarcely held them deare:
Hee higher flies, hee soares; hee spends his Blood
To doe his universall Countrie good.
Lett other Heades, which meaner are, and lower,   25
Provide, take Care, and scrape for three or foure;
Under an Empire, *Bainham* will not move:
Great Britaine is the center of his Love.

[folio 40]

[50]

On a packet of Letters, drowned in
their comming from his Friend beyond sea.

Ere since the Deluge (when a spreading rheume
Spoild the whole Earth's faire face) I dare presume,
By force of Water there was never done
A stranger Mischiefe, than this present one:
What tell yee mee of Shippes, or Men, or Plate,   5
Or jewels, that have felt the self-same fate?
As if the ruine of a totall Land
Could countervaile Lines written in his hand.
   Ah! how I hate that slabby Element,
That heape of faithlesse waves, whose Strength is spent   10
Onely in being weake, and letting sinke
Such things, as it should carry to the brinke.
Hang mee, if ever I againe drinke water;
My liquour shall bee nought but Wine herafter:
I will contrive it so, ere I have done,   15
My flesh shall bee as drie, as is my Bone;
And to beginne, now forthwith I will squize
Good store of trickling moisture through my Eies.

[folio 40ᵛ]

[51]

His rewarding a Musician.

Crown'd with May-flowrs, by night ther came to mee
 An harper; and desir'd that Hee
Might play: which done, Now what's your Hire? quoth I.
 Hee, looking upp into the Skie,
Bade mee *Arión* and *Ariadné* viewe,   5
 And sayd, What men gave, hee scarce knewe,
But hee knew that the gods noe lesse than Heaven
 Unto the HARPE and CROWNE hadd given.
Laughing to heare him so profoundly crave,
 I sayd, I scarce knew what Gods gave,   10
But men ne'r to the Harpe and Crown gave more
 Then they were wont to give the poore,
And that's a farthing: so I flang him downe
 A token with the Harpe and Crowne.

F = Folger MS. V.a.170, pp. 314–15

Title: *rewarding*] entertaining of F.
1 *mee*] /me/ F.
3 *I*] /I/ F.
6 *And sayd*] Saying F.
9 *him . . . profoundly*] the rogue so neatly F.
12 *the*] to F.
13 *flang*] threw F.
14 *token*] farthing F.

[folio 41]

[52]

An epitaph on a dis-
-contented man.

World, thou once fled'st; and I did follow thee:
World, now I flie; and thou shalt follow mee.

[folio 41ᵛ]

[53]

An eglogue betweene a Carter and a sheapard, made on Master *Michaël Oldis--worth's* Comming into the country.

Carter.	Now a Botch take thee, *Tom*: where hast thou beene
	These hundred yeares? Why (man) thou mightst have seene
	One that shines braver then a Summer's day;
	I scarce know whom: but I heard *Tahah* say,
	Not all the Horses in my landlord's teeme 5
	So many Vertues have, as are in Him;
	The nobles bragge (hee sayes) and Statesmen boast
	That goodnesse amongst Courtyers is not lost.
Sheapard.	Marry I thought 'twas something, when old *Guerim*
	Left singing, and ranne home-wards. I could heare him 10
	Downe in a Vallie, neare a litle Brooke,
	(As hee leant on the noddle of his crooke)
	Suck sorrowes from the Pleasures of the Yeare,
	And there grieve most, where most hee ought to cheare.
A shepard's	"Thou happy Earth (quoth hee) though nipping Cold 15
Song.	"Wrinkled thy skinne, and caus'd thee to looke old,
	"Though raging Windes did pierce thee, and the spight
	"Of hoary Raine did change thy greene to white,
	"Yet now againe fresh Youth adornes thy face,
	"And blest Delight straws flowrs in every place; 20
	"But (woe to mee!) my sadd Misfortunes bring
	"An endlesse Winter, without hope of Spring,
	"My sighes are alwaies blustring, and my head
	"With everlasting Frost and Snow is spredd:
	"Noe thawing Joy, noe Heate to ridd my heart 25
	"Of chill Despaire, no Cure to ease my Smart.
	"Yee torrents, though your banks yee oft orepasse,
	"And rudely wash away the meadow-Grasse,
	"Yet when warme Sunnes return, the grounds waxe drie,
	"And grow more fertile by your injurie; 30
	"But ah! my Teares, with their rebellious force
	"Drowning my cheekes, doe never cease their course:
	"Or if they stopp a While, they onely shew mee
	"How wither'd I am, while they thus bedeaw mee.

"The fields, though with the wounds of ploughs they bleed,   35
"Are well apayd, when they newe Harvests breede;
"But I, for all my pangs and restlesse minde,
"Nought but a Croppe of Scorne and Hatred finde.
"Fire dissolves pitch, and Water falling often
"Melts stones; but neither her hard Breast will soften.   40
                                        Wherfore

[folio 42]

"Wherfore both Fire and Water I'l consume,
"And quench my hott affection with cold rheume.

Carter   Old *Guerim* is the Creditt of our times;
                  Hee charmes his Sheepe with such transcendent rymes,
                  That hee drawes rural *Nymphs* from out their Bowers   45
                  To make him Garlands of their sweetest flowers:
                  And heard-groomes, flocking round to hear his Skill,
                  Thinke that his Layes are done too quickly still;
                  When hee beginnes, they seeme in mirth to flowe,
                  When hee concludes, they seeme to mourn for Woe.   50

Sheepheard   But in an angry moode the foole forswore
                  To sing of Love and Beauty any more;
                  Hee shakes off Women, and applies his Penne
                  To paint the worthy acts of famous Men:
                  Well are they spedd, whose Praises hee shall write,   55
                  Whose quill can nought but tarbox-Lines endite.

Carter   Nay, *Tom*, believe mee, *Guerim* can doe well,
                  Tahah commends him; and our *Ralph* can tell,
                  That gallant man, whom wee were speaking of,
                  His verses tooke, and did nor frown, nor scoffe: 60
                  I think, I have the Paper in my pocket;
                  Why dost thou laugh? I preethee doe not mock it.
                  "Accept our paines, great Sir, and daigne to read
                  "Things simple, as the place where they were bredd.
A sheap-heard's   "What though wee cladd our Meaning in low wordes?   65
Complement   "Humilitie with Highnesse best accordes.
                  "Dales becomes mountaines, and the stouping neck
                  "Suits fairest with the lofty lordling's beck:
                  "They doe but shew their dimnesse, which shine bright
                  "To you, and to a Torch a Candle light;   70
                  "Darknesse and Shade most fitts the Sunne, since Hee

"Besides himselfe sight-worthy nought can see.
"*Pan* crown your mighty partes, Sir: you can doe
"More than some Doctors, and some Captaines too:
"Tut, you scorne trifles, you can write and reade,   75
"And if you please, an Army you can leade;
"But this to mee appeares the strangest thing
That you can, when you list, behold the King.

The ende of the
eglogue.

[folio 42ᵛ]

[54]

To a Lady, that sang and
played on the Lute.

You wonder why of late the Spheares
Doe never sound, nor please our eares.
The truth is (Madam) modest they
Hearing how well you sing and play,
Doe cease their Musick, and stand still   5
To listen to your better Skill.

[55]

Which verses I thus altered, 1644.

To his musicall Valentine
Mistris Anne Henshaw.

The sphears were once harmonious Sphears;
But now they never please our eares:
Lady, your Lute makes them stand still.
    For, modest they
      Nor sing, nor play,   5
But listen to your better Skill.

BODLEIAN MS DON. C. 24: POEMS   99

[folio 43]

[56]

On the birth of James duke of Yorke.

Why dost thou weepe, blest babe? Thy happy Birth
Was not ordayn'd for Sorrow, but for mirth: These verses
Behold, how Court and Country both are gladd,   were printed at
                                                                    Oxford *
And none, besides thee, in the realme is sadd;
O shed noe Teares, unlesse from Joy they flow,   5
Then will wee all shed tears, as fast as thou.
Thou litle know'st in what good plight thou art,
Else sure thou wouldst not take it thus to heart:
Why, though thou mightst have chosen thine owne fate,
Thou noe way couldst bee in a better state.   10
Thy father is a King, so truly brave,
The angels faine his Companie would have,
And, were it not that God our ile does love,
Hee, long ere this time, had been crown'd above.
Thy mother is a Queene, in whose pure breast   15
So many sacred Vertues make their nest,
Her selfe above her Country wee advance,
And having *Marie*, wee regard not France.
Thy brother and thy sister are a paire
So wondrous witty, so exactly faire,   20
That had wee not a stedfast Hope of Thee,
Wee scarce knew who their parallell could bee.
The province, which receives thee, is so farre
From being vext with Famine, plague, or Warre,
The paradise, from whence thy Soule first came,   25
Is either very like it, or the same.
What canst thou wish for? Choiser things than these
Are noe where to bee gott in Lands, or Seas:

1633a = Vitis Carolinæ Gemma Altera sive Auspicatissima Ducis Eboracensis Genethliaca
Decantata ad Vadaisidis. Oxford, 1633. sigs. I4ᵛ–K1.

TITLE: om. 1633a.
13   does] doth 1633a.
18   regard not] the less need 1633a.
25   The paradise] Ev'n that sweete place 1633a.

Why then are there two raine-bowes in thine eyes,
When there is but one raine-bow in the skies?   30
    But ô, I am mistaken all this While.
Thou, by thy good Will, wouldst doe nought but smile,
Yet wanting other Boones to give the Peeres,
Instead of gemmes thy nakednesse droppes teares,
Which being spredd amongst the Lords and Earles,   35
Great Britain is enritcht with thy newe pearles.

+In Vitis
Carolinae
Gemma altera.
Oxon. 1633. 4°
sign I 4,b [all in
later hand]

31   this] the 1633a.

[folio 43ᵛ]

[57]

To his aunt, the la-
-dy Litcott of Molesey.

Madam, you are so happy, that you vexe
All womankind; the others of your sexe
Decay through age, and fade: whilst onely You
As you grow older still, grow still more newe.
Your veines as fresh, your Eies as bright appear,   5
As you, this very day, but sixteene were;
When wee thought that your Winter was halfe donne,
Nor autumne yet, nor Summer is begunne.
Sure Nature takes a certaine kinde of pride
In keeping you thus alwaies like a Bride,   10
To shew that (at the least) in this one thing
Shee can maintaine an everlasting Spring.

[folio 44]

[58]

On an envious man.

What *good* so-ere GOD gives mee, still the DEViLL
Gives Coscus just the contrary in evill:
By chance I rose to HONOUR, and straight Hee
Striving to undermine and legg-downe mee,
Tript upp his owne heeles. Honour gott mee FAME,   5
And hee, by plotting how to blurre my name,
Grew ignominious. Fame mee purchas'd WEALTH,
Which hee opposing both by Lawe and Stealth,
Brought himselfe poore. Wealth furnisht mee with PLEASURE,
Whilst hee in torment lay for Want of treasure.   10
Pleasure, in short space, made mee wondrous fatt,
In short space Hee grew wondrous leane therat;
At last, I did but laugh, and Coscus cryed;
I was *well*, hee fell *sick*; I liv'd, hee dyed.

F = Folger MS. V.a.170, p. 135

---

2   *Coscus*] Crastu F.
4   *Striving*] Thinking F.
6   *hee*] /he/ F.
       name] [n *over* s]ame F.
8   *opposing*] maligning F.
10   *treasure*] tr/e/asure F.
11–12 *fatt . . . Hee*]   Fatt
                          In short space. He F.
13   *Coscus*] Crastu F.

[folio 44ᵛ]

[59]

An Ode.

What meane my Armes? what would they have?
  They must be tutor'd, now I see.
    Fooles, they of late are grown so madd,
    They thinke some Solace may bee hadd
By clipping onely part of Thee.   5
      To tast good things, and but to tast
      Is worse by farre, than still to fast.

O, could they compasse all thy limbes,
    And wholly fully thee embrace,
    Could they in rounding knotts enfold   10
Thy feete, and at the same time hold
    Thy thighes, thy Middle, and thy Face,
      They would bee like some precious Boxe,
      Wherin a Prince his jewels lockes.

But then too, as a Boxe conceales   15
    Those things which lie within its lidd,
    So thy unmatcht and wondrous feature
    Which (like the Sunne) delights each creature,
    Would under their thick veiles bee hidd.
      And what a pity 'twere to shade   20
      That light, which for the World was made?

Noe course is left mee, but to wish
    I would my Armes a Lanterne were;
    That so both I might Thee enjoy
    At full, and yet none else annoy: 25
    But, like a lucid chrystall Sphear,
      At once, Thee to my private Heart
      And to the Universe impart.

[folio 45]

[60]

ITER AUSTRALE, 1632.
Or,
A journey southwards.

As we walkt *Westminster*, a barge we spy'd
Rowing with wheeles, with wheeles and nought beside;
Now the World turnes: shortly wee shall not faile
To see a Wagon goe with Oares and Saile.
    Behind the Abbey lives a man of fame;   5   Westminster-
With awe and reverence wee repeat his name,   abbey.
Ben Johnson: him wee saw, and thought to heare
From him some Flashes and fantastique Guere;
But hee spake nothing lesse. His whole Discourse
Was how Mankinde grew daily worse and worse,   10
How god was disregarded, how Men went
Downe even to Hell, and never did repent,
With many such sadd Tales; as hee would teach
Us Scholars, how herafter Wee should preach.
Great wearer of the baies, looke to thy lines,   15
Lest they chance to bee challeng'd by Divines:
Sure future Times will, by a grosse Mistake,
Johnson a Bishop, not a Poët make.
    Away to *Thisselworth*. There, shall Wee
My unkle Sir *Giles Overbury* see;   20
And Mistris *Old'sworth*, who as frankly gives
As does her Husband: one, than whom there lives
Noe squire of cleaner Handes, or cleaner Tongue;
For, *Michaël Oldsworth* never did man Wrong.
More I might say: but in so nice a mater   25
To tell the bare Truth onely, were to flatter.
O that I were noe Scholar, for his sake,
That so what-ere concerning Him I spake
Might bee believ'd: but now each Verse of mine
In his behalfe, is counted A strong line.   30
Speak for mee, other men; speak for me all   Michaël
Yee Oxford-witts, who him *Mecoenas* call: Oldisworth be-
Hee is a true *Mecoenas*, and doth keepe   ing Secretary to
That name alive, and will not lett it sleepe;   the Chancelour
Were it not so, that Hee loves Book-men yet,   35 of Oxford was a
                                                    great favourer of
                                                  scholars.

BODLEIAN MS DON. C. 24: POEMS

The word *Mecoenas* had grown obsolete.
    Where are we now? At *Arborvill* neare *Reding.*
Brave lanes, brave roomes, brave Meat, brave Drink, brave Bedding,
Nay, and brave people also here wee finde,
Brave people both in Bodie, and in Minde.   40
Their old ones are most wise, most kind; their yong
Most beautifull, most nimble, and most strong:
Noe fault they have, but this; they doe belive
                                        Bellarmin's

[folio 45ᵛ]

Bellarmin's doctrine. O how much wee grieve
To thinke that 'tis such worthy persons doome   45
To bee deluded (if noe worse) by Rome!
How-ere their Faith, their Diet pleas'd us well
Not onely with its Tast, but with its Smell;
The neighbring Garden, by a secret arte,
Sweet savours to our Dishes did impart: 50
And wee could scarce tell, if wee should have chose,
Whether to bee all Palate, or all Nose.
The neighbring Garden was a place so wrought,
As Skill and Nature both had thither brought
Their chiefe endowments, and stood there to trie   55
Which should bee judg'd to have prioritie.
Colours, as many as the dazeled Eies
Or frantick Braines of Painters can devise;
Sents new and strange: some of the weeders sweare
The rootes of all the Flowrs perfumed were.   60
On this side Arbors, hedges, Plotts of greene,
On that side Mounts and Walks were to bee seene;
But wee did most admire the curious Order:
There was a Commonwealth in every border.
    Drawne hence in pompous Coaches, wee surveigh   65
What workmen *Sir John Backhous* had in pay:
Sir John was hee, who with his quick'ning bounty
Rais'd the dead limbes of poore folks through the County,
And gave them Leggs and Armes of flesh and bone,
Which had before or earthen ones, or none.   70
O yee hard Masters, who doe rogue and knave them
Whom yee beat from your gates; what would yee have them
Doe with themselves? they have such weak thin fleeces,
That should they labour, they would fall in pieces.

Their carcases doe want not onely Foode,   75
But well-nigh whatso-ere besides is good:
They want both Strength and Health; thay want a Soule
Which may their drouping faculties controule.
Yea, they want ev'n themselves: they have noe feete
To goe and begge of Strangers in the streete;   80
They have noe Hands to take an almes at home,
Though scraps or pottage to their doors should come;
So much they have not, as a paire of Eies
To see and mend their owne Calamities.
Well-fare that tender and soft-hearted Knight,   85
Who makes it, as it were, his whole Delight
To rescue from the grave these ghosts, which may
                                          Him

[folio 46]

Him with their after-industrie repay.
For him they digg, they pray; hee maugre Nature
Through sundry new-made channels leads his water;   90
And leades it so, that ere the Yeare bee ended
By halfe in halfe his Mannor will bee mended.
      Let him enjoy his Vertues; whilst wee post
By land to sea: and now wee are almost
At *Portsmouth*. O god! there was such a Paire   95
Of sisters, as wee never sawe so faire:
Sydney must pardon us; these Dames in troth
Passe his *Philoclea* and *Pamela* both.
The elder is already matcht, and findes
Squire *Burch* a right good Husband in two kindes: 100
Happy is hee, who shall the yonger take,
And her his constant Bedd-fellow shall make.
I know not why, but still mee thinks that Shee
Should never lesse then some great Dutchesse bee;
This I grant, shee is my friend *Bacon's* sister,   105
And a king once, by way of Honour, kisst her.
      Within a furlong of the quiet Shoare,
Where neither Windes nor Waters use to roare,
There stands a pleasant solitary House
(They call it *Chillings*) shelter'd with the boughes   110   Chillings
Of circling elmes; next which, an ancient Grove   standeth sixe
Beares off the summer: hither wee did love   miles from
To come, and muse, and talke, and laugh, and play,   Portsmouth and
                                                                            sixe miles from
                                                                            South-hampton

BODLEIAN MS DON. C. 24: POEMS

Because our friend Dick Bacon (as men say)
Ere hee from England went, was wont to doe so;　　　115
And hee too built such Arbors here, as Whoso
Is pleas'd or Shippes, or Tempests, to descrie
May have the whole Maine subject to his Eie.
O how wee feare that this was that curst place,
Which tempted him beyond sea; whilst the grace　　　120
Of forraigne Prospects sent him, in a trance,
From *Spaine* to *Italie*, from thence to *France*.
Our selves, wee must confesse, tooke much Delight
Spying *New-forrest*, and the *ile of Wight*:
But heav'nly *Chillings*, and the Dwellers there,　　　125
And their sweet manners (though they Papists were)
So wanne us, that Wee counted all houres vaine,
Wherin wee did not somthing from them gaine.
Their servants and their slaves they us'd like frends,
Their friends like Princes; not for their owne endes　　　130
But 'cause they honour'd these, and they lov'd those:
In maters of Dispute, they alwaies chose
Rather then wrangle, to chaine upp their Tongue,
And so gott Praise, although they held the Wrong.
　　　　　　　　　　　　　　　　　　They

[folio 46ᵛ]

They never sware. for why? they still spake troth,　　　135
Their naked Word was taken for an Oath;
And with the Poore they did so kindly deale,
Noe neighbour ere had any Need to steale.
　　Wee at *Southampton* have as dainty Fish,
And of as diverse sortes, as wee can wish:　　　140
But ere wee dine, wee wander upp and downe
To prie into the fashions of the Towne.　　　　　　　　　　　South-hampton
Without the gate, painted on either hand
Sir Bevis and *Sir Ascapart* doe stand;
Before them sitts a lyon made of wood:　　　145
And they stare on him so, as if they stood
On purpose, to keep out that Beast of sinne,
Lest hee should chance to mischiefe those within.
There is but one good Street, in which is store
Of faire Maides, some say; but of faire shops, more:　　　150
Wares are dogg-cheape; ô might *Southampton* bee
In *London*, it would grow rich presently.

What shall wee doe? Wee are againe invited
To *Chillings*, where wee erst were so delighted;
Are wee againe invited? lett us goe: 155
Some men are such, that when you doe not know
Which way to pay them for their past Goodwill,
Your onely Thanks is, to oppresse them still.
Two daies more here wee sport, and then provide
For our Returne: but as a fondling Bride   160
Kisses, and clippes, and hugges her dearest spouse,
To stay him; so the couple of the House
Plotted a thousand stratagems to hold us,
And in an open Auditorie told us,
Wee should bee well-come there, if wee would stay   165
Not for a month, or Yeare, but ev'n for ay.
Learn, learn to handle Guests, yee Northern partes,
And at the least-wise gett you Southern hearts;
Yee thinke it much, when one hath brought a Gift,
If for a Draught of beere yee lett him shift: 170
And when by chance yee bidd a friend sitt downe
To suppe with you, yee doe so swell and frowne
That serving-men can hardly discerne whether
Yee suppe asunder, or yee suppe together.

[folio 47]

[61]

On a Lover.

That youth, whom you see walke before
The front of his curst Mistris doore,
Is noe whitt wett, though hee bee faine
To undergoe a Showr of Raine;
The reason is, within him lie   5
Such fires, as him all over drie.

[folio 47ᵛ]

[62]

An epitaph on Master Little
of Abingdon.

Behold him here to dust and ashes turn'd
Who in his life with zeale and Charity burn'd:
Witnesse the Church, the Crosse, the Hospitall
Repaird at most of his Charge: witnesse all
Those later Rites, which beautifie the towne,   5
Such are, the Mace before the Mayor, the gowne
For aldermen, and Privilieges many
Which hee ('tis strange!) gott without loosing any.
Witnesse himselfe, who foure years was a Mayor,
A burgesse forty two; who dealt so faire   10
That hee was once made of the Parliament:
Who, where hee gayn'd, was just; free, where hee spent.
    Reader, if none of all these Witnesses
Will serve thy Turne, take one more; witnesse Blisse.

[folio 48]

[63]

To one of my acquaintance.

The widow, which thou marry'dst, being dead,
A yong and handsome damsell thou dost wedd:
Thy policie, in both kindes, I approve;
Some things thou dost for Mony, some for Love.

[folio 48ᵛ]

[64]

To Sir *Giles Fetiplace*, high
sheriffe of *Glocester-shire*. 1633.

Sir, all the Wishes, which an humble Friend
May send to the high Sh'riff, I to You send.
The joyes of Harvest-men, when they have reapt
Their long expected Croppe, bee on You heapt;
The joyes of *Christmas*, which is to the Yeare   5
As to a Ring a pearle, and breedes good Cheare,
The joyes of brides and Bride-groomes the first night,
When they at once doe trouble and delight,
The joyes of such a rich man, as despaires
Of having sonnes, and yet at last getts heires,   10
The joyes, which Conquerours conceive, when they
Are told the Newes, how they have wonne the day,
The joyes of Princes, when they are made Kings,
A martyr's joyes, when in the fire hee sings,
The joyes, which you deserve, to you bee given,   15
The joyes of a cleare Conscience, and of heaven.

These verses I made ex tempore upon the Command of my Father.

BODLEIAN MS DON. C. 24: POEMS

[folio 49]

[65]

To B.R. a Dissembler.

Thought wee that all the World was false, but You,
And finde wee now that all, but You, are true?
Would wee scarce credit any Bishop's oath,
Taking your naked word; and shall the Troth
Of poëts grow to such Repute, that (if   5
You are noe Poët) they gaine our Beliefe?
Of late our very Shop-men, when they tell
Their customers how they doe use them well,
Are payd the totall summe: but wee had neede
Misdoubt our Faith, when You repeat the Creede.   10
Good lord! what means your inconsiderate Tongue
To doe her neighbring Members so much Wrong,
As dwelling just between your Braines and Heart,
To jarre, and not agree with either part?
Take heed lest shee devise some kinde of Plott   15
Against your other limbes: why may shee not
Your comely Legge into suspicion bring,
That 'tis some patcht-upp artificiall thing?
Why may shee not prove how your Face is faire
Onely by Paint? or how instead of Haire   20
You weare a perywigge? when what is best
Deceives us, wee guesse ill of all the rest.
Was it for this, wee us'd to bring you home,
And early in the Morne againe to come

F = Folger Ms. V.a.170, pp. 285–86

Title:	B.R.] *om.* F.
4	*your*] thy F.
6	*You are*] Thou art F.
8	*how*] that F.
11	*your*] thy F.
16	*your*] thy F.
17	*Your*] Thy F.
18	*'tis . . . patcht-upp*] it is but some F.
19	*your*] thy F.
23	*you home*] thee whome F.

Ere you were upp? was it for this, wee chose   25
You master of our Stage-plaies, and our Showes?
Wee were too blame in teaching your greene age
How to performe the sly Tricks of a stage;
Why did wee lett you act? alas, wee feare
That you did learne how to dissemble there.   30
    See now how well I love you! After all
Thee my Acquaintance, thee my Friend I call;
Though thou hast justly lost thy Clayme in mee,
Yet will I alwaies challenge Right to Thee.

---

26   *Stage-plaies . . . our*] playes, our Masques, and F.
27   *your*] thy F.
        age] aye F.
32   *my*] mine F.

[folio 49ᵛ]

[66]

On a Race.

In vaine men came to see *Tharuleot* runne,
    For, hee too sodaine was for humane sight;
Hee scarcely had began, when hee hadd donne,
    And did at once take horse, goe through, alight:
Many him standing at both endes have seene,   5
But never any saw him ride betweene.

[folio 50]

[67]

To Mistris Thorold of Arborvill.

Blest creature, laugh at my Mistake. When I
Behold your childrens Faces, and there spie
Lillies and Roses, I beginne to feare
You have noe Flowrs, but those which doe grow here:
Yet straight againe (ô foolish!) when I see   5
Your garden, and the Beauties which there bee,
I feare, you have noe issue; all your Blisse,
All your Delight, I feare, consists in this.
For why? can you at once doe two things well?
Can you in this Bedd, in that Bedd, excell?   10
To breed faire slippes, is nothing; to breed faire
Daughters, is common: to breed both, is rare.
Wonder of fruitfulnesse, who ever knewe
Any thus doubly happy, besides You?

[folio 50ᵛ]

[68]

An immoderate Love.

Still art thou sick, dear Youth? 'Tis my great griefe
That I at all can yeeld thee noe Reliefe;
Yet thus much I'l doe for thee, I will trie
Whether or noe it bee a paine to die.
Sure 'tis noe paine; Hell hath already sent   5
All the paines on thee, which it can invent:
Sure 'tis a paine; if Death should painlesse bee,
How soone wouldst thou from this badd Life bee free?
But I will slay my selfe, to cleare the Doubt:
'Tis done; so, now the truth I have found out.   10
    Dear youth, 'tis paine to die; but then againe
To die for thee, deare Youth, it is noe paine.

[folio 51]

[69]

For a discontented Scholar of Ox-
-ford, 1632, these following verses
were written while the King
was at Woodstock.

To *Michaël Oldisworth*, Esquier.

In seeing You, Sir, I have seene the Court.
'Tis now enough; I wish noe ampler sporte.
You are to mee the King, queen, prince, and Lordes:
The rest are but a troupe of pompous wordes.
The progresse may to some a number seeme,   5
One man to bee the Progresse I esteeme;
And when they talk of Parks, and stags, and houndes,
I into You alone contract these soundes.
Though twenty thousand Soules at Woodstock bee,
What are those twenty thousand Soules to mee?   10
They are noe Friends of mine, nor doe they Love mee.
'Tis my ill fortune, if they are above me.
Give mee a man whom I may call my owne:
I meddle not with such as are unknowne.
Suppose now that the Sun and Moon should shine   15
On many people's heades, but not on mine,
Or that the Constellations should with-hold
Their force, and leave mee darklong and acold,
Thinke you that I would worship Sun and Moone?
Noe: I would see them both extinct as soone.   20
Or that the Constellations should out-brave mee?
Yes, lett them doe mee good, if they will have mee.
One litle Star, who gave mee Light and Heate,
Him I would honour, more than all the greate.

BODLEIAN MS DON. C. 24: POEMS   119

[folio 51ᵛ]

[70]

On the picture of Beauty.

Here joyn'd you see white Snow, and purple Fire;
The one doth move, the other quench Desire:
Feare not or Freezing, or excessive heate,
The worst that can fall out, is but Cold sweat.
   O who of such a mixture can complaine,   5
Where still the Cure is equall to the Paine?

F = Folger MS, V.a.170, p. 313

Title: *On the*] On the picture of yong Master Bacon, as it is sett upp beyond sea, and
           entiled. The F
2   *doth*] does F.

[folio 52]

[71]

On a Bagge of Perfumes
given him by a Friend.

Aske mee noe more the Cause why Oxford-Winde
Sweeter than spik-nard, and than myrrhe, wee finde,
Or why our fresh and odoriferous Aire
May with *Arabian* frank-incense compare;
The fragrancie, which in this silk-bagge lies,   5
Might ev'n turne Sodom to a Paradise.
    Yet hee, which gave mee this, as much excells
The choysest steam of such compounded Smells,
As *Nature* excells *Arte*: his panther-Breath
Hath oft preserv'd a Citizen from death,   10
Whilst, comming where the Plague was, hee putt downe
That tyrannous Disease, and clear'd the Towne.

F = Folger MS. V.a.170, p. 331

---

1   *more*] mor[e *over* r] F.
4   *May*] My F.
5   *fragrancie*] Frankinsence F.
8   *steam*] steames F.

[folio 52ᵛ]

[72]

To an acquaintance.

The angels doe so wish for thee,
And strive to have thy conmpanie,
That till wee doe thy Letters reade,
Wee alwaies feare lest thou art dead;
Then lett us from thee often heare,   5
That so wee may not often feare.

[folio 53]

[73]

A lover's fancie.

How wise, how good, how faire art Thou, my dear!
Whose onely fault is, that thou art not here:
Yet is thy Absence very small Annoy;
For why? thee in my selfe I can enjoy.
Give mee but such a Bodie, such a Minde,   5
As I already have, and I will finde
Ten thousand wayes to make my *Genius* sport,
Whilst in conceipt thy matchlesse shade I court.
As oft as Day shall breake, I will suppose
I see thy wondrous Brightnesse: when I close   10
Mine eies, or lett my Head stoup downe, I'l thinke
It is on Thee, that I thus nodde, or winke.
Thy breath shall yeeld mee aire: and as oft as
Any pure Odours through my nostrils passe,
I'l straight crie, Sure my sweetest lately went   15
Along these coasts, for, this is right her Sent.
Noe word shall scape my Tongue, but what is spoken
In some sort, unto Thee: and for a token
That those men, which kisse least, are most in love,
With touches voyd of Lust my lippes I'l move.   20
My folded Armes shall never change their places,
But when they seeme to answer thy Embraces;
Embraces not prophane, but chast and holy:
And by a new-found Art, bequeathing wholly
My selfe to Thee, what thing so-ere is mine   25
I'l hugge that thing, that thing, I'l vow, is thine.

[folio 53ᵛ]

[74]

On Mistris Summer, who dyed in child-bedd.

Wake, wake deare creature. Does it not suffice
That for one Labour thou hast rested twice?
Thou in the Bedd, and in the Grave, hast laine:
'Tis high time now to stirre, and rise againe.
Upp, upp, and come abroad. Thy tedious Sleepe   5
Does make thy very new-born Daughter weepe:
The litle Infant cries, to thinke that Shee
Should of her Mother thus forsaken bee.
Shee is worse us'd, then is the Fawne or Lambe,
Who though they want a cradle, have a Damme.   10
Doe not, ô doe not barre her from the Teat.
Poore girle! 'tis too too soone to weane her yet.

These verses were written at the request of a Londoner.

[75]

On the death of both Mistris Summer and her Childe.

Now wee perceive why mortals have two Eies:
'Tis 'cause in such like Woes they might weep twice.
A paire of griefes just fitts a paire of crosses:
Too small are single Teares for double Losses.
    Mourn, *London*, mourn. Loe! she that was the Head   5
Of all religious Citizens, is dead.
Shee was noe fickle zelot, who by Turnes
Is good and badd, now freezes, and now burnes:
Who one day goes to heare a godly Text,
And goes to heare a bawdy Play the next: 10
Who somtimes hates a ribond or a lace,
And somtimes loves to weare a painted face.
Shee was a constant matron, still devoute,
Whose shining Lampe of faith was never out:
Her life made Sermons; and shee sham'd the Preacher   15
By doing better things than hee could teach her.
Where-ere shee went, there Temples were in vaine;
Each man was holy where her Worth did raigne:

And had it not beene so, that shee had dyed,
Paul's church had scarcely beene re-edifyed.   20
    The mother was but just gone, when the Daughter
Was too too mannerly, and follow'd after;
As if the Babe had thought it some Dishonour
To lett her goe alone, and wayted on Her.
Farewell, blest Soules. This riddle yee shall have   25
Writt for an Epitaph upon your Grave:
"Here lies a couple, who a While were one,
"And when they once were two, then they were none.

[folio 54]

[76]

To a Lady, looking out
of a window.

Madam: they say, when-ere
You doe abroad appeare,
 The weather then is faire;
But when your selfe you hide,
And within doores abide,   5
 Then cloudy is the Aire.
The sunne n'er shewes his face,
But when You come in place;
 O doe not, doe not stay:
But yeeld to our Request,   10
And straitwayes make us blest
 With a cleare joyfull Day.

[folio 54ᵛ]

[77]

On the death of Sir
Rowland Cotton.

Were he but one brave person, and noe more,
Wee scarcely would the Losse of him deplore,
But hee was many: and in Him alone
Whole multitudes of worthy men are gone.
Strange! strange! hee was so variously skill'd   5
Hee seem'd with soules of all kindes to bee fill'd;
Had hee beene sundred into partes, you might
Of every limbe of his, have made a Knight.
His working braines would well a *Ralegh* make,
His face a *Sydney*, and his heart a *Drake*.   10
His handes might, by themselves, have serv'd for Forces,
If wee had wanted Ord'nance, foote, or Horses;
His diverse-Tongues to *Babel* had allusion,
Onely hee spake them all without confusion.
His very leggs perform'd such wondrous things   15
As were the Talke of two great Western kings,
When hee those *Danes*, which were to *England* sent
To shew their *Leaping*, by foure foot out-went.
  Mighty prince *Henry*, if thou now hadst liv'd
For this thy darling how wouldst thou have griev'd!   20
But lie thou still, and in thy tomb-stone sleepe:
'Twere ill, if wee did call thee upp to weepe.
Under thy brother *Charles* wee better thrive
Then that wee should wish thee againe alive.

[folio 55]

[78]

On an Arbour made by Master Ri-
-chard Bacon, on the sea-shoar
opposite to the ile of Wight.

When I approacht that happy place,
 Where once my Friend was wont to rest,
Each object was so full of grace,
 Mee thought, I was all over blest:
What-ere I saw, what-ere I felt,   5
What-ere I heard, what-ere I smelt,
My senses told my Soule, that Shee
Just thus in Paradise should bee.

The plants there, polisht by his hand,
 So greene, so tall, so upright grow,   10
And in such dainty order stand,
 As if their Authour they did know:
Their barkes are faire, their stocks are strong,
Their leaves are sweet, their twigs are long;
And ev'ry branch, and ev'ry limbe   15
Retaines a certaine Touch of Him.

Noe jutting Stumpe, or testy Thorne,
 Noe clownish Bramble dares dwell nigh;
But all base Shrubbes, which there are borne
 Doe learn good manners straight, and die: 20
If any Broome there happes to bee,
It chandges to some better Tree;
Furz too and Thistles, in fewe daies,
Doe turne to Eglantine and Baies:

The sand forgetts its barrennesse,   25
 And by an unexpected Spring

F = Folger MS. V.a.170, pp. 322–26

---

14 *long*] [strong *del.*] /long/ F.
16 *Touch*] *om.* F.

Produceth hearbes and flowrs, noe lesse
    Than those which Gardens use to bring:
Still to the Water holding true
The grasse maintaines his wonted hue,   30
And for the Sea's sake, will bee seene
Cladd in noe Livery, but greene.

The waves soak through the Earth, and strive
                                 To

[folio 55ᵛ]

    To leave their saltish dreggs behind,
That to these Rootes they may derive   35
    Newe moisture of a fresher kinde:
The gentle Aire, in modest sort,
Does with the Woodbine's tresses sport;
And whisp'ring Windes, in calmer Gales,
Beare to the Myrtle's eare soft tales.   40

The royall Sunne, in gorgeous wise,
    Oft comes a suitor to this Bower,
But shee does coily Him despise,
    And keepes her selfe in her owne power.
Nor cares shee, though hee, at her doores,   45
Her favour and goodwill implores;
Shee will not such a Foole bee made
As yeeld to Him her virgin Shade.

Shee hath variety of Seates,
    Some high, some low, some old, some newe,   50
That which way ere the Weather beates
    With ease you may its force eschew:
Some hold that Tempestes therfore sigh
Because to Her they come not nigh;
And for the same Mishappe, that Raine   55
In teares of sorrow does complaine.

---

38   *sport*] sprtoe F.
45   *cares*] eares F.
53   *Tempestes:* Tempestes [*over . . . erased*].

BODLEIAN MS DON. C. 24: POEMS   129

Wheat, rye, and other Graines doe love
    By this good Neighbour to reside;
And therfore seldome they remove,
    But for the most part, here abide: 60
Groves likewise, and whole Troupes of wood
Are at a Call; as if they stood
Like yeomen of her Guard, to arme
If there rose any feare of Harme.

At hott times Shee keepes Deaw within,   65
    To coole Her both by day and night;
But when the Winter does beginne,
    Those chill Droppes she dismisseth quite:
Frost never nippes her; and although
Her garrets sometimes take-in Snow,   70
                                    Yet

[folio 56]

Yet where her Hall and Parlour lies
Such hoary inmates shee defies.

The ruder Cattle are pent out,
    Lest they should croppe those buds of hers;
But fawnes and kiddes may play about,   75
    And lambes, and Hares, and grasse-hoppers:
The nightingale here yeelds such Choise
Of musick from one litle Voice,
That till you doe its bodie see
You would it guesse a Quire to bee.   80

Ships, boates, and Castles you may spie
    If you desire a Prospect neare;
Or if you farther cast your eie
    Rockes on the other side appeare.

---

61   *Groves*] [< . . . > *del.*] Groves F.
75   *play about*] pla[. *altered to* y] abaut F.
77   *here*] there F.

Alas! I grant, here wants one Sight: 85
Or else, with all your Heart, you might
For ever in this Arbour sitt;
Here wants Himselfe, who planted it.

---

85   *here*] there F.
86   *Heart*] H[<.> *altered to* e]art F.

[folio 56ᵛ]

[79]

To the builders or Repairers
of Paul's Church in London.

'Tis true, Stone-temples can noe more containe
The lord, than Nut-shels can eclose the Maine;
But if on earth God chooseth any place
Which with his presence hee doth chiefly grace,
Goe on, and bee yee sure (Sirs) that where-ere   5
His PROGRESSE is, his constant COURT is here.

[folio 57]

[80]

A Paradoxe.

To one whom hee both extremly lo-
-ved, and extremly hated.

Thou best of good things, thou of badd things worst,
O how thou blest art, ô how thou art curst!
Thou sweetest bitter, I can scarce debate
If I should love thee more, or more thee hate.
Thou neither, and thou both, I doe not knowe   5
Whether to call thee FRIEND, or call thee FOE/./
Thou art the author of my greatest joyes:
Thou art the author of my chiefe Annoyes.
What-ere haps to mee well, it springs from thee:
From thee it springs, what-ere haps ill to mee.   10
Were it not for thee, I my selfe would kill:
Were it not for thee, I would yet live still;
At high Noone thou dost blinde mee like the Night:
By thee, I see at mid-night, as by light.
Without thee, Pleasure is a paine to mee: 15
Paine to mee is a pleasure, without thee.
Thou art the Sawce which rellishes my Meat:
Thou art the Bane, which poisons what I eate.
Thy horrid Furies oft mee waking keepe:
Thy smiling graces lull mee oft asleepe.   20
When through thy Ice I freeze, Cloaths warm mee not:
When through thy flames I burn, Cloaths are too hott.
Wine is no wine, unlesse to Thee I drinke:
Wine is noe wine, if I on Thee doe thinke.
In thoughts, words, deedes, thou mak'st mee to mistake: 25
In thoughts, words, deeds, thou mee exact dost make.
My yong God thou art, thou art my yong Devill;
To good thou draw'st mee, thou mee draw'st to evill:
And when I ill doe, and when I doe well,
Thou art my Paradise, thou art my Hell.   30

---

11   *not*: /not/

[folio 57^v]

[81]

On Nobility.

From heav'n, noe doubt, wee are descended all:
For why? who may not god his Father call?

[folio 58]

[82]

To his Friend beyond sea.

Come, come: thy Stay, mee thinks, is such a thing
As doth our Kingdome out of order bring:
What else but Jarres and Tumults can here bee,
When thou art gone, our Love, our Harmonie?
Some goodnesse, wee confesse, was left behind   5
At thy departure; but now none wee finde:
Vertues thou didst bequeath to us good store,
But wee have spent those, and now begg for more;
Wee sinne so roundly, that of late the Devill
Letts us alone to tempt our selves to evill.   10
Our magistrates have found a crafty way
To punish faults in other folkes, that they
In their owne Wickednesse may beare noe Losse,
But to themselves all Vices may engrosse.
Our ladies plainly laugh their Lordes to scorn;   15
Noe man knowes, wherabouts his Wife was born:
Paynting they, fetch their Bodies and their Faces
Not from the same Shire, but from sundry places.
    Why write I satyres? O, I am afrayed
That to thee I the slanderer have played;   20
Griefe for thy absence, makes my Verses flowe
Crosse to my Reason. All the World does know
If Vertue any where bee to bee found
Under the Moone, it is on English ground.
But thy Remembrance causeth us to moane,   25
As if along with thee all Worth were gone.

[folio 58ᵛ]

[83]

To Citizens.

Sirs, all the World confesse, yee love your wives
Farre above or your Riches, or your Lives;
Yet them yee spoile: ô strange! that which men most
Affect, they soonest suffer to bee lost.
Yee spoile them, not that with your fawning Speeches   5
You make them proud, and apt to weare the breeches;
Nor that you give them Coine, and bidd them doe
Like gentle-women, and like Ladies too:
But that yee lett them lie so long in bedd
Till they grow pale, and to White change their Redd;   10
While twixt a paire of sheets they spend the day
Their blood, for want of stirring, turnes to whey.
    Good lord! how many tallow Skinnes wee meet
At *London*, in each parish, in each Street?
Walk from the *Towre* to *Wesminster*, and yee   15
Scarcely a ruddy Cheek, or Lippe, shall see;
Like moyst'ned Snow, or like a sullyed peece
Of chalke, or like the country-man's soft Cheese,
Or like this Paper, on which now I write,
Just so their Faces look, ghastly, and white.   20
They have such wither'd veines, that some folkes say
They never blush after their wedding-day;
Noe kind of Shame, noe angry mood, noe Praise
Can a fresh colour in their faces raise:
And (which torments them worst) Paints cannot hide   25
Their palenesse, but it ev'n through Paints is spy'd.
Oft hath an honest Chapman meant to buy,
And comme into a Shoppe, when by and by
Seeing a Ghost, which askt him what hee lackt,
Hee grew afrayd, and straight away he packt.   30
Is not this madnesse, to have such a Wife
As shall bee dead ere shee hath lost her life?

[folio 59]

[84]

On the Commencement at Cam-
-bridge. 1632.

Cambridge, though in thy Praise wee dare not write,
Yet since some wrong'd thee, wee will doe thee Right.
There were, who either stole, or made a Jeast,
And sayd forsooth Thy meat so ill was drest
As scholars were the cookes; thy learned guere   5
So ill was penn'd, as cookes the Scholars were.
False, on my knowledge: 'tis as false as Hell;
In faith thy Gownes and Aprons both did well.

BODLEIAN MS DON. C. 24: POEMS

[folio 59ᵛ]

[85]

To a gentle-woman that de-
-lighted too much in her garden.

Look what a litle shredd of earth it is,
Wherin you place your Joy, and fixe your blisse:
I thought that you so good had beene, and wise
The totall Globe could not your minde suffice.
Fie, come away. Think but how vile and base   5
They are, who labour alwaies in one place;
None but A Prisoner or a Mill-horse sure
To doe the same, as you doe, would endure.
You see, the Plough-men, though they sweat and moile,
Are yet so happy as to change their Soile,   10
And though perchance they meet with some choise Plott
(Like that, which you now till) yet doe they not
Stay there, but freely walk on, and proceede
As if they wrought for Pleasure, not for Neede.
The delving Foxes, and the toyling Moles,   15
Doe follow you perhaps in scratching holes,
But sure they scorne to bee besotted so
As never from the self-same holes to goe.
The muck-hill Cock enjoyes a richer Ground
Then any in your Quarters can bee found,   20
And yet hee often findes a time to play,
Whilst shamlesse You stand toiling here for ay.
   Why, you doe kill your selfe, and doe endure
More weathers, then the Hearbs which you manure:
Lett it bee cold, or hott, or wett, or drie,   25
Or night, or day, yet on the earth you lie.
I tremble when I think how oft you have
Beene digging, and providing your owne Grave.
I tremble when I think how oft you meete
Wormes crawling upp and down your Arms and Feete.   30
Who knowes, alas! who knowes how soon you may
Bee layd too deeply in these beddes of clay?
Who knowes how soon these Sprigs may mourn for You,
And bee made moist with Tears, instead of Deaw?
I should bee loath to see you die, and weare   35
Such flowrs, such knots, such borders, as grow here;
Mee thinks, those borders, knots, and flowrs, which are
Now on you, doe become you better farre.

[folio 60]

[86]

On London Waies. 1632.

The common Rodes about the realme are worse
Than can be conquer'd well by any Horse;
But as you nearer to the Court repaire
The rodes are alwaies even, wide, and faire:
If by the owners wee may judge of things,   5
Those high-wayes are the people's, these the King's.

[folio 60ᵛ]

[87]

To his friend beyond sea.

Wee know not (dearest) in what part
Or corner of the World thou art;
But this wee know, what-ever place
Holdes thee, it noe way can bee base.
Thy goodnesse is of such a force,   5
That though the Natives were farre worse
Then vipers; by its onely power
They would turne honest in an houre.
Wee sooner may conceive a Night
There, where the Sun gives perfect light,   10
Than think those people can bee naught
Who are by thy Example taught.
If any thing thou see awry
It straight is mended by thy Eie;
And is corrected by thine Eare,   15
If any thing amisse thou heare.
Vice shuns thee, as the Meteors flie
From those fires, which them purifie.
Noe filth dares tarry any where
Within the compasse of thy Spheare.   20
    What sayst thou? I confesse, my Muse
Speakes false: but I must Her excuse,
So alike Thou and Vertue looke,
My muse for Vertue thee mistooke.

[folio 61]

[88]

On the Christmas at Cosham
in Wilt-shire. 1632.

As those, which for a While in Heav'n have been,
Relate not what things they have heard and seene,
But onely in a silent joy admire:
So wonder I, and so I reach noe higher.
   Sir *Edward Hungerford*, that more than Knight,   5
To all at once imparts both Heat and light;
Throughout his Palace, wee can hardly see
Or brighter Lampes, or warmer Fires, than Hee:
And though in ev'ry roome hee keepes good Cheare,
Yet hee himselfe is still the best Dish there.   10
Hee rules us so, as yong Kings rule their Courts:
Hee lengthens our Delights, extends our sports,
Stoppes the Approach of Night, and will not lett
Our mirth for eighteen houres together sett;
As hee were some newe Sun: whose wondrous raies   15
In midst of Winter made long Summer-Daies.
   It holds not thus for two weekes, but for ay:
Here are noe bounds of Feasting, or of Play.
Guests doe not come and goe, but tarry ever:
Their year may sometimes end, their Christmas never.   20
December is but one month other-where:
December is noe lesse then twelve months here.
I scarce know what the Innes of court yee call,
But sure this single House excells them all:
And if it had its right, each novice Heire   25
To Cosham, not to London, would repaire;
Fooles, as they are! which fare ill, and pay deare,
When they might fare well, and pay nothing here.

F = Folger MS. V.a.170, pp. 282–83

Title: *the*] his **F.**
          in . . . 1632] *om.* **F.**
15   *raies*] raise **F.**
17   *not thus*] thus not **F.**
          for] *om.* **F.**
18   *bounds*] b/o/undes **F.**

[folio 61ᵛ]

[89]

To Master *M.B.* the whilst his
picture was drawing.

Wee would (blest Youth) that thou shouldst never goe
From England, but wee cannot have it so,
Our kingdome is too litle, to containe
The many Wonders of so great a Braine:
Thou dost well therfore, thus to leave behind   5
The living copie though not of thy minde
Yet of thy Bodie; that at least-wise wee
Might in this sort enjoy the halfe of Thee.

[folio 62]

[90]

On Master Swaine, who deceas-
-ed upon good friday.

Swain dy'd that day as Christ dy'd. O that *Swain*
That day, as Christ arose, might rise againe.

Master Swain
lies buryed in
Christ-church.
Oxon.

[folio 62ᵛ]

[91]

To his litle Brother
Giles Oldisworth.

So yong? so small? and yet so good a Poët?
Deare infant, I am wondrous proud to know it.
Lett mee weepe over thee; I cannot choose
But strangely melt away, and sweetly loose
My selfe in thy Embraces: ô, I must   5
In love doe that, which others doe in Lust.
    Kisse mee; kisse mee againe: from these same lippes
It is, that such delightfull Musick skippes;
From these same lips. Take heed, lest with the choise
And strong Enchantments of thy powrfull Voice   10
Shortly thou ravish Virgins, and beginne
To make Maides wish thee old enough to sinne.
Numbers worke much on females: diverse times
Those who resist Gold are ore-come by Rymes.
    Give mee thy hand; this white and slender Hand   15
Hath but one match or fellow in the land,
And that too is thy owne: this pretty paire
Of handes, write Verses so exact and faire,
That many Strangers doe mistake thy Age,
And ask when thou wilt sell Plaies to the stage.   20
Trust mee the issues of thy childish Penne
Might well bee fatherd on our ablest Men.
    But why do I forgett the other part
Of thee? for, Thou but half of thy selfe art;

F = Folger MS. V.a.170, pp. 316–17

---

5   *thy*] the F.
9   *choise*] /choise/ F.
14   *who*] which F.
16   *or*] of F.
17   *thy*] thine F.
20   *stage*] staye F.
22   *fatherd*] featherd F.
      ablest] gravest F.

Robin is hee who makes thee upp complete: 25
Till he comes, we may spell thee; but as yet
Wee cannot reade thee, or thee putt together.
Yet because yee are twins, I care not whether
I speak to Him, or Thee: you two were gott
And borne at once; and wherfore should I not   30
So speake to one, as if I spake to both?
Robin and *Gilёs*, to tell the very troth,
Seeme not each like to each, but each the same,
And are disjoyn'd in nothing, but in Name.

28   *yee*] you F.

BODLEIAN MS DON. C. 24: POEMS

[folio 63]

[92]

For an Innes of courts man.

To his Mistris.

Dearest: I call you so, because I spend
More on you, than on my entirest Friend;
You and your Maid have both learnt tricks to crave
And gett from mee, almost what-ere I have:
If by a crafty Chance it comes to passe   5
That you or Shee doe hide your Looking-glasse,
Shee weeping comes to mee, and sayes 'tis broken,
Whence by mee straight a new one is bespoken;
If any trifles (as a Watch, or Gemme)
Fancie you, forthwith I must purchase them.   10
    I pray you now, forbeare. You answer, Why?
You know, Sir, nothing Wee to You denie.
Do not you so? this one Boon grant mee then,
Never to aske me any thing agen.

F = Folger MS. V.a.170, p. 327

Title: *For . . . man*] *om.* F.
13   *grant*] gra/n/t F.

[folio 63ᵛ]

[93]

On Abraham Cowley the
yong poët laureat.

Ben Johnson's wombe was great; and Wee
Did doubt, what might the issue bee:
But now hee brings forth to his praise,
And loe, an Infant crown'd with Baies.

F = Folger MS. V.a.170, p. 312

---

4   *an*] and F.

BODLEIAN MS DON. C. 24: POEMS   147

[folio 64]

[94]

To Mistris Katharine Bacon.

You doe well, Fairest, that although so many
Sue to you, yet you never yeeld to any;
You were not made for wedlock: You are one
By all to bee desir'd, attayn'd by none.
'Tis pay enough for those who come and court,   5
If you vouchsafe to lett them make you Sport;
And if they once but happe to move your laughter,
They are for ever bound to serve you after.
What man is hee, who hath so litle Witt,
That hee will not confesse himselfe unfitt   10
To match with you? and thinke it farre more pride
To wish You, then to wish the Moone, his Bride?
Your partes are numberlesse: wee may as well
Reckon the Beauties of the skie, or tell
How many Stars there bee, as count your graces;   15
And should a single mortal's rude Embraces
Compasse you wholly? Should those limbs of Heaven
Which were too much for all, to one bee given?
Noe: if indeed some new Trick wee could finde
How to distribute You amongst Mankinde,   20
If wee could sunder you without your harme,
And give this Prince a legg, that Duke an arme,
If wee could turne your fingers into wives,
And make your Haires save longing gallants Lives,

H = British Library Harley MS. 6918, fol. 91–91^v.
R$_2$ = Rosenbach MS. 1083/17 [Phillips MS. 8270], fols. 85^v–86

Title	*To . . . Bacon.* To a Mistres **R**$_2$
3	*were*] are **H**
7	*once . . . your*] chance but once to make you **R**$_2$.
9	*who*] that **R**$_2$.
17	*those*] thes **H**.
18	*were*] are **H**, **R**$_2$.
20	*amongst*] among **H**.
21	*sunder*] sever **R**$_2$

Then might you bee unvirgin'd: and then Wee   25
Quite round the Earth might happy Husbands see;
Then might the very Naile of your least Toe
Bee lady to an upstart Knight, or so.
But now (alas!) there is noe other way,
You and the phoenix must lack mates for ay.   30
    Believe it, sweetest, if you had your due,
Noe lesse then half the World should marry You.

---

26   *Earth might*] world should **R**₂
        see] bee **H**, **R**₂.
29   *there is*] ther's **R**₂.
32   *half the*] the whole **R**₂.

[folio 64ᵛ]

[95]

On the transparencie of Master Took-
er's house at Strettam.

If, as
This way you passe,
Quite through the window-Glasse
You spie what is, shall bee, and was
Done in this house; lett it not you amaze: 5

Trust mee,
Who-ere they bee
That live so well, as Hee,
Neede never care who comes to see;
The workes of Light affect not Secrecie.   10

[folio 65]

[96]

A satyre.

On occasion of Master   his
departure out of England.

If both my Eies doe full of water stand,
One weepes for Him, the other for our Land,
One weepes for Him, because hee was my friend,
The other for our land, which did offend.
    Wee well may think that somthing went amisse,   5
When hee us left, who our good angell is.
Confesse, great Britain: ô what hast thou done,
To fright away thy best and fairest Sonne?
Hast thou hatcht Cowards, who doe seeme well bredd
Because they lie warme, and are richly fedd;   10
Who with soft females have so much to doe,
That they themselves become soft females too;
Who never heare a Trumpet or a Drumme,
But when to Stage-plaies or to Showes they come?
Hast thou sett flocks of soules to Priests, who feed   15
Men so, as if men were but sheepe indeed;
Who shine, like those false Night-lampes on the way,
Not to direct folks, but to make folks stray?

F = Folger MS. V.a.170, pp. 305–6

Title: *A . . . his*] On yong Master Bacons F.
1   *of*] /of/ F.
6   *hee*] hee hee F.
14   *they*] thy F.
16   *Men*] them F.
17   *the*] th[y *altered to* e] F.
18   *stray*] st[<.> *altered to* r]ay F.

BODLEIAN MS DON. C. 24: POEMS   151

Hast thou rais'd Armies, who uphold our Foes?
Or chosen States-men, who &c.   20

---

20   *who &c*]   who our Realmes oppose?
                All is not right: thou sure hast done some ill,
                Else loving Bacon would have dwelt here still.
                Farewell now all our hopes. We thought to bee
                As learned and as honest as is Hee.
                Had hee staid longer with us hee by fitts   25
                Would have refind our Hearts, and cleared our witts
                But hee goes from us, and our good partes faile
                Just by degrees as hee away does saile.
                Wee plainly feele our selves growe worse and worse
                Yet wee must rest content, and take our course.   30
                Why should wee build Temples, or found schooles?
                Wee are ordayned to bee both Knaves and Fooles. **F**

[folio 65ᵛ]

[97]

For a Lover, standing by
a Smith's shoppe:

An Ode.

Marke this same Smith, how with his Bellowes hee
    Augments the flame, and propagates the Fire:
Just so I blow, and so my lungs use mee,
    With puffing Sighs encreasing my Desire.
O, had I tooles as good as his, by Arte   5
Soft I would make my Mistris iron heart.

Still mark him, how with Water hee revives
    The coales, and frames a kind of burning Raine:
Just so I droppe; and so my Weeping strives
    To quench my inward Heat: but all in vaine.   10
Would I were such a VULCAN, as is hee;
Then VENUS sure would better favour mee.

BODLEIAN MS DON. C. 24: POEMS 153

[folio 66]

[98]

To all his Acquaintance.

My mates, I give you here to understand
If any of you lacks or House, or Land,
Lett him repaire to mee. I scorne to use you
Like many of your Kindreds, who abuse you;
Nor will I torture you, like fretfull Lordes,   5
And pay you all your Wages in sharpe wordes:
Nor will I deale with you, as Beggars deale
With their poore friends, and teach you how to steale.
Desire of mee an hundred thousand poundes,
Desire of mee or Shippes, or Plate, or groundes,   10
Or any thing; I care not what you want:
You shall not say that ever I was scant.
    Why? what is my Estate? To tell you true,
I stand in greater Need, than most of You;
But I would still have my Companion such,   15
That hee should worthy bee to aske so much.

F = Folger MS. V.a.170, pp. 326–27

---

4   *Kindreds*] Kindred F.
6   *And*] Who F.
       you] you[r *del.*] F.
7   *you*] *om.* F.
15   *Companion*] Companions F.

[folio 66ᵛ]

[99]

For a Lover, whose Mistris con-
-cealed her selfe from him.

Appeare
My deare;
Thou dost doe ill,
To lie hidd still:
For, whilst thou thus dost lurke,   5
Thou all things settst on worke,
And mak'st the universall World
In seeking after Thee, bee hurld.
Appeare: noe creature ere can quiet bee,
Or take its Rest, till it hath found out Thee.   10

The Skie
Does flie,
Searching each where
If thou art there,
And oft, for griefe, it raines   15
And in sadd Sighs complaines,
And oft, for anger, rends a Cloude
And lightens too, and roares aloude.
Appear: noe creature ere can quiett bee,
Or take its Rest, till it hath found out Thee.   20

The Fire
Stepps higher,
And rais'd by Love
It lookes above,
To trie if Thou bee not   25
About heav'n somwhere gott.
And failing of thee, it returnes
And chafes, and fumes, and smoaks, and burnes.
Appear: noe creature ere can quiett bee,
Or take its Rest, till it hath found out Thee.   30

Springs move,
Brookes rove;
                        Deawes

[folio 67]

Deaws come and goe,
Seas ebbe and flowe:
Their course fewe Waters stoppe 35
Till they with sweating droppe;
And through much Labour, growing weake
At last they melt their Grease, and breake.
Appear: noe creature ere can quiett bee,
Or take its Rest, till it hath found out Thee. 40

The sunne
Does runne
From clime to clime;
And at noe time
Hee shutts his drowzy Eies, 45
But watches still, and pries:
Yet 'cause hee speedes not, hee is faine
Each morning to beginne againe.
Appear: noe creature ere can quiett bee,
Or take its Rest, till it hath found out Thee. 50

And now
If thou
Art sought by these,
Then what small Ease
Doe I enjoy? who would 55
(If possibly I could)
Divide my selfe in foure, and send
East, west, north, south, for my Shee-friend.
Appear: noe creature ere can quiett bee,
Or take its Rest, till it hath found out Thee. 60

156 BODLEIAN MS DON. C. 24: POEMS

[folio 67ᵛ]

[100]

To Master Michaël Oldisworth
comming to Oxford, 1633.
March 30.

Were it (Sir) any other time, You should
Bee quite as welcome as our Chanc'lour could:
But since 'tis Lent, except you would grow leane,
Wee must confesse, wee wonder what you meane.
Here is nor Flesh, nor Fish. You might doe well,   5
If you your Horses and your Men would sell:
Else such a dreadfull Famine will ensue,
That wee shall scarce abstaine from eating You.
Nay, take you Heed. Wee *Cannibals* are faine
Our guests within our mawes to entertaine: 10
And those, which hither ride in hope to eate,
At once are both our Strangers and our Meat.
Thinke you that all the favours, which good You
In former yeares have done the learned crew,
Shall save you from our Teeth now? Noe indeed: 15
Our patrons still must feed us at our Neede.

F = Folger MS. V.a.170, p. 313

Title: *To*] On the right worshipfull F.
         comming] his comming F.
         1633] om. F.
13   *the*] those F.

[folio 68]

[101]

Amorous Dreames.

Oft in my Sleep I think thee (dearest) neare mee,
Oft I thee call, though thou dost seldome heare me;
Oft folded in my gladsome armes thou art:
Oft thou dost lie close joyning to my Heart.
Yet do I never see thee. Why, I pray?   5
All this is done by night, and not by day.

[folio 68ᵛ]

[102]

To an over-modest Ladie.

Madam, when I beganne to honour You,
And use those Ceremonies, which were due,
You stood so silent, that I fear'd lest I
Went to adore a piece of Imag'rie:
Yet I proceeded; I had rather bee   5
To you a Papist, than unmannerly.
Nor had I done amisse, if there were all:
But (see how quickly Protestants may fall!)
After I thus had found the way to erre,
And playd the superstitious Worshipper,   10
I heard and sawe a Miracle; for, You
At last did utter some Wordes, though but fewe.
Thus turnes my Faith, this my Religion breakes:
I am converted now a Statue speakes.

BODLEIAN MS DON. C. 24: POEMS   159

[folio 69]

[103]

To his Friend beyond sea,
March 26. 1633.

How haps it that the Spring so long does stay?
Must wee endure this Winter-time for ay?
When wee expected Leaves, and Grasse, and Flowers,
Behold here Frost, and Haile, and Snow, and showers.
Is it because the Sunne does from us bend,   5
And goes where hee may oft'ner see my Friend?
Or is it 'cause the Stars, and Skies, which Love
To gaze upon my Friend, doe slower move?
Oh noe: 'tis 'cause my Friend himselfe's not here.
Things would grow better, if hee present were.   10
The sun, the stars, the skies compar'd to Him
Are neither warme, nor bright, but cold and dimme.
Hee 'tis that should adorne our ile, and make
The earth to weare newe Liv'ries for his sake.
Hee 'tis that should shine on us, till each Tree   15
And every Ground became as gay as hee.
Had wee the least reflection from his face,
Wee should noe Beauty lack in any place.

F = Folger MS. V.a.170, pp. 283–84

Title: *To . . . 26*] On the backwardnesse of the / Spring March 25 F.
1   *that*] om. F.
18   *place*]   place.
          Come away dearest; dearest, come away.
          How happes it that the Spring so long does stay? F.

[folio 69ᵛ]

[104]

To the faire Mistris Burch,
at his first sight of her.

Divinest: wee confesse, when wee did viewe
Your picture, wee were loath to looke on You:
The shadow was so debonaire, that Wee
Fear'd lest the substance might inferiour bee.
Who would believe that Nature could excell   5
Art then, when Art had playd her game so well?
To finde a Ladie, which out-went such Paynt,
Were, on the earth, to find an heav'nly saint.
    Thus (doubters, as we were!) wee scarce could feign
That which now to our Eies appears most plaine: 10
Wee never thought, in all our daies, to see
Your like againe, when you your selfe were Shee.

The picture of
Mistris Burch
was in London
but shee her
selfe lived by the
sea-side

BODLEIAN MS DON. C. 24: POEMS   161

[folio 70]

[105]

On his Majesty's going
to Scotland. 1633

Whether or noe the King to Scotland goes,
Is a maine pointe of doubt. You say, hee does;
I say, hee does not. Kings doe never goe   These verses are
(Within their proper Realmes) or to, or fro;   in print.
Nor are they like to Men, now here, now there,   5
But like to Gods, are alwaies every where.
Will you deny, the Soule is in the Heart,
If you descry it in some other part?
Or will you say, the Leggs and Thighs are dead,
As oft as Life is in the Neck and Head?   10
Sure the great Body politique would perish,
If the same Spirit did not each limbe cherish.
Hath mighty *Charles* been absent all this while,
From noe lesse place, than halfe of this great ile?
And went he thither not till now? What then   15
Shall we determine of the Irish-men?
They have (alas!) small Hope to see him ere,
Unlesse that Hee bee seene already there.

F = Folger MS. V.a.170, p. 318

1633 = *Solis Britannici Perigæum. Sive Itinerantis Caroli Auspicatissima Periodus.* Oxford, 1633
[STC 19033] Sigs. M4–M4ᵛ. [The text is in italic, with roman for emphasis.]

TITLE: *On . . . Scotland*] On the present Newes F.
1633] *om.* F, **1633**.
3   **gloss**: *om.* F, **1633**.
4   *to*] two F.
       fro] f[<.>]ro F.
8   *you descry*] once you meete F.
10   *As . . . as*] Because that **1633**.
11   *Sure . . . great*] Surely the F.
14   *great*] vast **1633**.
17   *They*] the F.

Believe't, our monarch spreads, and at one time
Fills both the Northern and the Southern clime.   20
So farre, as any of his people bee,
The aire it selfe is less diffus'd, than Hee.

---

20   *Northern*] Southerne F, **1633**.
        Southern] Northerne F, **1633**.
22   *Hee*]   hee.
            To Edenborough rides hee? Noe, hee tarries
            At Dublin, London, Edenborough, Paris. **F**

BODLEIAN MS DON. C. 24: POEMS   163

[106]

On his Majesty's being
in Scotland.

What did your Highnesse meane, to tarry forth   This is in print.
So long, amongst the countries of the North?
Was it to passe the Summer in coole aire,
And keepe your body fresh, and newe, and faire?
'Tis true; your Love to England grew so hott,   5
It might have bredd a Fever, had you not
By this same Change of Dwellings, found a Way
Wherby its force to temper and allay.
O lett us learne of our Discreetest King
                                                    To

[folio 70ᵛ]

To use a Moderation in each thing.   10
Or was it to advance the Scottish glorie,
That when their chroniclers shall write the storie
Of this your Entertainment, and shall tell
How bravely things were carry'd, and how well
You liked all their Doings; they may say   15
That you at last were loath to part away?
'Tis very right: a good Prince is so blest
Hee alwaies thinks, the present place is best,
And every where hee findes such store of Love,

F = Folger MS. V.a.170, pp. 331–32
1633 = *Solis Britannici Perigæum. Sive Itinerantis Caroli Auspicatissima Periodus.* Oxford, 1633
       [STC 19033] Sigs. M4ᵛ–N1. [The text is in italic, with roman for emphasis.]

---

1   gloss: *om.* F, **1633**.
7   *Dwellings*] dwelling F.
9–10   *O . . . thing*] *om.* **1633**.
12   *Chroniclers*] chronic[h *altered to* l]ers F.
16   *loath*] lo/a/th F.
18   *Hee alwaies*] That he still **1633**.
19   *Love*] Loves **1633**.

He n'er is troubled, but in his Remove.   20
Or was it to enrich them with your bounty,
Spreading both gold and silver through each county,
That so, as many men, as could not see
Your selfe, might with your image solac'd bee?
Yes, 'twas to doe this, and 'twas to doe more: 25
Your gifts and graces reacht beyond the Poore
They stream'd into the Clergie, and did blesse
Those angels, with Encrease of Holynesse.
They crown'd the Nobles, whom-to they imparted
Such height of Worth, as made them royall-hearted.   30
Your vertues flew about in such large measure,
Men fear'd that You had quite consum'd your treasure;
But you have yet to spare, when all is donne,
Being immense and boundlesse; like the Sunne,
Who, though hee fills the World with Heat and Light,   35
Is not the colder, is not the less bright.

---

20   *in . . . Remove*] with this remove F; when he removes **1633**.
24   *image solac'd*] Stampe delighted **1633**.
27   *They*] The F.
29   *whom-to they*] and to those **1633**.
32   *that*] least **1633**.
35   *hee*] hee [the *del.*] F.
36   bright] bright, **F**.

BODLEIAN MS DON. C. 24: POEMS

[107]

On his Majesty's coming
from Scotland.

Yee maides of honour, goe and tell the Queene   This is in print.
Now her triumphant Husband may bee seene;
Lett her noe longer lead a Widow's life,
She is againe becomme a happy wife.
    Ah, how shee starts, good Ladie! Did you ere   5
Behold a Turtle, when her mate is neare?
Just so shee quivers, and begins to trie
If shee upon a Male can cast her eie

                               Her

[folio 71]

Her chast and modest Soule is so severe,
It knowes not whether more to hope or feare.   10
Should it now prove another, shee would die,
And then (ô traytor!) in what case were I?
But I am certaine. Take the Newes from mee,
And tell her, that I pawne my life, 'tis Hee.

F = Folger MS. V.a.170, pp. 331–32
1633 = *Solis Britannici Perigæum. Sive Itinerantis Caroli Auspicatissima Periodus.* Oxford,
     1633 [STC 19033]. Sigs. N1. [The text is in italic.]

---

5   *not indented* **1633**.
       you] yee **1633**.
14   *Hee*]   Hee
       Nic. Oldisworth Ct Church **1633**

[folio 71ᵛ]

[108]

For a Lover

To his absent Mistris.

From thee I nothing heare; yet I can tell
That thou (deare Soule) art both alive and well:
Sea, heav'n, and Earth in perfect health I see;
Sea, heav'n, and earth are but great partes of Thee.
The moving Orbes keepe one tune day and night,   5
Whence I doe gather that thy pulse beats right;
Springs yeeld fresh Water, Rivers ebbe and flowe,
By this, thy veines runne spritefull blood, I knowe:
Hee is not worthy to enjoy the Light,
Who doubts the piercing clearnesse of thy sight;   10
Behold, the single Sunne does blaze and shine,
What then does that same double Sun of thine?
Have I not learnt that all the glist'ring Skies
Are onely Raies reflected from thy eies;
And if they sometimes cease from being bright,   15
That 'tis when thou dost sleep, and wink up Light.
    Lutes, poëts, rhetoricians, brides, and spheares
Tell me, why sound they, if Thou hast noe eares?
Or why doe Eunuchs learn to play and sing,
If thou noe more canst thy attention bring?   20
Shouldst thou grow deafe, and loose thy aëry Sense,
Sure all sweete Noyses straight would vanish hence,
And all Windes would depart, and wee should have
Noe more Breath, than would sigh thee to thy Grave.

[folio 72]

[109]

To a Curtezan.

Lean, slender, gracil, wither'd, lank, and thinne,
How canst thou, preethee, make a shift to sinne?
There is noe Ring of such a litle size,
Through which wee may not well draw both thy Thighs:
Thy armes are like two twiggs; thy ribs doe sawe   5
Thy lovers Breasts, and make their skins look raw.
Thy knees resemble picked dartes: thy Haire
Is as invisible, as is the Aire.
Thou in those holes maist creepe, where Crickets lie,
And ore the toppes of Steeples swiftly flie: 10
Oft have wee known thee on a feather ride,
Oft on an upper Sun-beame sitt astride.
   Now thou demandest why wee thus abuse thee:
Truly wee doe it onely to excuse thee.
All others of thy Trade, wee must confesse,   15
Doe open penance; nor deserve they lesse:
But thou noe humane Punishment dost merit,
Thy lusts are not the lusts of Flesh, but Spirit.

[folio 72ᵛ]

[110]

For a Gentleman.

On the embracing of his Friend.

Lett us alone, yee mortals, and permitt
Us two for ay to bee thus sweetly knitt;
Lett us alone: wee bidd you all adieu,
Trouble not Us, untill we trouble You.
In nought, but in our selves, wee place our Quiet,   5
As for the World wee totally defie it.
Possesse thy yellow heapes, thou man of gold,
And purchase Livings more than can be told,
Onely give Us our Love: whilst thou art poore
Amidst thy Plenty, wee in Want find store;   10
Noe treasure is so boundlesse as a Friend.
Hee n'er can lack, who hath a man to spend.
Tumble thy gawdy wenches, thou spruce Ladd,
Whose highest Aime is, never to bee sadde,
Drink, sleep, use Games, make Feasts, dance Masks, see Plaies, 15
And when in pleasure thou hast passt thy daies,
At last confesse that Wee have hitt the right:
Chastly to joyne soules, is the chiefe Delight.
Enjoy thy Crowne, great *Turke*, and raigne as farre
As any Empires worth the having are,   20
Stretch out thy Scepter over Landes and Seas,
Throw down, build upp, destroy, save what thou please,
Yet doe not envie us: and thou shalt see
It will bee long, ere wee doe envy thee.

BODLEIAN MS DON. C. 24: POEMS 169

[folio 73]

[111]

For a gentleman.

To yong Master *Henry Gresley.*

Were I in heav'n, Hall, or were I with Thee,
    (Thy presence is a heav'n to mee)
By visions, not by wordes, I would disclose
    Why thee, on earth, my Friend I chose.
The saints would ravish'd bee, to learn my Story,   5
    And thinke, it added to the glorie;
The angels would admire a mortal's Love,
    And wish that they had such above.
First, I would shew thee how thy pleasing face
    Promis'd an Heart enrich'd with Grace,   10
Through thy faire eyes, I could espie within
    Much vertue, and scarce any Sinne.
This made mee looke so oft, and gaze on thee,
    That I thy inward Worth might see;
More of the Priest I had, than of the Lover,   15
    And did high Mysteries discover.
I saw a Witt divine, which did not follow
    But did out-goe, the sage *Apollo,*
Thy oracle was blinde in noe man's case,
    Best-sighted in thine owne it was;   20
Ripe were thy braines: thou seemedst to most men
    A youth of threescore yeares and tenne.
I saw a Modestie, which did invite
    And yet did hinder, my Delight;
Thou wert so holy, thou to sleepe, or drinke   25
    Wouldst blush, and it too carnall think:
Oh, how thy noble Blood mounted, and flam'd,
    When to thee first I Friendship nam'd!
Pure friendship 'twas; and 'tis: else I should sure
    The hell of losing thee endure.   30
I sawe a Conscience, which did scorne to feare,
    It was so upright, and so cleare;
To men thou gav'st their dues: but to the Lord
    Thou didst thy very selfe afford.

Hence sprung thy Peace, thy Mirth, thy jolly Rest: 35
    The whole Yeare seemes to Thee one Feast.
Nothing ere vext thy soule, but profer'd Wealth,
    Newe honour, or continuall Health,
That which made others proude, did humble Thee.
    Thou, with this World, couldst n'er agree.   40
                                      What

[folio 73ᵛ]

What saw I else? a rare internall Beauty,
    Which to keepe secret, is my duty;
Some superstitious Fooles would thee adore,
    Should I lay open all thy store.
While I thus view'd thy Inside, I beganne   45
    To count thee somthing more then Man:
In each parte, as thy Bodie, so thy Minde
    Strait, sweete, heroïck I did finde.
Tell me, yee Cherubins, who dwell in Light,
    Have I done well? is my Choise right?   50
Have I on goodnesse my affections plac'd,
    And by a proxy God embrac't?
Have I my JESUS, in my *Harry*, lov'd?
    Is friendship now Devotion prov'd?
If yea, then *Christ* smiles on our mutuall Troth,   55
    And is a third Friend to us both.
An unity here is, if noe Trinity,
    I, thou, and Christ: Christ, thou, and I.

[folio 74]

[112]

An hymne to God.

O thou All, conforme my Minde
　　So thy goodnesse to embrace,
That it may noe Pleasure finde
　　But in wondring at thy grace.
　　　　Things below　　　　　　　　　5
　　　　Lett mee knowe:
　　　　Lett mee love
　　　　Things above.

[folio 74ᵛ]

[113]

On the death of his deare friend
Master Richard Bacon.

[Blank]

[folio 75]

[114]

On Sir *Thomas Overbury*
and his poëme.

This knight was never marryed in his life,
    What wondrous creature is his WîFE?
Yet I admire Her not: one of my owne
    I hope to have, shall putt Her downe.
Shee, alas, by Man's art was made: god can   5
    Make better Wives, then ere could Man.
I grant, shee's like her Authour, wise and good,
    But shee's not (like him) flesh and blood.
An issue lett her bee rare and divine,
    I never wisht this issue mine: 10
When I doe finde a Daughter full of Witt,
    And each way to my humour fitt,
To such a one I would not bee the Father,
    Why? I would bee her Husband rather.

[folio 75ᵛ]

[115]

At the Command of his reverend
diocesan Godfry Goodman
Bishop of Glocester.

A translation of the *Te deum laudamus*
after the tune of the 100 Psalme.

God, ô our god, wee praise thy name:
    Thee for the chiefest Lord wee know.
To thee, ô Father still-the-same,
    The totall Earth does homage owe.

To thee all Angels reare their Voice,   5
    The heav'ns, and each celestiall Power;
Cherub and *Seraphin* rejoyce
    To chant this Song to thee each houre,

OF SABBATH, HOLY, HOLY, HOLY
    LORD GOD /./ So great's the majestie   10
Of thy dread presence, that thy glorie
    Fills the earth below, fills Heav'n on high.

That faire and glorious Companie,
    The twelve Apostles thee doe laude.
That goodly large Societie   15
    The clear-ey'd Prophets thee applaude.

Those hosts, which did for thee expire,
    The martyrs, thine admirers bee.
And like an universall Quire
    The Christians, through the world, praise thee.   20

Thee, one in three, and three in one,
    The father, who vast Sway does beare,
Thine honour'd, true, and onely Sonne,
    The holy Ghost the Comforter.

BODLEIAN MS DON. C. 24: POEMS

Thou, *Christ*, the King of glorie art,   25
    The father's everlasting Sonne;
When thou began'st to take man's part,
    The virgin's wombe thou didst not shunne.
                    When

[folio 76]

When thou hadst blunted *Death's* sharpe sting,
    To all men thou free Leave didst give,   30
Who pleas'd, might bee an heav'nly King,
    If first hee truly did believe.

Thou now on god's right hand dost sitt:
    Thou wilt sitt Judge of quick and dead,
O then thy dear-bought Servants quitt,   35
    For whom thy precious blood was shedd.

Grant them such endlesse Happynesse,
    As thy triumphant Saints enjoy:
Thy people save, thine heritage blesse.
    Governe and lift them upp for ay.   40

Wee day by day extoll thy name.
    World without end wee thee adore.
Lord, keepe us this day free from blame.
    Mercie, thy mercie wee implore.

Thy mercie so to Us afford   45
    As wee doe putt our Trust in thee.
In thee I trusted have, ô Lord
    Confounded lett mee never bee.

[folio 76ᵛ]

[116]

A divine Rapture.

Scorn, scorn to grovle on the earth, my Soule,
All here is base, thou seest, all here is foule;
Look upp to heav'n (thy country) mount, and flie
Above the bright vault of the spangled Skie:
Converse with holy Angels, and acquaint   5
Thy knowledge with the manners of each Saint;
And when thou com'st to God, there, ô there rest
In thy beginning, middle, Ending blest.
    Then, if thou canst, come down again, to doe
(As thou wert wont) like Men, and devils too;   10
Noe, fie! noe: triumph over Sinne and Hell,
And instruct others to doe, say, think well.
I know, thou n'er wilt after mony duck:
What is a litle white and yellow Muck?
And what is Honour, but that very thing   15
Thou now hast, being next the supreme King?
Pleasures tast bitter of the Hoppe and Leaven,
Onely except these thy Delights in heaven.
And I forewarn thee to beware of Friends:
Friends, for the most part, seek but their own endes.   20
Praise is the best of humane goodes: yet that
(Alas!) too is not worth the ayming at.
In short, what-ever is below the Moone
Like the Moone, blotted is, and wanes as soone.
Goe, center thee in GOD: there, ô there rest   25
In thy beginning, Middle, Ending, blest.

[folio 77]

[117]

His Farewell to *Poëtrie*.

Goe, gett thee back to heav'n, thou sacred Fire
Which faine wouldst mee with melodie inspire;
  Here is noe Worke for thee,
  Thou canst noe goodnesse see:
  When *Vice* shall ende her Raigne,   5
  Then hither come againe.
 Now each man strives to hide his name,
 That hee may therby hide his Shame;
 Noe other Praise their Actions crave
 But silence, darknesse, and the Grave.   10
  Out of the Earth they peepe,
  And in they forthwith creepe;
  Poore wormes! lett them alone:
  They joy thus to bee gone.
Thou art too cruell, if thou bring'st to light   15
Those which putt all their confidence in Night.

[118]

Poetry's Answer.

Straight, straight I will goe back to heav'n. But here
Does one* of such heroïck Worth appeare,   * Master
      That ere I hence depart   Michaël
      I needes must shew my Art,   Oldisworth
      And in a matchlesse Storie   5
      Labour to spreade his glorie.
  Who knowes but I was hither sent
  Just for the very same Intent?
  Dreame not that I was bidd, in vaine,
  Onely to come, and goe againe.   10
      My office is to sing
      Of some egregious thing,
      Which when thy World shall heare
      They may at once forbeare
To wallow in their wonted Lustes, and strive   15
By noble Deedes to keepe their Fame alive.

                      His

[folio 77ᵛ]

[119]

His Reply to *Poëtrie*

Doe, shew thy Art. But yet half way upp flie,
That so thy Straines may bee divine and high.
    If thou below should'st crawl
    On this grosse earthly Ball,
    The rellish of the place   5
    Would make thy Musick base.
  Above the Cloudes exalt thy flight;
There shalt thou find both Heat and Light:
There thou mayst thundering Speeches make,
And colours from the Raine-bow take.   10
    There single thou mayst sitt,
    As in a throne of Witt;
    And thence droppe down a Booke,
    On which who-ere shall looke,
Shall wonder, and confesse Thou wert so hallowed   15
Thou scornedst or to follow, or bee followed.

ADDITIONAL POEMS
FROM
FOLGER MS. V.a.170

page 277

[AP1]

To the sacred Majestie
of his dread soveraigne
King Charles.

Treason, my liege. Your keeper, Coventree
In earnest offers to chandge Seale with mee.
Treason. Yet I confesse, Hee should not loose
Much by it. There is litle oddes to choose.
Mine is as solid gold, as ere the Dutch   5
Tooke from the Spanish, and wellnigh as much.
It scornes to vye with Cheap-side. It weighs downe
The weightest thing in England, next the Crowne,
It weighs downe all your treasure. You neede call
A parliment betimes: or else you shall   10
Shortly heare Weston crye, Prodigious thing!
Behold a Boy growes richer then the King.
More, more then gold. It sparkels with such pearles
As countisses are wont to steale from earles
                                        You would:

page 278

You would suppose, the Jewells of the East   15
Mett to outbrave the Metalls of the West.
What saies your Highnesse? will you take this fee
To bate the Commons of a Subsidie?
The bores would thanke mee. They had rather spend
Whole hecatombes to glutt some private frend   20
Then give their Country almes. I tell you true,
I will not parte with it, unlesse to you.
It is so neate, a man may sooner spye
Faults in the dainty carving of the Skie,
Or want of beautie in Queene Maries face   25
Then the least Cutt, or Touch, out of his place
The very Heralds, which first did us give
Dead creaturs, now confesse our Coate doth live.
There lyons walke belowe, whilst one above
Standes in full state. They seeme to seeke his love, 30
And fawne on him. But hee beares forth a sheild

By warre to winne away their crimson Field.
And doubtlesse, had not you all Blood forbad
Their crimson Field more crimson would be made.
In sooth, they looke so sprightfully all foure   35
Quaking I oft expect when they will roare.
Mee thinkes the silver Printes at Amsterdam
And Leyden, might doe well, if ore they came
To waite on the Stampe and learne how to better

                                            Theyr cunning

page 279

Their cunning in the draught of every letter.   40
Nay, might not Duchmen themselves learne of it
How to refine their judgement? and their Witt?
In time might teach their Poets to write Sence
Many in Oxford are of late turned wise.
By wiping it once onely ore their eyes.   45
Which makes mee thinke, the Popes bulls, if they were
Seald with noe other Type, could never erre.
Nor care I though mee Puritanes detest.
This signe, and call it The marke of the Beast.
I know, they would insult, if any brother   50
For synceare love should send them such another,
And were they not within your statutes pent
Would sweare that It weare a Third Sacrament.
O fate! how noble! ô, how rich am I!
I have enough to raise a familie.   55
See, here are Armes: and here are Gemmes good store
What man of all your courte needes seeke for more
    Yet one thing I wish, for the Givers sake,
When I shall dye, the goddes would please to take
It upp to them, and place it for a Signe   60
Amongst the other lampes which nightly shine,
And when your Majestie above shall rayne,
To lett it triumpe in the newe Charles wayne.

---

41   *learne*: l[a *altered to* e]arne

page 284

[AP2]

On the picture of the Virgin
feeding her babe.

Rejoyce yee that are borne anewe.
See, Christ himselfe becomes like you,
Whilst sitting in his Mothers lappe
Hee scornes nor Swathes, nor Milke, nor Pappe
These are his Cloaths his Meate, and Drinke.   5
Dwell here a while, and yee will thinke
His infancie endures for aye,
And all the yeare is Christmas day.
If Abram, Moses, and the rest
Of holy men, were counted blest   10
Because hee saw Christ, as hee was
Farre off, in a prospective glasse,
How happy then, how blest are wee
Which face to face our Jesus see?

page 292

[AP3]

On a paire of hand-
some children.

Who can denye, the world is at his prime,
When skilfull Nature, in so litle time,
Can perfect such rare workes? Two babes at nurse
So faire, that riper Beauties all seeme worse.
Theyr eyes, like Sunnes, such yellow beames reflect   5
As guild theyr glistring haire. Theyr lippes are deckt
With redder Corall then theyr Pipes have any.
Theyr teeth resemble Pearles, and though not many,
They stand in rankes. The white and damaske rose
Joyne forces in theyr Chinne, theyr Eares, and Nose   10
But in theyr lovely Cheekes and lovelyer Browe,
They parte theyr colours and assunder growe.
Naked Apollo, whilst hee was a boy,
Or undresst Venus, ere shee grewe so coy.
Was but an ilde Tipe, and silly shade   15
Of these their limbes. Limbes so exactly made
That though the kinges of both their Realmes were dead
Theyr bodies would shewe well, without a head.
Tempt mee noe more to goe and see the ladies
At Naples, Rome or Venice. In these babies   20
I can behold what-ever peece of heavn
The godds above to mortall wights have given
Hee bright is, as shee: Shee, as hee. This paire
Can with noe other, but themselves, compare.
Hee doth command your love shee doth invite it.   25

page 293

Here you are conquerd: there you are delighted.
You know not which is best to take alone.
You are constrayned or both to choose or none
You yeeld to him, if once to Her you yeeld.
Though but one fights yet Two doe winne the field.   30

---

12   *They*: They[r *del.*]

BODLEIAN MS DON. C. 24: POEMS

page 300

[AP4]

To his Enemie.

Thou worst of all good fencers, Wilt tho feele
How much my Penne wounds deeper then thy Steele
Thou shalt If there bee any way to cause
Thee hang thy selfe, thou shalt. Noe dread of lawes
Noe friends request, no recompense, noe Bribe   5
Shall hold mee off: but I will so describe
Thy partes, that thou shalt thine owne person hate
And seeke an Halter, and growe desperate.
Know then all people, which desire to see
The picture of my foe, this is Hee.   10
And if you thinke I lye: at leastwise knoow
That this is Hee, or I would have him so.
  My foe is one, that were it not for those
Fewe scrapps of Understanding, which hee showes
In bawdy talke, might sinne without controule   15
For, noe man would beleeve hee had a Soule.
Hee scarce knowes how at once to kisse his hande
And make a legge. His face six houres doth stand
In the same posture. With his Eyes hee heares
Hee with his Nose speakes, and sees with his Eares   20
Hee lookes nor farther than the shells of things,
And counts none blest, but Emperours and kings
His grave is, Armes acrosse, Thighes loosely spredd,
With a negleetive waving of his head
Rude multitudes of indigested humors.   25
         People

---

4 *thy*: th[e *altered to* y]
21 *than*: th[. *altered to* a]n
22 *counts*: cou/n/ts
24 *negleetive*: *stet.*
27 *there*: th[. . . *altered to* er]e

188   BODLEIAN MS DON. C. 24: POEMS

page 301

People his fancie; and such borish tumors
Fill upp his hearte, that there is left noe roome
For neate Concepts, though they by chance should come.
Hee is your ape: and whatso-ere you doe
You shall be sure to have him doe so too.   30
Hee tells you what you told him, and affordes
You noe discourse, but your repeated Wordes
Hee dares not thinke his owne thoughts, nor permitt
Himselfe to understand himselfe his witt.
Is such a Coward, and so prone to erre   35
That till you backe it will never stirre.
Not so much as his hope, or his Affection,
Or his Feare, but is under your correction.
Hee still beares cloudy weather in his lookes
And though for nothing else hee studies Bookes   40
But how to learne to laugh, he nought doth doe
In mirth, but what seemes glude on, and sett to.
Aske him the least thing and hee makes a Doubt
And where the path is straitest, goes about.
In any Saying, bee it nere so true,   45
Contradict him, and hee to answer you
Will contradict himselfe. His reason breakes
The whilst he mendes it. And too when hee speakes
Hee spawles, hums scratches coughs: enough to make
The teeth within an asses jawbone shake.   50
                                                Take heede

page 302

Take heede, yee blacke gownes, take heede how yee heare him
If I may counsaile you aproach not neare him
One speech of his would so bedull your schoole
That you for ever after would live fooles.
Where lye his Gutts, thinke yee? The truth to tell you   55
In his scull. Where lye his Witts? in his belly
Whoere knockes out his Braines, had (as good cracke
Old rotten Nutts, which pith and kernells lacke

---

41   doe: /doe/ [know del.]
51   heare him: /heare him/

BODLEIAN MS DON. C. 24: POEMS

Hee slumbers standing, working, climbing, walking
Running, attiring, playing, feeding, talking   60
Oft have I markt him at the Boord sitt dumbe,
And hold betweene his finger and his thumbe,
His trencher and his mouth, one bitt of meate
Till all the other victualls have bine eate
What will hee doe? If hee were to bee bought,   65
An owle were of more price. Sure hee for nought
Butt for to serve some fellow Dolts, is fitt,
Some heavy Lordes: whose greatest shew of witt
Is this, that they still putt tricks on thir Elves,
Lest all men might seeme wiser then themselves.   70

---

64   *bine*: b[<.> *deleted*]ine

page 303

[AP5]

An Ode

Prethee away, Love: what a foole thou arte,
Against my Councellour to be thus tarte,
If, thou wilt needes wound, wound some meaner parte.
   But tis thy Arte
   To fixe thy darte   5
   Just in my hearte
That so what should most cure, might most breed smarte.

---

7 *smarte*: /smarte/

BODLEIAN MS DON. C. 24: POEMS

page 314

[AP6]

On an Ewe
that was drowned.

The wolf pursude an ewe; a Dogge, the wolfe;
Till at last, the Ewe fell into a gulph
Nor did it grieve her, that shee perisht so
Better feele any death, then feele a foe.
Yet in the waves another Wolfe there was   5
Which would not lett the Ewe so fairely passe
But caught her, and devoured her. All in vaine
The dogg-fish helpt, when shee before was slaine
Alas! what will yee doe, poore wretched sheepe?
Nor sea, not Land you safe from wolves can keepe   10
I thinke, you must to heaven. But oh I feare
The wolfe too is a Constellation there.
So that where-ere you goe, yee must still dye
For why? the Dogge starres dwelling is not nigh.

---

14   *nigh:* /nigh/

192   BODLEIAN MS DON. C. 24: POEMS

page 321

[AP7]

To a friend of Sir
Thomas Overburyes.

Sir you are one of those, who dare commend.
A worthy though a lamentable Friend;
Your tounge is so triumphant, when it saies
Any thing in dead Overburyes praise,
That wee could wish you alwayes might survive   5
If but to keep his Epitaph alive.
    Oh, you doe nobly to maintaine the Truth:
If second you. Sir Thomas was a youth
That had a Mint of Witt, a mint of money,
And master was of both that gathred honey   10
From others gall, and made himselfe good sport
To see how he was envyed in the Courte;
That lovd King James, because King James lovd him
And for noe other reason. That sawe dimme
In maters of selfe profitt and selfe honnor,   15
That where hee mett a whore, cryd out upon her,
Although shee were a Ladie, or a Countesse,
That did not scatter but well place his Counties,
That with his manlike Beauty, as he went
Ravisht beholders; that held nought misspent   20
Or to relieve the Poore or grace the Church;
                                   That oft

page 322

That oft would plundge into a willing lurch
Rather then lett the mighty and the strong
Doe thier weake litle harmelesse Neighbours wrong
That knew what twas to bee a favorit,

---

14   *sawe dimme*: see Commentary.
15   *of selfe*: of [f *for* s]elfe
16   *hee*: /hee/
23   *then*: [. . . *del.*] then
24   *wrong*: [. . . *del.*] /wrong/

COMMENTARY

[Dedication]

Title: *Wife*. Nicholas Oldisworth married Mary Chamberlayne sometime in 1640. The parish records of Coln Rogers are not extant; if they had been, we might know the exact date of the marriage. Mary died without having remarried in 1684 at Batsford, about a mile north of Bourton-on-the-Hill. For further details of her life, see pp. xxii–xxiii. For biographical data in general, see John Gouws, "Oldisworth, Nicholas," in ODNB, 60 vols. (Oxford: Oxford University Press, 2004), vol. 41: 698–99.

5–6 *marryed . . . yeares*. This is confirmed by the memorial to Mary Oldisworth in Tewkesbury Abbery; see p. xvii–xxiii.

13–15 *in those very dayes. . .virginlike contentments*. Mary married late, at the age of twenty-nine; see p. xxii.

17–21 *Time . . . Play*. Cf. [96], 9–14. Oldisworth probably has in mind the years of Charles I's personal reign.

29 *Oxford*. Charles I made Oxford his capital in 1642. He left it for the last time on 27 April 1645.

33 *two little daughters*. All their children were born at Bourton-on-the-Hill. Mary, the first daughter, was baptized on 6 January 1641; the second, Francis, was baptized on 11 June 1642 and buried 28 November 1643; the third, Margaret, was baptized on 8 February 1644 (that makes her only a year old when the poems were transcribed). See Gloucester Record Office, Bourton-on-the-Hill Baptismal Record, MS. PFC 54 in 1/1, pp. 19–20.

43 *Willington*. Oldisworth died on 25 March 1645 at Willington, Warwickshire, about eleven miles as the crow flies from Bourton-on-the-Hill. The next day he was buried in the nearby church at Barcheston.

194   BODLEIAN MS DON. C. 24: POEMS

44 gloss *Treaty of Uxbridge.* Negotiations between royalist and parliamentary emissaries were conducted at Uxbridge between 30 January and 24 February 1645.

[1]

Copies of this poem appear in Bodleian MSS. Eng. Poet. e. 97, pp. 147–148; Ashmole 47, fols. 107–108ᵛ; and Firth e. 4, pp. 104–5. It first appeared in print in *Wit Restor'd,* ed. Sir John Mennes and James Smith (London, 1658), 79–81. It was printed from Bodleian MS. Don. c. 24 (then in possession of Percy J. Dobell) in *Ben Jonson,* ed. C. H. Herford and Percy and Evelyn Simpson, 11 vols. (Oxford: Clarendon Press, 1925–1952), 11: 396–98. See D. Hugh Craig, ed., *Ben Jonson: The Critical Heritage, 1599–1798* (London and New York: Routledge, 1990), §35, "Nicholas Oldisworth on Johnson, 1629," 141–43. (Cf. also A. H. Nethercot, "Milton, Johnson, and the Young Cowley," *Modern Language Notes* 49 [1934]: 158–62.)

The unique readings of the holograph at lines 23, 30, and 44 suggest that Oldisworth revised the poem at a later stage. The original version of the poem, read by Jonson, is slightly cruder and more extravagant. The extent of Oldisworth's revisions is revealed by the change of title, and the variants at lines 3, 11, 13, 23, 30, 33, 54, and 56.

The poem might be one of several responses to Jonson's "Ode to Himself" on the failure of *The New Inn,* for which see *Ben Jonson,* ed. Herford and Simpson, 11: 333–46. Jonson sent a copy of the poem to the Earl of Newcastle. See [60], 5–18, for Oldisworth's encounter with Jonson in 1632.

For other metapoetic poems, see [42], [117], [118], and [119].

Title *Ben Johnson.* Jonson died on 6 August 1637.

1 *Die . . . Johnson.* Oldisworth here evinces an early instance of the anxiety of influence usually attributed to Romantic and post-Romantic writers.

19 *Latine . . . long.* The Westminster School curriculum was based on the study of Latin. In 1629, Oldisworth would have completed his first year of study at Oxford.

20 *dispute . . . tongue.* Jonson is thus established as the figure through whom vernacular poetry achieves "classic" status.

31 *lit'rature.* humane learning; "letters."

37–38 *the Stars . . . Life.* Stellification was a commonplace of seventeenth-century poetry of praise; see Alastair Fowler, *Time's Purpled Masquers: Stars and the Afterlife in Renaissance English Literature* (Oxford: Clarendon Press, 1996), esp. chap. 2,

Commentary 195

but Oldisworth is more likely to think of the stars in Zodiacal terms as "Fate" or "Fortune," which allows poets an afterlife in their works: by not dying, Jonson is presented as claiming a literal immortality.

42 *length of dayes.* In 1629 Jonson was fifty-six or fifty-seven.

53 *Rhodian colossus.* Chares of Lindus' statue of Helios on the island of Rhodes described in Pliny, *Naturalis Historia* 34.41, was considered one of the Seven Wonders of the ancient world. It was thirty-two metres (105 feet) high, and stood on a hill above the city, not astride the harbor entrance. It fell in an earthquake in 228 or 226 B.C. Pliny notes that even in its fallen state it was remarkable.

[2]

This poem, with suitable alterations, was addressed by Matthew Bacon, Richard's brother, to his friend Clement Harby; see British Library MS. Sloane 396, fol. 4–4ᵛ.

Title *his Friend beyond sea.* Richard Bacon, Oldisworth's contemporary at Westminster, was admitted to the English College at Douay on 8 September 1629, aged eighteen; see *The Douay College Diaries: Third, Fourth and Fifth (1598–1645)*, 2 vols., ed. Edwin H. Burton and Thomas L. Williams (London: Catholic Record Society, 1911), 1:277–78. According to *The Douay College Diaries*, Richard Bacon (alias Robert Boyer) was the son of Richard Bacon of St Dunstan's-in-the-West, Fleet Street, a dealer in medicine, and his wife Jane. Having attended Westminster School, he was elected a King's Scholar in 1626; see G. F. Russell Barker and Alan H. Stemming, *The Record of Old Westminsters . . . to 1929*, 2 vols. (London: Chiswick Press, 1928–1929). On his admission to Douay, he was said to have spent the previous year at Cambridge (although there is no record of his matriculation). This is confirmed by [15], 15, and the gloss to [15], 80. At Douay, where Bacon taught rhetoric, he was joined by his brother Matthew in 1632 (*Douay Diaries*, 1:305). In 1636 the two brothers fled Douay to escape the plague, but Richard died soon after in the Carthusian monastery at Nieuwpoort in Flanders; see Matthew Bacon's autobiographical account in British Library MS. Sloane 464, fols. 4–5.

    Oldisworth wrote several other poems to Bacon: [5], [31], [50], [70], [78], [82], [87], [96], [103], and [113]. See Paul Hammond, *Figuring Sex Between Men from Shakespeare to Rochester* (Oxford: Oxford University Press, 2002), 32 and 38, and John Gouws, "Nicholas Oldsiworth, Richard Bacon, and the Practices of Caroline Friendship," *Texas Studies in Literature and Language* 47 (2005): 366–401. Cf. Oldisworth's hyperbolical use of the four elements in poem [5] below.

1–2 *Time . . . Sea.* Cf. Oldisworth's use of the four elements in poems [5] and [32] below.

[3]

Title *Master Michaël Oldisworth.* Michael Oldisworth (159[?]–1645?). On 10 June 1611 Oldisworth graduated B.A. from Magdalen College, where he was granted a fellowship. After proceeding M.A. in July 1614, he became secretary to William, Earl of Pembroke, the Lord Chamberlain. The Earl's influence led to his election to Parliament as the member for Old Sarum in January 1624. He was re-elected in 1625, 1626, and 1628. When the Earl as Chancellor recommended that Oldisworth should be one of the University's parliamentary representatives, Oxford refused to comply. On the Earl's death in 1630, Oldisworth was unemployed, but in October 1637 he succeeded one Taverner as the secretary to Philip Herbert, Earl of Pembroke and Montgomery, William Herbert's brother, and his successor as Lord Chamberlain. Oldisworth identified himself with his new master's fortune. It would appear that he himself was always inclined to support the parliamentary cause, and was later thought to have ensured that Philip Herbert's loyalties lay in the same direction. Robert Herrick's "To the most accomplisht gentleman Master Michael Oulsworth" (*Poems*, ed. L. C. Martin, [Oxford: Clarendon Press, 1956], 329) pays tribute to him. Michael Oldisworth married Susan Poyntz on 26 April 1617.

Oldisworth wrote several other poems to his cousin: [25], [33], [53], and [100].

18 *courtship.* Oldisworth frequently expresses his distrust of duplicity inherent in conduct at court and of the deferences and ingratiations associated with rank; see, for example, [4] below. Rather than being a conventional satiric pose, this distrust could well be connected with his family's sensitivity to the fate of Sir Thomas Overbury. See "The Semantics of Courtship," in Catherine Bates, *The Rhetoric of Courtship in Elizabethan Language and Literature* (Cambridge: Cambridge University Press, 1992), chap. 2, pp. 25–44.

[4]

For Oldisworth's distrust of rank, see [19] and the note to [3], 18 above.

[5]

Title *Friend beyond sea.* For other poems to Richard Bacon, see the notes to [2]. The variant readings of the Folger manuscript indicate that it was copied from an early version of the poem.

14 *Earth . . . Fire.* Cf. Oldisworth's hyperbolical use of the four elements in poem [2] above.

24 var. This passage adds nothing to the poem, and was probably omitted for aesthetic reasons.

var. 2 *loose both Calis and Ree.* Calais, the last English possession in France, was lost in 1558, at the end of Mary I's reign. In 1627 the Duke of Buckingham led a disastrous expedition to the Ile de Ré, in support of the Huguenots.

var., 4 *Take . . . survives.* The scansion of this line is defective. It is short of one syllable.

[6]

Title *lord Haies . . . Carlile.* James Hay, Earl of Carlisle, Viscount Doncaster, Baron Hay (d. 1636), one of James I's favorites, was noted for his extravagance and splendid hospitality. Unlike some of the other Scots who came south with James I, he was good-natured and made no personal enemies. He was not politically astute, but at a personal level his shrewd, observant common sense predominated. Between 1616 and 1628 he was dispatched on six diplomatic missions to France and one to Germany (on the 1624 mission to Paris he helped negotiate the marriage of Henrietta Maria with the future Charles I). After 1628 he no longer enjoyed the confidence of Charles I.

The use of the plural first-person pronouns in the Folger manuscript suggests that the original version of this poem might have been written on behalf of a group or community.

3 *joy . . . Favour.* I have been unable to trace records of any connection between the Earl and Oldisworth. It might be that Michael Oldisworth served as an intermediary between Lord Carlisle and his would-be client, and conveyed reports of a favorable response to his younger relative. The aspirant poet's hopes of patronage were not entirely misplaced, since the Earl (then Viscount Doncaster) had befriended John Donne from 1608 until the poet's death in 1631; see R. C. Bald, *John Donne: A Life* (Oxford: Oxford University Press, 1970), 160–62, 272–73, 395–96, 431–523, and *passim.* Donne had acted as Chaplain to the Earl on his embassy to Germany in 1619.

[7]

Title: *To . . . his Patron.* See headnote [6] above.

[8]

Title: *Recovery . . . 1632.* On 17 December 1632, the Venetian ambassador reported that the King had what might be smallpox. A week later he wrote that the king was recovering. See *Calendar of State Papers, Venetian* 23 (1632–1636), 47, 49–50.

1 *vice-chanc'llour Duppa.* Brian Duppa (1588–1662) was Vice-Chancellor in 1632 and 1633 (*The Historical Register of the University of Oxford* [Oxford: Oxford University Press, 1900], 26]. He was educated at Westminster and Christ Church. In 1628 he became Dean of Christ Church, succeeding Richard Corbett, who had been promoted to the see of Oxford. In November 1626 he married Jane Killingtree. He was responsible for *Jonsonius Virbius* [*STC* 14784], a collection of poems by thirty writers marking the death of Ben Jonson in 1637.

1 gloss *Master Osbolston.* Lambert Osbaldeston (1594–1659) was elected to a scholarship at Christ Church after his early education at Westminster. In 1621 he held a joint patent for the headmastership of Westminster School, which was renewed to him alone in January 1626. In 1629 he became a prebendary in the church of St. Peter at Westminster (Westminster Abbey). In 1638 he was deprived of his church preferments because of a libel against Archbishop Laud.

3 *When my . . . sing.* The University commemorated the King's recovery from what was supposedly smallpox with the publication of *Musarum Oxoniensium pro rege suo soteria* (Oxford, 1633) [*STC* 19035]. The volume contained English poems by Jasper Mayne, William Cartwright, Jerameel Terrent, and T. Lockey, all of whom had some association with Christ Church.

13 *Ryott . . . Ease.* Charles I was renowned for his personal moderation.

17–18 *His heav'nly Bodie . . . spheares.* The apotheosis of Charles I is conventional.

27 *Travell'd . . . Spain.* In 1623 Charles, then Prince of Wales, travelled through France to Spain hoping to gain the hand of Philip IV of Spain's sister.

Commentary   199

[9]

Title The seal referred to is probably the same as the one mention in "To his sa-
cred Majestie of his dread sovereigne King Charles," Additional Poems [1]. See the
note to lines 6–7 below.

The variant readings of the Folger manuscript are those of an earlier version.

6–7 *Where . . . Tower.* The heraldic elements are very similar to the Oldisworth
coat of arms. Mary Oldisworth's monument at Tewkesbury carries the arms of
Oldisworth impaling Chamberlayne; the Oldisworth portion is described in Wil-
liam Dyde, *The History and Antiquities of Tewkesbury From the Earliest Periods to
the Present Time*, 2nd ed. (Tewkesbury: Dyde and son, 1790), 27: "Gules, on a fesse
argent, three lioncels passant-gardant purpure." See also the description in Addi-
tional Poems, [AP1], 29–32.

[10]

25 *stiff necks*. Cf. Psalm 75:5.

30 *prostrat*. levelled with the ground (OED, *prostrate* a, 1b [1677]).
      skirre. skirr, move rapidly.

35 *Indian Figge*. Banyan tree.

[11]

Oldisworth wrote several poems on behalf of others; see [20], [64], [74], [75], [92],
[97], [99], [108], [110], and [111]. Vicarious poems of this sort shed light on the
way in which poetic communities functioned. They are different in kind from ven-
triloquist poems such as [14].

The variant readings of the Folger manuscript are those of an early version
of the poem.

2 gloss *Master Chandler*. The Rector of Coln Rogers parish church.

39 *Sodaine, and cruell*. Cf. John Donne, *The Flea*, l.19: "Cruel and sudden." This is
one of the few verbal echoes in Oldisworth.

[12]

Title *Shottover*. A prominent ridge three miles south of Oxford, Shotover Hill formed part of the Royal Forest of Shotover and Stowood. Disafforestation occurred after the Restoration; see *A History of the County of Oxford*, vol. 5, ed. Mary D. Lobel (Oxford: Oxford University Press, 1957), 275.

[13]

Title *Separatist*. This label was loosely attached to the followers of Robert Browne (Brownists)—Independents and Congregationalists—who were at the forefront of the struggle against Charles I and Archbishop Laud.

8 *painted Sepulcher*. Cf. Matthew 23:27, where hypocritical Pharisees are described as "whited sepulchres."

10 *mortifie . . . members*. Cf. Colossians 3:5.

15 *Chine*. backbone.

20 *Snaffling*. speaking through the nose.

[14]

This is the first specifically religious poem in the collection. For other vicarious and ventriloquist poems, see the headnote to [11] above.

16 *setts . . . lower*. Cf. 1 Samuel 2:8 and Luke 1:52, which forms part of the Magnificat in the Order for Evening Prayer in *The Book of Common Prayer*.

[15]

The variant readings of the Folger manuscript are those of an early version of the poem.

Title *1631*. This poem appears to precede Oldisworth's incorporation at Cambridge after having obtained his B.A. in 1632.

1–2 *Wee . . . Palaces*. Oldisworth appears not to have visited Cambridge before 1632; see [84].

6 var. *Thy . . . face*. Cf. 1 Cor. 13:12.

Commentary 201

15 *Three years since.* See the note to the title of [2] above.

17–18 *(Bacon . . . Grave.* Francis Bacon, Viscount St Albans, died in 1626.

26 *the Butler's books.* The college record of amounts owed for food and drink.

64 *Ennius.* Quintus Ennius (239–169 B.C.), author of the *Annales*, was Virgil's predecessor as a writer of Latin epic.

68 var. *councells.* Councils of the early church.
   Fathers. Fathers of the early church.

77–78 var., 2 *your . . . eares.* the "y" might not be erased. Cf. [28], 91 var., where the Folger scribe uses the same spelling.

80 **gloss** Bacon played the role of Flavia in Thomas Vincent's Latin play *Paria*, performed before the king on 3 March 1628. The play was published in 1648 (Wing H170); see Alan H. Nelson, ed., *Records of Early English Drama: Cambridge* (Toronto: University of Toronto Press, 1989), 912, 959. For a modern edition, see *Paria*, ed. Steven Berkowitz (Hildesheim: Georg Olms, 1990).

102 *great Carlile . . . legat.* See the notes to [6] above.

109 *tell Rome.* This is a reference to either Bacon's Catholicism or to his residence in the city.

112 **gloss** *Master Vincent.* Thomas Vincent, the author of *Paria*, was a Westminster scholar who matriculated at Easter 1618, took his B.A. in 1621–1622, his M.A. in 1625, and B.D. in 1632. He was elected a fellow in 1624, and became minister of St. Edward's, Cambridge, in 1631. Soon after, he became Vicar of Blyth, Nottinghamshire, where he died on 28 September 1633.
   fuit . . . &c. This may be translated as: "There was indeed in that young man a certain very extensive liberality of mind, combined with an external comeliness of body, by which means he easily drew to himself the gaze and affections of everyone. His nature was adaptable and acute, his learning not the usual sort."

[17]

Title *Sir Edward Hungerford of Cosham.* Sir Edward Hungerford (1596–1648), the parliamentary commander, lived at Corsham, Wiltshire from 1625 until 1645, when he removed to Farleigh Castle. In 1620 he married Margaret, the daughter of William Hollidaie or Haliday; she died in 1672. Hungerford was deputy lieutenant of Wiltshire in 1624, and sheriff in 1632. He was elected MP for Chippenham in January 1620, and sat in both the Short and Long Parliaments in 1640. He was made a Knight of the Bath in 1625.

For Oldisworth's visit to Corsham in 1632, see [88].

[18]

New year's poems and gifts were part of social convention; see, for example, Thomas Carew, "A New-Year's Sacrifice," "A New-year's Gift: To the King," and "To the New Year: For the Countess of Carlisle," and "New Year's poem": Steven W. May and William A. Ringler, Jr., *Elizabethan Poetry: A Bibliography and First-line Index of English Verse, 1559–1603*, 3 vols. (London: Thoemmes Continuum, 2004), 2104. For a discussion of Herrick's New Year poems see Janie Caves McCauley, "On the 'Childhood of the Yeare': Herrick's *Hesperides* New Year's Poems," *George Herbert Journal* 14 (1990): 72–96.

Title *lady Hungerford*. See [17] **Title** note above.

13–18 *winter . . . last*. The seventeenth-century commonplace of a woman walking in the snow can also be found in Strode's "On a gentlewoman walking in the snow"; see *Poetical Works of William Strode (1600–1645)*, ed. Bertram Dobell (London: Bertram Dobell, 1907), 41–42. Dobell draws attention to a similar poem in *Wits Recreations* (1640): "I saw faire Flora take the aire." Strode's poem was probably "the single most popular English lyric in the 17th century" (Peter Beal, *Index of English Literary Manuscripts*, II.2, 352). Beal (402–7) records eighty-eight copies in manuscript, and it was frequently reprinted in miscellanies.

16–17 **var.** See the note to lines 13–18 above.
And . . . belowe. The earlier version is open to indecorous reading.

21 *Which . . . abound*. This line is not indented in the manuscript, unlike the third line in each of the other stanzas.

[19]

For other poems expressing a distrust of rank, see the headnote to [4] above.

1 *viscount*. Oldisworth might not have any particular person in mind. The most recent elevation was that of Edward Conway, who was created Viscount Conway of Conway Castle in 1627.

Commentary 203

12 *thirty pounds.* This would appear to be the standard fee paid to the Heralds' Office for a coat of arms. In Jonson's *Every Man out of his Humour*, 3.4, Sogliardo boasts that the patent for his flamboyant arms cost him £30.

15 *like . . . coat.* In *Every Man out of his Humour*, 3.2.29–30, Jonson delivers the same jibe at pretentiously complicated heraldry: Sogliardo's coat of arms is described as "of as many colours, as e're you saw any fooles coat in your life" (alluding to Joseph's coat, Genesis 37:3 and following).

15 *Archy's.* Archibald Armstrong (d. 1672), the jester to both James I and Charles I, wore traditional fool's motley; see Enid Welsford, *The Fool: His Social and Literary History* (London: Faber, 1935), 171–79.

[20]

Title I have been unable to identify Mistress E.W. For poems written on behalf of others, see the note to **[11]** above.

1 gloss *Mistris K.B.* This is presumably Richard Bacon's sister Katharine; see **[29]** below.

[21]

This and the following poem form a pair, suggesting that he regards the Petrarchan motifs of the present poem as aristocratic.

[22]

The poem is yet another variation on Christopher Marlowe's "Come live with me and be my love."

[23]

Title *Mistris Dorothie Litcott.* She was the daughter of Sir John Lytcott, of Molesey, Surrey, and Mary, the daughter of Sir Nicholas Overbury. She is thus Nicholas Oldisworth's cousin.

1 gloss *sonne . . . Offly.* John Offley, of Isleworth, Middlesex, matriculated at Trinity College, Oxford, 16 October 1635, aged sixteen. In 1638 he was a student of the

Middle Temple. On 13 July 1641 be obtained a license to marry Dorothy Lytcott. His father was knighted on 25 April 1615.

[24]

This and the previous poem are intended to be read as a contrasting pair.

Title The ugly or deformed female is a conventional topic; see, for example, Shakespeare's Sonnet 127, John Donne, "The Comparison" and "The Anagram," and Sir John Suckling, "The Deformed Mistress".

38 *Jakes.* latrine.

[25]

For other poems to Michael Oldisworth, see the note to [3] above. The variant readings of the Folger manuscript clearly reveal Oldisworth's painstaking revision of his poems.

[26]

Title In writing this fantasy, Oldisworth might have had in mind lines 289–322 of Richard Corbett's "Iter Boreale"; see *The Poems*, ed. J.A.W. Bennett and H.R. Trevor-Roper (Oxford: Clarendon Press, 1955), 41–42. The poem is deliberately juxtaposed to the following brief poem on "walking abroad".

17–22. *Sheapards . . . seven.* The shepherds err in assuming the validity of the Ptolemaic, geocentric model of the universe.

[27]

The Petrarchan motifs of this complimentary epigram heighten the contrast between it and the previous poem. The poem can be seen as a response to Strode's enormously popular "On a gentlewoman walking in the snowe" ("I saw faire Cloris walke alone"); see the note to [18], 13–18.

8 *three sunnes . . . appeare.* The Petrarchan hyperbole suggests that each of the lady's eyes adds a sun to the skies, but Oldisworth's allusion to the legend of the three suns associated with the Nativity further heightens the conceit. For possibly

Commentary   205

the earliest documentation of the legend, see Jacobus de Voragine, *The Golden Legend: Readings on the Saints*, 2 vols., ed. William Granger Ryan (Princeton: Princeton University Press, 1993), 1:40. The phenomenon of parhelia was thought to precede momentous events.

[28]

The poem contrasts town and country life. The version of the poem in the Folger manuscript is more personal and less polished. The references to Osbaldeston and Westminster School in **106 var**. are particularly valuable.

Title *his honoured Cosin, Mistris Susan Oldisworth*. The wife of Michael Oldisworth; see [3], [60], 21–36 and notes. Her departure from London might have been occasioned by her husband Michael Oldisworth's loss of employment; see the headnote to [3].
    Thisselworth. Isleworth, Middlesex, nine miles southwest of London, on the left bank of the Thames. Sir Giles Overbury had a house there (cf. [60], 19–20); see the map of Isleworth village and Syon House in 1635, *A History of the County of Middlesex*, vol. 3, ed. Susan Reynolds (London: Constable, 1962), facing p. 90.

10 gloss *Brainford*. Brentford.

20 *collops*. pieces of meat.

40 *A crowd*. Oldisworth occasionally uses a majuscule "a" for the indefinite article.

43 *sowne*. swoon.

45 gloss *Doctor Richard Holsworth*. Richard Holdsworth (1590–1649) was active in London from 1624. He was elected Professor of Divinity at Gresham College in 1629, and Master of Emmanuel College in 1637. Twenty-one of his sermons were published in *The Valley of Vision* (1651) [Wing H2403 and H2404].

47 var. *feeding . . . Hony-combe*. For the topos of poets being fed on honey, see Theorcritus, *Idyll* 1.146–47, and Gregory Crane, "Bees Without Honey, and Callimachean Taste," *American Journal of Philology* 108 (1987): 399–403.

48–49 *Bone . . . man-and-wife*. Cf. Genesis 2:23.

54 *Tom Thumb*. Presumably this is a bag pudding of the traditional kind into which Tom Thumb fell while his mother was preparing it: ingredients such as meat, suet, oatmeal and seasoning stuffed in the entrails of an animal and boiled.

82 *Mulsack.* I can add nothing to Oldisworth's gloss.

91 var. *Eares . . . F.* Cf. [15], 77–78 var.

94 *in . . . lie.* within hearing of St. Mary-le-Bow's bells; that is, within the bounds of the city of London.

106 var. line 1. *Foure yeares ago.* There is no record of Oldisworth's admission to the School.

> line 3 *Osbalston.* Lambert Osbaldeston (1594–1659), Headmaster of Westminster School from 1622 until 1639; see General Introduction, pp. xvii–xix.

> line 5 *Augustus blisse.* The Augustan Peace. The general peace in the ancient world during the early years of the Christian era was later interpreted by the church fathers as providential; see *A Variorum Commentary on the Poems of John Milton*, vol. 2, *The Minor English Poems (Part One)* (London: Routledge and Kegan Paul, 1972), 73–74.

> line 10 *Two . . . yong Friends.* Presumably Oldisworth is referring to himself and Richard Bacon.

> line 11 *field . . . Tuttle name.* Tothill Fields, southwest of Horseferry Road, were built over in the nineteenth century.
>> *gamsters.* players of games or frolicsome, merry persons (see *OED* "gamester", 1 and 4. It is unlikely that Oldisworth intends "gamblers" or "lewd persons" (senses 3 and 5).

> line 24 *jogge.* jolt, disturb, take aback.

> line 42 *frizzled.* metaphorically, covered with curls or frills, hence "with dense foliage."

> line 47 *feeding . . . Hony-combe.* For the topos of poets being fed on honey, see Theocritus, *Idyll* 1, 146–147, and Gregory Crane, "Bees Without Honey, and Callimachean Taste," *American Journal of Philology* 108 (1987): 399–403.

> line 47–48 *feeding . . . dumbe.* Cf. Proverbs 16:24.

113 *Colnrogers.* Coln Rogers, Gloucestershire, where Robert and Muriel Oldisworth had their home.

122 var. line 4. *winnow-sheete.* a large cloth used for winnowing corn.

Commentary   207

[29]

The link between this and the preceding poem is the phrase "in eache streete."

Title *Mistris Katherine Bacon.* One of Richard Bacon's sisters. See [20], **1 gloss** above.

[30]

Title *Cosham.* Corsham, Wiltshire.

2 gloss. *Hulbert's monument.* There are two memorials to Thomas Hulbert on the south side of the chancel at Corsham, one on the wall, the other directly below it on the floor.
    Sir Edward Hungerford. See [17] above.

16 *Sh'riff.* sherrif.

[31]

Title The friend is presumably Richard Bacon. See the note to [2] for other poems to Bacon.

[32]

Title *Hampton-court* The poem is an exercise in prosopopeia; see the Introduction, p. xxxviii.

5 gloss *Prospects.* outlooks, vistas.

15 *Earth . . . Fire.* Cf. Oldisworth's use of the four elements in poems [2], [5], and [99].

[33]

This complimentary poem takes the form of a dream-vision, which opens with an unusual representation of the loss of sensation. The variant readings of the Folger manuscript are those of an early version of the poem.

Title *his cosin.* For other poems to Michael Oldisworth see the headnote to [3].

24 var., 1–3 *tricke . . . hoarse.* These lines do not rhyme. Either Oldisworth's work on the poem was still in progress, or the copyist has misread his source.

39–40 *my Hearse . . . verse.* For the custom of attaching verse to a poet's bier, see Henry King, "Upon the Death of my ever Desired Friend Dr. Donne Deane of Paules" (*The Poems*, ed. Margaret Crum [Oxford: Clarendon Press,1965], 76): "Each quill can dropp his tributary Verse, / And pin it, with the Hatchments, to the Hearse" (lines 7–8); and Milton, *Lycidas*, line 151.

57 *droppe . . . Overbury's blood.* Oldisworth repeatedly reveals his self-consciousness of his Overbury heritage.

[34]

Title *Moore.* On the presence of Africans in London in the first half of the seventeenth century, see Imtiaz Habib, *Black Lives in the English Archives, 1500–1677: Imprints of the Invisible* (Aldershot: Ashagate, 2008), 121–170. Habib emphasizes the significant size of the black population in the area of Westminster.

1 *black wench.* John Aubrey, *Brief Lives*, ed. Oliver Lawson Dick (London: Secker and Warburg, 1960), 86, records that Davenant contracted syphilis from a "black handsome wench" of Axe Yard, Westminster, in 1630. Most biographers understand "black" to mean "dark-haired", influenced, no doubt, by the assumption that few people of African descent were to be found in Early Modern England. Oldisworth's poem supports Habib's contrary view.

[35]–[36]

This pair of epitaphs demonstrates the two main forms of the genre which aims at vivid description or representation (*enargia*). The first is a form of ethopoeia, in which the deceased person establishes his or her character by addressing the reader directly, and the second is a form prosopographia, in which the author pays tribute to the deceased in order to move the reader. The two poems are linked by the complex interconnections between "Play" in the first line of the first poem, and "Platforme" in the last line of the second poem, which invite associations of the commonplace notion of mortal life as a temporary stage-play (see William Shakespeare, *As You Like It*, New Variorum Edition, ed. Richard Knowles ([New York: Modern Language Association of America, 1977], 130).

Commentary   209

[35]

Title *Thomas Bacon.* Presumably, a brother of Richard Bacon.

1 *at Play.* Engaged in playing entertaining and amusing games, but also, given the last line of [36], playing (only temporarily) a role on a stage.

3–4 *Then . . . companie.* The reader is invited to respond as if partaking in the child's past-times and so as being of the same company, but also as if to a comedy and not a tragedy.

[36]

6 *Platforme.* Elevated structure, pedestal (of an angelic statue), and, given "Play" in [35], a stage.

[37]

1–2 *English. . .Wolves.* England rejoiced in the distinction of being the only European country where wolves had been hunted to extinction by the end of the fifteenth century; see William Camden, *Britannia* (1610) [*STC* 4509], sig. 3K1; and Keith Thomas, *Man and the Natural World: Changing Attitudes in England, 1500–1800* (London: Allen Lane, 1983), 273.

[38]

Title Oldisworth here does a free translation of the first twenty-three lines of Aristophanes, *Ecclesiazusae.* The earliest separately printed translation of the play appears to be by Rowland Smith, *The Ecclesiazusai or the Female Parliament* (Oxford: J. H Parker, 1833).

3 gloss *Doctor Duppa.* See [8], 1n.

10 *In . . . burne.* This line is not indented in Bodleian MS. Don. c. 24.

20 *They . . . show.* This line is not indented in Bodleian MS. Don. c. 24.

[39]

3 gloss *Mistris Duppa.* See [8],1n.

4 *Hermophradit.* This is Oldisworth's spelling.

37–38 *Vesta . . . give.* The goddess Vesta's chastity was proverbial. Her temple in Rome was served not by male priests who shaved (hence "shorn-haire Orders"), but by the Vestal Virgins. See H. D. Brumble, *Classical Myths and Legends in the Middle Ages and Renaissance* (Chicago: Fitzroy Dearborn Press, 1998), 346–347.

53–54 *Amazons . . . round.* The Amazons were a mythical race of female warriors. Oldisworth's references are not without irony, since in epic at least, "Amazons exist in order to be fought, and ultimately defeated, by men in an Amazonomachy"; see Simon Hornblower and Antony Spawforth, eds., *Oxford Classical Dictionary*, third edition revised (Oxford: Oxford University Press, 2003), 69.

55 *Europa . . . Landes.* Europa was the mythical figure abducted by Jupiter in the form of a bull. I have been unable to locate a source for Oldisworth's suggestion that Europa accomplished a feat which won twelve lands (the countries of Europe, perhaps).

56–57 *by vertue . . . founded.* Carthage was founded by Dido.

57–58 *Carthage . . . shame.* Oldisworth appears to be referring to the Punic Wars (264–146 B.C.) between Carthage and Rome, and to Hannibal's invasion of Italy in the second of these wars. He deliberately suppresses the fact that Rome was the eventual victor.

71–72 *Sibylls . . . God.* In the pre-Christian era ten (on other counts, twelve) mysterious female figures, or sibyls, were thought to be endowed with oracular powers. Some of the prophecies were later taken to predict the birth of Jesus. The prophecies appear to have ceased at about the time of the Christian area, but in Rome a collection of prophecies were consulted at times of great crisis until as late as 362 A.D. (See Simon Hornblower and Antony Spawforth, eds., *The Oxford Classical Dictionary*, third edition revised [Oxford: Oxford University Press, 2003], 1400–1401.) These manuscripts were destroyed, and the surviving prophecies attributed to the sibyls are of Jewish and Christian origin. In later ages there was an ongoing debate as to whether the prophecies were of demonic origin, even though they could be aligned with Christian events. For a near-contemporary discussion of sibyls which might reflect Oldisworth's passing interest, see Thomas Heyward, *ΓΥΝΑΙΚΕΙΟΝ or Nine Bookes of Various History Concerning Women* (London, 1624) [*STC* 13326], 77–94. For the later sibylline tradition see Anke Holdenried,

Commentary   211

The Sibyl and Her Scribes: Manucripts and Interpretation of the Latin 'Sibylla Tribur-
tina,' c.1050–1500 (Aldershot: Ashgate, 2006); and for Early Modern interest in
the tradition, see Jessica L. Malay, "Jane Seager's Sibylline Poems: Maidenly Ne-
gotiations Through Elizabethan Gift Exchange," *English Literary Renaissance* 36
(2006): 173–193.

85 *fore-fathers.* The scansion requires this to be disyllabic: fore-fa'rs.

115–116 *wee . . . noe.* Cf. "Women have no souls," Tilley, W709. The debate on
whether women have souls arose from commentaries (wrongly attributed to St.
Ambrose) on 1 Corinthians 11: 1–12 and 14; see Helen Peters, ed., *John Donne: Par-
adoxes and Problems* (Oxford: Clarendon Press, 1980), "Problem VII: 'Why hath
the common opnion affoorded woemen Soules,' 28–29. See also *A New Argument
Against Women (1595): A Critical Edition,* ed. Clive Hart, second edition, 2 vol-
umes (Clacton-on-Sea: Gilliland Press, 2002), 1:1–19 and 2:251–64 (Appendix 2:
Further references to the *Disputatio nova* and to the belief that women have no
souls).

126 *Husband . . . Wife.* Cf. Ephesians 5:23.

[41]

The consistent revision of "thou/thy" to "you/your" perhaps reveals Oldisworth's
attempt to make the poem more formal and less personal.

Title *Sir B.R.* Not identified. There is no obvious connection between this poem
and [65], "To B.R. a Dissembler."

2 *THE COMPLETE GENTLEMAN.* The first edition of Henry Peacham's *The Com-
pleat Gentleman* appeared in 1622 [STC 19502], and the second in 1627 [STC
19503].

6 *translated.* Cf. *OED, translate,* v. I.1.b: "to carry or convey to heaven without
death."

[42]

For other metapoetic poems, see [1], [117], [118], and [119].

3 *The Sweeden king.* Gustavus Adolphus.
      gloss *1630.* The poem was written some two years before Gustavus Adolphus's
death at the battle of Lutzen on 6 November 1632. The king's death prompted at

least two other calls for poetic responses: Dudley, Lord North's "An Incentive to our Poets upon the Death of the victorious King of Swedeland" in *A Forest of Varieties* (London, 1645), Part 1, p. 75, and in *A Forest Promiscuous of Several Productions* (London, 1659), Part 1, p. 72; and Aurelian Townshend's "Elegy on the death of the King of Sweden: sent to Thomas Carew" in Bodleian MS Rawl. poet. 209 and St. John's College, Cambridge MS S. 23, and reprinted in *The Poems and Masques of Aurelian Townshend*, ed. Cedric C. Brown (Reading: Whiteknights Press, 1983), 48–49. Carew's response, "In answere of an Elegiacall Letter upon the death of the King of Sweden from Aurelian Townshend," (Thomas Carew, *Poems* [London, 1640], 126–30) celebrates the halcyon days of the early years of Charles I's personal rule that Oldisworth nostalgically recalls in the dedicatory epistle to his wife. For the texts of Carew's and Townshend's poems see Thomas Carew, *The Poems*, ed. Rhodes Dunlap (Oxford: Clarendon Press, 1949), 74–77 and 207–208.

28 *Natt Butter.* Nathaniel Butter (d. 1664), the news writer, began in 1605 to compile and publish news pamphlets, but it was not until 1622 that he began to issue reports at frequent intervals. He was satirized by Ben Jonson as "Cymbal" in *The Staple of News* (1625). In 1630 he began a series of half-yearly volumes of foreign news. Butter did in fact publish some poems on the death of Gustavus Adolphus in *The Swedish Intelligencer: The Third Part* (London, 1633) [*STC* 23525], sigs. ¶1–3¶4.

37–38 *Corbett . . . bishoppe.* See Introduction, p. xx.

43–44 *thing . . . sing.* Oldisworth himself stopped writing verse once he took orders. See the title-page of *A Recollection of Certaine Scattered Poems* and the dedicatory epistle to his wife, p. 5–6.

[43]

Title *Niobe.* According to the Greek myth, Niobe, the mother of many children, boasted that she was superior to Leto (Latona), who had only two, Apollo and Artemis. To avenge the insult, Apollo killed all Niobe's sons, and Artemis, the daughters. Excessive grief turned Niobe to marble which continued weeping. Cf. Ovid, *Metamorphoses*, 6.146–312. See H. D. Brumble, *Classical Myths and Legends in the Middle Ages and Renaissance* (Chicago: Fitzroy Dearborn Press, 1998), 244.

Commentary   213

[44]

Title *Mistris Strange.* Not identified. Jane Hungerford, sister of Sir Edward, was married to Robert Strange. Oldisworth's paternal grandmother was Margaret Strange (married to Joseph Oldisworth of Coln Rogers).
   Summerford. Presumably, Somerford in Wiltshire.

22 *Rochet.* a linen vestment usually worn by bishops.

[47]

Title *greene Sicknesse.* See *OED*: "an anaemic disease which mostly affects young women about the age of puberty and gives a pale or greenish tinge to the complexion; chlorosis." See Introduction, p. xxxviii. Oldisworth's poem is in some ways not unlike Edward, Lord Herbert of Cherbury's two greensickness poems (both entitled "The Green-Sickness Beauty"); see *Poems English and Latin*, ed. G. C. Moore Smith (Oxford: Clarendon Press, 1923), 67–69. Though Herbert's poems treat the woman with respect, their main concern is to celebrate her beauty. Oldisworth's poem, on the other hand, is consolatory rather than eulogistic, and his tone is avuncular and personal rather than elegantly witty and courtly.

25 *Looke . . . gemmes.* Pliny, *Natural History,* 37.16.62–63, extols the virtues of looking at green and through green *smaragdi* (often mistranslated as emeralds). See also Theophrastus, *On Stones,* 23–27, ed. and tr. Earle R. Caley and John F. C. Richards (Columbus, Ohio: Ohio State University Press, 1956), who comment (100) that σμαραγδος is better understood as green quartz in the form of "plasma or prase."

38 *toilsome Dutch.* Oldisworth appears to have in mind the Germans (Deutsch), who were stereotypically hardworking, rather than the Netherlanders; see Peter Heylyn, *Microcosmos* (Oxford, 1625) [STC 13277], sig. S8.

39 *Switzers.* Having expelled the Habsburgs, the Swiss were proverbial for their rejection of monarchy; cf. Fulke Greville, *Prose Works*, ed. John Gouws (Oxford: Clarendon Press, 1986): "The Switzers swollen with equality; . . . enemies . . . to monarchies" (50).

43 *muzzles.* (humorously) faces.

[49]

Title. Alexander Baynham, the son and heir of Joseph Baynham of Westbury in Gloucestershire, was married to Elizabeth, the daughter of Arnold Oldisworth (which makes her the sister of Michael Oldisworth); see the complex marriage settlement, dated 1 May 1611, Gloucester Record Office, MS D33/271. There is no mention of an Alexander Baynham in the casualty lists of 15–25 August 1632 for the siege of Maastricht; see PRO, SP 84/144, folios 233–237 (fol. 233 mentions a Lieutenant Raynham as being "hurt").

Siege of Mastrich. 1632. In July and August 1632 the Spanish garrison of Maastricht was besieged by Dutch forces under the command of Prince Frederick Henry of Orange.

3 *Sweeden's king*. Gustavus Adolphus, killed in the Battle of Lützen on 6 November 1632.

the Palsgrave. Frederick V, Elector Palatine, died in Mainz on 29 November 1632.

16 *kickt-off . . . Manors*. Alexander Baynham inherited extensive properties on the death of his father, Joseph, in July 1613, but they were soon heavily encumbered and had to be sold off; see, for example, Sir John Maclean, "The History of the Manors of Dene Magna and Abenhall, and their Lords," *Transactions of the Bristol and Gloucester Archaeological Society*, 6 (1881–1882): 134–45, 184.

20 *Children*. By 1623 Alexander Baynham had four children.

[50]

Title *Friend beyond sea*. For other poems to Richard Bacon, see [2].

[51]

5 *Arión*. Arion the poet, having been thrown overboard, was rescued by a dolphin charmed by his lyre playing. Apollo, the god of singers, later stellified his harp as the constellation Lyra. See H. D. Brumble, *Classical Myths and Legends in the Middle Ages and Renaissance* (Chicago: Fitzroy Dearborn Press, 1998), 36–38.

Ariadné. Ariadne, having been deserted by Theseus, was rescued by Dionysus, who, when she died, turned her wedding crown into a constellation, Corona Borealis, the Northern Crown. See H. D. Brumble, *Classical Myths and Legends in the Middle Ages and Renaissance*, 35–36

Commentary   215

13 *farthing*. The standard design in the reigns of James I and Charles I for farthing tokens —with a crowned harp on the reverse—was stipulated in a proclamation of 19 May 1613. Since the reign of Elizabeth I, tokens— pieces of stamped metal issued by private persons or companies—were used to remedy the scarcity of small coin. See C. Wilson Peck, *English Copper, Tin and Bronze Coins in the British Museum, 1558–1958*, 2nd ed. (London: Trustees of the British Museum, 1970), 19.

[52]

Title *discontented man*. Oldisworth might have in mind the plight of his cousin Michael between 1630 and 1637 (see the headnote to [3] and above [69]). This might explain why this poem precedes [53]. The poem is a reminder that death comes to all, despite their worldly ambitions. In some ways it can be seen as a re-action against the *beatus ille* motif so common in Early Modern writing. Robert Herrick's "Discontents in Devon" (*Poetical Works*, ed. L. C. Martin [Oxford: Clarendon Press, 1965], 19) provides a more conventional reaction to the tradition, for which see Maren-Sofie Røstvig, *The Happy Man: Studies in the Metamorphosis of a Classical Ideal, 1600–1700* (Oxford: Basil Blackwell, 1953). The figure of the melancholy malcontent is common on the Jacobean stage, and is satirized in the Theorphrastian Character of "A Discontented Man" in John Earle, *Microcosmography*, ed. Harold Osborne (London: University Tutorial Press, 1933), 19–20. It appears in the first four editions of *Micro-cosmographie. Or, a peece of the wold discovered* (1628) [*STC 7439–7441*].

[53]

Title *Michaël Oldisworth's*. For other poems to Michael Oldisworth see the head-note to [3].

4 *Tahah*. I have not been able to attach any significance to this name.

9 *Guerim*. Unidentified.

56 *tarbox-Lines*. A derogatory term for unsophisticated, rustic, even crude, verse. A tarbox was used by shepherds for the tar to salve sheep wounds.

[55]

Title *altered 1644*. This is one of the few indications that Oldisworth wrote or re-vised poems after the mid-1630s.
   Mistris Anne Henshaw. Not identified.

[56]

The variant readings of the earlier, printed version draw attention to Oldisworth's painstaking process of revision.

Title *birth . . . Yorke.* James, Duke of York, was born on 14 October 1633.

4 gloss *These . . . Oxford.* See *Vitis Carolinae Gemma Altera* (Oxford, 1633) [*STC* 19035], sigs. I4ᵛ–K1.

[57]

Title *his aunt . . . Molesey.* Mary Overbury married Sir John Lytcott (d.1641) of Molsey, Surrey; see [23] above. There is a monument to him in East Molsey church; see *The Victoria History of the County of Surrey,* vol. 3, ed. H. E. Malden (London: Constable, 1911), 454.

[58]

2 *Coscus.* There is no obvious reason for the name. In Donne's *Satire II,* the target is a bad poet and worse lawyer named Coscus.

4 *legg-downe.* trip.

[60]

Verse narratives of a journey probably derive from Horace, *Satires* 1.5. The most obvious immediate source for Oldisworth's poem is Richard Corbett's "Iter Boreale." Many other instances of the genre were produced in the seventeenth century; see J. A. W. Bennett and H. R. Trevor-Roper, *The Poems of Richard Corbett* (Oxford: Clarendon Press, 1955), 118–19.

1 *we.* There is no indication of who accompanied Oldisworth.

1–2 *barge . . . wheeles.* I have not been able to find records of this early paddleboat.

5–18 *Behind . . . make.* This account of Oldisworth's encounter with the aging Jonson has been misattributed to Michael Oldiworth in *Ben Jonson,* ed. Herford and Simpson, 1:113, n.1. See also Oldisworth's tribute to Jonson in poem [1].

Commentary 217

8 *guere.* discourse, doctrine, talk (*OED*, "gear" sb. 11a.); cf. [84], 5.

19 *Thisselworth.* Isleworth; see [28] and notes.

20 *Sir Giles Overbury.* See [28] and notes.

21 *Mistris Old'sworth.* This is presumably Michael Oldisworth's wife, Susan; see the note to [3].

24–36 *For . . . obsolete.* This defense of his cousin probably arises from the fact that Michael Oldisworth had been out of office for two years; see the headnote to [3].

30 *strong line.* If the evidence gathered by George Williamson in "Strong Lines", in *Seventeenth Century Contexts* (London: Faber, 1960), 132–47, is representative, Oldisworth's use of the term is unusual at this time. Normally, the term seems to have been used to valorize the strenuous style of Donne, Jonson, and their followers. Here it is used pejoratively to refer to the discreditable exaggeration of academic verse.

32 *Mecoenas.* Caius Maecenas (d. 8 B.C.), the friend and trusted counselor of Augustus, was regarded as the archetypal patron. He is chiefly remembered as the patron of Virgil, Horace, and Propertius.

37 *Arborvill.* Arborfield, Berkshire.

39–46 *brave people . . . Rome.* Oldisworth is strangely reticent about identifying his hosts, perhaps because of their religious affiliations; but see the note to 49–64 below.

44 *Bellarmin's doctrine.* Robert Bellarmine [Roberto Francesco Romolo Bellarmino] (1542–1621), the Jesuit theologian, and professor of controversial theology at the Collegium Romanum, was the leading apologist for the Roman Catholic position. Oldisworth might have in mind a particularly hard-line Counter-Reformation stance as manifested, for example, in Bellarmine's argument against Roman Catholics taking the Oath of Allegiance.

49–64 *neighbring Garden . . . border.* The garden described here was probably the work of the Mistress Thorold referred to in [67]. It is possible that she was a member of a recusant family.

65 *pompous.* magnificent, splendid.

66 *Sir John Backhous.* The son of Samuel Backhouse (d.1621) who had obtained the lease of Swallowfield Manor from Sir John Lytcott (for whom, see the headnote to

[23]). In 1615 Sir John Backhouse married an heiress, Flower, or Flora, Henshawe, and was made a Knight of the Bath at the coronation of Charles I. He was a Royalist, and his estates were sequestered. According to the inscription on his monument erected by his widow in Swallowfield church, he was imprisoned, and died in 1649. He was succeeded by his brother William (1593–1662), the Rosicrucian philosopher; see *The Victoria History of the County of Berkshire*, vol. 3, ed. William Page *et al.* (London: Constable, 1923), 269.

98 *Philoclea and Pamela.* The heroines of Sir Philip Sidney's *The Countess of Pembroke's Arcadia.*

100 *Squire Burch.* Not identified.

106. *king . . . her.* I have not been able to discover any occasion when either James I or Charles I might have kissed the elder of the Bacon sisters.

110 *Chillings.* The manorhouse at Chilling Farm on the coast between Warsash and Titchfield in Hampshire has long since been demolished. It was probably owned by Thomas Wriothesley, Earl of Southampton (1608–1667), who succeeded to the title in 1624. See [78] for another poem about the Bacon home.

114 *Dick Bacon.* Richard Bacon; see [2] and notes.

116 *such Arbors.* See [78].

129 *servants . . . slaves.* Oldisworth's distinction between servants and slaves provides clear evidence of the institution of slavery in Caroline England, something routinely denied by historians of the period. Imtiaz Habib, *Black Lives in the English Archives, 1500–1677: Imprints of the Invisible* (Aldershot: Ashgate, 2008), provides ample evidence to confirm not only Oldisworth's reference to slaves in rural Hampshire, but also his reference to the presence of people of African descent in London (see poem [34] and notes).

144–45 *Sir Bevis . . . wood.* The tenth-century legend of Sir Bevis of Hampton, son of Guy, Earl of Southampton, became popular from the fourteenth century onwards; certain details held a special significance for the inhabitants of Southampton. For an historical account of the legend of Sir Bevis and Ascupart, the giant who submits to the knight and becomes his page, see Jennifer Fellows, "Sir Bevis of Hampton in Popular Tradition," *Proceedings of the Hampshire Field Club and Archaeological Society* 42 (1986): 134–45. Adrian B. Rance, "The Bevis and Ascupart Panels, Bargate Museum, Southampton," *Proceedings of the Hampshire Field Club and Archaeological Society* 42 (1986): 147–53, provides illustrations of nineteenth-century engravings of the original panels, 326 x 99 cm. (now in the

Commentary   219

Bargate Museum, Southampton), as well as a photograph (c. 1870) of the Bargate
showing the panels and a pair of leaden lions which replaced the original wooden
ones in 1743 (Oldisworth writes as if there was one lion only). Rance suggests that
the panels may have been part of a display of civic pride occasioned by the visit to
Southampton by the Emperor Charles V in 1522. He cites (149) what he takes to
be the earliest account of the panels and lions, a record of a visit by a Lieutenant
Hammond in 1635:

> I entered at the North Gate thereof with no little feare, betweene the
> Jawes of 2. ramping Lions, and two thunderign [sic] warriors, Exipat,
> the fearefull gyant on the one side and braue Beuis of Southampton on
> the other, if aboue them had not been plac'd our late renowned, vertu-
> ous Queen, Elizabeth to daunt their courage and quell their Fury, and
> to suffer peaceable Passengers to haue quiet and safe entrance.

149 *one good Street.* Cf. Samuel Pepys's account of his visit in 1662: "The towne is
one most gallant street"; *The Diary,* ed. Robert Latham and William Matthews, 11
vols. (London: Bell, 1970–1983), 3:71.

[61]

The poem is a form of *paraclausithyron,* a poem before or next to the door (of a
scornful beloved). For Classical antecedents, see Catullus 67; Horace *Odes* 3.10
and 3.26; Tibullus 1.2; Propertius 1.16; Ovid *Amores* 1.6. See also Frank O. Copley,
"The Suicide-Paraclausithyron: A Study of Ps. Theocritus *Idyll* XXIII," *Transca-
tions and Proceedings of the American Philological Association* 71 (1940): 52–61;
and Aristophanes, *Ecclesiazusai,* lines 960–76 (Oldisworth translated the opening
lines of the play; see [38]).

[62]

Title *Master Little of Abingdon.* Francis Little (?1554–1631). His "A Monument of
Christian Munificence," a manuscript dated 20 September 1627, was edited for
publication in London and Oxford, 1871, by Claude Delaval Cobham.

3–4 *Hospitall . . . Charge.* Little was a governor of Christ's Hospital, Abingdon,
1592–1630, and Master 1596–1598.

9 *foure . . . Mayor.* He was Mayor of Abingdon 1592–1593, 1598–1599, 1606–1607,
1617–1618.

220   BODLEIAN MS DON. C. 24: POEMS

11 *once . . . Parliament.* He represented the Borough of Abingdon in the Parliament
of 1597.

[64]

Title *Sir Giles Fetiplace.* Sir Giles Fetiplace of Poulton, d.1641. For poems written
on behalf of others see [11]n.

[65]

Title *B.R.* Not identified. There is no obvious connection between this poem and
[41], "On Sir B.R.".

26 *master . . . Showes.* If there were better records of theatrical productions and
shows at Westminster School and Christ Church, this line might help us identify
"B.R.".
     Stage-plaies . . . our. The Folger manuscript variant might indicate that Old-
isworth's revision attempted to bring the poem up to date, and so not obviously
connected with the University or the Court.

[66]

1 *Tharuleot.* A character in Oldisworth's "Chronicle of Europe", in Bodleian MS
Don.c.24, fols. 88–91^v.

[67]

Title *Mistris Thorold.* This is possibly Frances Thorold commemorated in a plaque
now on the wall at the south west end of the nave of Arborfield church:

     Blessed are the dead which dye in our Lord
     Heere lyeth the body of Thomas Haward Gent:
     with Anne his wife & Frances there
     onely child, who was married to William
     Thorold Esq[uire] & had issue by him 7
     Son[n]es & 7 daughters
     this Thomas Haward dep[ar]ted the 24th of
     November A[nno] D[omi]ni 1643.

Commentary   221

According to Elias Ashmole, *The Antiquities of Berkshire*, 3 vols. (London: Mears and Hooke, 1723, repr. 1791), 2:385, the brass plate was fixed to a gravestone near the entrance to the chancel in the original church. If William Thorold had been a recusant, it could possibly explain why his wife was buried with her parents. For Oldisworth's visit to Arborfield, see [60], 37–64.

[69]

Title Presumably Michael Oldisworth is "discontented" because of his loss of office after the death of his patron, William Herbert, Earl of Pembroke; see the headnote to [3] and [52] above. The poem is part of a consistent valorization of personal virtue over public status.

9 *Woodstock*. The royal palace at Woodstock, near Oxford.

18 *darklong*. darkling or in darkness. *OED* ("darklong" *adv.*) records three instances of "darklong" dated 1561, 1577, 1620.

[70]

Title *On the picture of Beauty*. The title of the poem, and even the poem itself, would generally lead readers to believe that feminine beauty is being described. The title of the Folger version, however, radically alters the perspective of the poem. Given the other poems in the collection, the "yong Master Bacon" of the Folger manuscript is more likely a reference to Richard than to Matthew Bacon. There is no obvious explanation why the picture should be described as "sett upp beyond sea" (Richard Bacon was already abroad)—unless, of course, Bacon himself is thought of as a picture or representation of beauty. (For other poems to Richard Bacon see the headnote to [2].) Alternatively, one could suggest that the picture referred to is one of Matthew Bacon, which his elder brother carried with him in his travels. In which case, the picture is one referred to in [89].

[71]

8 *steam*. odorous fume.

9 *panther-Breath*. For the sweet breath of the panther which leads others to destruction, see Pliny, *Natural History*, 23.62; cf. Dryden, *The Hind and the Panther*, 2.228.

[72]

Title *acquaintance.* This poem might well be another addressed to Richard Bacon. Oldisworth expresses anxiety over the loss of letters from Bacon in [50].

[73]

16 *Sent.* scent.

[74]

Title *Mistris Summer.* Not identified. For poems written on behalf of others see [11] n.

[75]

Title See the headnote to [74].

20 *Paul's church.* Repairs to St Paul's began in 1633; see [79] and note. This reference provides a *terminus ad quem* for Mistris Summer's death.

[77]

Title *Sir Rowland Cotton.* Sir Roland Cotton of Bellaport in Shropshire matriculated from St John's College, Cambridge in about 1596, and was admitted to Lincoln's Inn on 13 June 1599. He was knighted in 1608 and represented Newcastle-under-Lyme in Parliament in 1605 and 1628, and Shropshire in 1626. His will was proved in 1634. In the volume of Latin and English elegies, *Parentalia spectatissimo Rolando Cottono* (1635) [*STC* 5870], most of the poems refer to Cotton's athletic prowess (as a wrestler rather than a leaper, but see Thomas Randolph's poem on sig. Cl^v: *Ad Danum quem Cottonus olim juvenis saltando exuperavit*), his linguistic abilities (in Greek and Hebrew), and his service to Prince Henry. Among those who contributed to the volume were William Strode, Owen Felltham, and Thomas Randolph, whose English poems also refer to Cotton as a leaper (sig. H1):

> For when he leapt, the people dar'd to say
> Hee was borne of fire, and were no clay.
> Which was the Cause too that hee wrestled so,
> 'Tis not fires nature to be kept below.

13–14 *diverse-Toungues . . . confusion.* Cf. Genesis 11:7–9.

Commentary   223

[78]

Title This poem probably stems from Oldisworth's visit in 1632 to Chillings recorded in "Iter Australe" ([60], 93–138 and 153–74; the arbor is referred to in lines 116–18). All signs of the arbor have vanished. As a poem relating an owner to his estate, this poem can be read as another country house poem influenced by Ben Jonson's "To Penshurst." For other poems to Richard Bacon, see the headnote to [2].

[79]

Title *Repairers of Paul's Church.* The restoration of St Paul's began in 1633 under the direction of Inigo Jones, with the support of William Laud, bishop of London and archbishop of Canterbury (from September 1633). See William Dugdale, *The History of St Pauls Cathedral in London* (1658), 157–70.

1–2 *Stone-temples . . . lord.* Cf. 1 Kings 8:27.

[81]

For other poems expressing Oldisworth's distrust of titles and social status, see the note to [4].

[82]

Title *his . . . sea.* For other poems to Richard Bacon see the headnote to [2].

17 *Paynting . . . fetch.* Oldisworth's comma after *they* is misleading. If there has to be a comma, it should be after *painting.*

[83]

Title *Citizens.* For other descriptions of Londoners, see [28], 53–98.

[84]

Title *Cambridge. 1632.* Oldisworth, having graduated B.A. in 1632, was incorporated at Cambridge in the same year. This poem may be related to that occasion. For another poem on Cambridge, see [15].

5 *guere.* discourse, doctrine, talk (*OED*, "gear" sb. 11a); cf. [60], 8.

[85]

It is possible that this poem is connected with the Mistress Thorold of Arborfield celebrated in [67].

[87]

Title *To . . . sea.* For other poems to Richard Bacon, see the headnote to [2].

[88]

Title *Cosham . . . 1632.* For other poems referring to Sir Edward Hungerford and Corsham, see [17], [18], and [30].

1–3 *As . . . admire.* Cf. 2 Corinthians 12:2–4.

[89]

Title *Master M.B.* Presumably, this is Matthew Bacon. He qualified as a medical doctor at Padua on 15 October 1642, and was admitted as an Honorary Fellow of the College of Physicians in December 1664; see William Munk, *The Roll of the Royal College of Physicians of London*, 2 vols. (London: Longman, Green, Longman & Roberts, 1861), 1:317.

his picture. See [70] and note.

Commentary   225

[90]

Title *Master Swaine*. Richard Swayne of Wimborne, Dorset, matriculated at Christ Church in 1632, aged 17. He died on 4 April 1634. His memorial is to be found on the west wall of the north transept of the Cathedral. See Anthony Wood, *The History and Antiquities of the college and Halls in the University of Oxford*, ed. John Gutch (Oxford: Clarendon Press, 1786), 484–85.

[91]

Title *Giles Oldisworth*. Giles Oldisworth (1619–1678) was born at Coln Rogers, educated at Westminster, and admitted to Trinity College, Cambridge, in May 1639. He graduated B.A. in 1642 or 1643. Having been deprived of his scholarship because of his royalist sympathies, he was incorporated M.A. at Oxford in July 1646. In 1645 he succeeded his brother to the living of Bourton-on-the-Hill. The only poems attributed to him are "Sir Thomas Overbury's Wife Unvailed" and those to be found in the allegorical narrative "A Westminster Scholar, or the Patterne of Pietie" (Bodleian Rawlinson MS. C. 422).

25 *Robin*. I have been unable to find any record of a twin brother. He is mentioned in Giles's "A Westminster Scholar, or the Patterne of Pietie." It might be that he is simply an alter ego for Giles.

[92]

Title The holograph acknowledges Oldisworth's surrogate authorship. This kind of information is lost in the Folger manuscript, as it is in most miscellanies. The practice of vicarious authorship was perhaps more common than we realize. For poems written on behalf of others by Oldisworth, see [11] n.

[93]

Title *Abraham Cowley*. Abraham Cowley (1618–1687), another of Lambert Osbaldeston's pupils, was educated at Westminster and Trinity College, Cambridge. His *Poetical Blossomes* was published in 1633, 1636, and 1637.

[94]

Title *Mistris Katharine Bacon*. Richard Bacon's younger sister; see [60], 101–6.

226   BODLEIAN MS DON. C. 24: POEMS

[95]

Title *Master Tooker . . . Strettam.* Maria Oldisworth, the sister of Michael Oldis-
worth, married Robert Tooker (Tucker), the rector (from 1631) of St Leonard's,
Streatham, at St Martin-in-the-Fields on 3 April 1627.

[96]

Title *Master . . . departure.* This could refer to either Richard or Matthew Bacon.
The Folger manuscript supplies the surname of the recipient. From Oldisworth's
wish that "we thought to bee / As learned and as honest as is Hee" (line 20 var.),
it would seem that he has the elder brother in mind. This poem also has much in
common with [82].

For other poems to Richard Bacon, see the headnote to [2].

15–16 *Hast . . . indeed.* Cf. Ezekiel 34 *passim.* Oldisworth's generalized sugges-
tion that the clergy neglect their pastoral responsibilities anticipates Milton's "The
hungry sheep look up, and are not fed" ("Lycidas," line 125). Given the context of
the poem, Oldisworth, unlike Milton, does not attack the hierarchy of the estab-
lished church, nor is he concerned to warn against the dangers of Roman Catholic
proselytism. These lines are, in fact, complexly nuanced, since the poem appears
to be addressed to someone who has left England to be trained as a Roman Catho-
lic priest.

20 var. *who &c.* Apart for reasons of political sensitivity in the 1640s, there is no
obvious reason for the suppression of the end of the poem in the holograph.

[97]

Given Venus's infidelity to Vulcan, it is tempting to attribute a complex irony to this
vicarious poem. In writing a poem for someone else in which the speaker wishes
himself as fortunate as Vulcan, Oldisworth is either inept or jesting at his client's
ignorance. There is little to justify a reading which sees Oldisworth as a possible in-
terloping Mars figure. See also Brumble, *Classical Myths and Legends*, 207–8.

For poems written on behalf of others see [11] n.

[99]

For poems written on behalf of others see [11] n. Cf. Oldisworth's use of the four
elements in poems [2], [5], and [32].

Commentary   227

[100]

Title *Michaël Oldisworth.* For other poems to Michael Oldisworth, see the head-note to [3].

2 *our Chanc'lour.* If this is a particular reference, it is to William Laud, who was Chancellor from 1630–1641.

[102]

The underlying conceit of the poem depends on Protestant oppposition to the sup-posed veneration of images by Roman Catholics.

[103]

Title *To . . . sea.* For other poems to Richard Bacon, see the headnote to [2].

[104]

Title *Mistris Burch.* Richard Bacon's elder sister; see [60], 99–100.

[105–107]

These three poems are included in the commemorative volume published by Ox-ford University, *Solis Britannici Perigæum* (1633), sigs. M4–N1. Charles I departed from London on 8 May 1633, arrived in Edinburgh on 15 June, and was crowned King of Scotland three days later. He left Edinburgh on 28 June and was back in London on 15 July.

[105]

The figure underlying the poem is that of the King's "two bodies," which was gen-erally used to justify Stuart absolute monarchy. Oldisworth's language appears to echo that of Edward Forset, *A Comparative Discourse of the Bodies Natural and Poli-tique* (London, 1606) [STC 11188], especially sigs. C2–C4, in which Forset likens the sovereign to the soul which is coterminous with the body. For a recent discus-sion of the topic, see Albert Rolls, *Documents Illustrating the Theory of the King's Two Bodies in the Age of Shakespeare: The Reports of Edmund Plowden and A Com-*

228   BODLEIAN MS DON. C. 24: POEMS

parative Discourse of the Bodies Natural and Politique by Edward Forset (Lewiston, Queenstown, and Lampeter: Edwin Mellen, 2006), 1–20.

Title The title of the Folger manuscript version provides evidence of the copyist's source. The original and the copy must have been produced in circumstances under which the immediate historical context was taken for granted. Copies made after the event would require a more descriptive title.

22 var. The final lines of the Folger version are omitted in both the early printed and later holograph versions. This would indicate that the Folger manuscript derives from the author's working papers. The ending of the later versions provides a measure of Oldisworth's skill and taste.

[106]

22–30 *gold . . . royall-hearted.* Having mentioned the King's largesse, Oldisworth then proceeds to pun on several words for gold and silver coins: *angels* (28), crowns [*crown'd*] (29), *Nobles* (29) and *ryals* [Royal-hearted] (30). The Angel was so called because St Michael slaying a dragon was on the obverse. It had no portrait of the monarch. The Noble was first issued in the reign of Edward III, but there is no record of any being issued in the reign of Charles I. Ryals were also not minted in this period. See Charles Oman, *The Coinage of England* (Oxford: Clarendon Press, 1931), 300–5 and Plate XXXIV; and C. H. V. Sutherland, *English Coinage, 600–1900* (London: Batsford, 1973), 165–68, and Plates 80–83.

23–24 *men . . . bee.* Cf. Oldisworth's claim in the dedicatory epistle (p. 5, lines 27–29) that he saw the king's face more often than the portrait of him represented on coins of the realm.

[108]

For poems written on behalf of others see [11] n.

[110]

Title The title suggests that the poem was produced under the same circumstances as the one following. For poems written on behalf of others see [11] n.

Commentary 229

[111]

Title *For a Gentleman.* I cannot identify the person on whose behalf this poem is supposedly written. For poems written on behalf of others see [11] n.

Master Henry Gresley. Henry, the son of John Grisley, of Shrewsbury, matriculated on 1 September 1634, aged seventeen. He was at Oxford until 1648, having graduated B.A. in 1638 and M.A. in 1641. He was rector of Severn Stoke, Worcesterhire from 1661, and prebendary of Worcester from 1672 until his death in 1680.

18–19 *did out-goe . . . case.* The female Pythian Oracle at Delphi was not blind, though she spoke in a trance. Oracular figures were proverbially blind, as for example Teiresias.

55–58 *Christ . . . and I.* Cf. Aelred of Rivaulx, *De Spirituali Amicitia* 1: "Ecce ego et tu, et spero quod tertius inter nos Christus sit" [Here we are, you and I, and I hope Christ makes a third with us]; see J.-P. Migne, *Patrologiae cursus completus [Partrologia Latinae],* 221 vols. (Paris: J-P. Migne, 1844–64), 195: 661A. Oldisworth probably did not have access to the Aelred text, but both would have in mind Matthew 18:20: "where two or three are gathered together in my name, there am I in the midst of them."

[113]

Apart from the title, folio 74^v is blank. There is no indication that this is Oldisworth's intention. He might well have intended to copy a poem at this point. If so, having left a single blank page, he must have known the poem's length.

[114]

Title *Sir Thomas Overbury.* Sir Thomas Overbury (1581–1613) was Oldisworth's maternal uncle. He was closely associated with Robert Carr, eventually the Earl of Somerset, one of James I's Scots favorites. Overbury is said to have nurtured the rough Scot in courtly ways, to the extent that Queen Anne called him Carr's "governor" or tutor. They parted company over Carr's infatuation with Frances Howard, Countess of Essex; see [AP7], 16–17n. His uncle's fate appears to have had great significance for Oldisworth; see the General Introduction, p. xvi. For another poem on Overbury, see [AP7].

his poëme. Overbury's ideal portrait, "A Wife," first appeared in print in 1614, and was reprinted sixteen times by 1637.

[115]

Title *Godfrey Goodman*. Godfrey Goodman (1583–1656) entered Westminster School in 1592, and was elected to scholarship at Trinity College, Cambridge, in 1599. He became Bishop of Gloucester in 1625. He was frequently reprimanded for his Roman Catholic sympathies which severely embarrassed Archbishop Laud and his supporters, but only in his will did he make a declaration of his allegiance to Roman doctrine.

[116]

The *contemptus mundi* motif of this poem prepares for the closing triptych.

[117–119]

For other metapoetic poems, see [1] and [42].

This set of poems alludes to the myth of Astraea's retreat from the earth. Astraea or Virgo, the goddess of justice, was the last of the immortals to depart, and in Christian terms her retreat figures the Fall. See H. David Brumble, *Classical Myths and Legends in the Middle Ages and Renaissance* (Westport, Conn: Greenwood Press, 1998), 38–39.

See John Gouws, "Religious Authority and Poetic Knowledge: The Alternative of Nicolas Oldisworth's Farewell to Poetry," *Southern African Journal of Medieval and Renaissance Studies* 17 (2007): 41–55, where I discuss the distinctiveness of Oldisworth's religious perspective on his poetry.

[118]

2 gloss. *Michaël Oldisworth*. See the headnote to [3].

Commentary   231

Additional Poems

[AP 1]

1 *keeper, Coventree.* Thomas Coventry, Lord Coventry (1578–1640), was made
Lord Keeper of the Great Seal in 1625.

2 *seale.* The seal celebrated in this poem might be the same one referred to in [9],
which also has three lions (line 7); see below (lines 29–30).

7 *Cheap-side.* Cheapside, north-east of St. Paul's Churchyard was associated with
wealth because of Old Change (where bullion was received for coining), and Gold-
smith's Row (with its fourteen goldsmith's shops).

11 *Weston.* Richard Weston, Lord Portland (1577–1635) was made Lord High
Treasurer in 1628.

19 *bores.* countrymen, husbandmen; cf. *OED,* "boor."

27–31 *Heralds . . . state.* The seal brings the armorial creatures granted by the Her-
alds' office to life. See [2] n. above.

37–8 *silver Printers . . . Leyden.* Most fine etching, which often appears silver, was
produced in the Dutch cities of Amsterdam and Leiden.

43 *In . . . Sence.* If there were a second line to this couplet, it is missing.

48 *Type.* Distinguishing mark or stamp; see *OED,* "type" n¹, 3.

49 *Marke . . . Beaste.* The mark of the Antichrist; see Revelation 16:2.

50 *brother.* Fellow Puritan.

52 *your statutes.* Oldisworth probably has in mind Article 25 of the Thirty-Nine
Articles which distinguishes between the two distinctly instituted sacraments,
Baptism and the Eucharist, and the five lesser sacraments that "have not like na-
ture of Sacraments with Baptism, and the Lord's Supper, for that they have not any
visible sign or ceremony ordained by God."

53 *Third Sacrament.* Puritans would have maintained that there are only two (as
opposed to the traditional seven) sacraments: Baptism and the Lord's Supper.

56–57 Cf. Luke 22:38

[AP2]

9–12 *If Abram . . . Farre off.* Cf. John 8:56 and accounts of the Transfiguration (Matthew 17:1–13; Mark 9:2–13; and Luke 9:29–36).

12 *prospective glasse.* Magical glass or crystal revealing future events. Cf. 1 Corinthians 13:12.

[AP3]

7 *Pipes.* Cf. *OED* "Coral" n¹, 3: "A toy made of polished coral, given to infants to assist them in cutting their teeth. The name was extended to toys of glass, bone, etc. used for the same purpose."

15 *ilde.* Presumaby this is a scribal error for "idle."
Tipe. Type, prefiguring, representative image.
silly shadow. Feeble, insignificant secondary representation.

17 *kinges . . . Realmes.* Oldisworth seems to mean that even without taking into consideration their heads (the kings or rulers), the bodies (or realms) of both children are beautiful.

[AP4]

This invective poem is a variation on the theme "The pen is mightier than the sword" (see William George Smith, *The Oxford Dictionary of English Proverbs*, 3rd ed., ed. F. P. Wilson [Oxford: Clarendon Press, 1970], 619).

10 *The picture . . . Hee.* The line is one syllable short, though the scansion is not radically defective: there are five beats, and an implied offbeat between "foe" and "this".

17–18 *at once . . . legge.* The enemy is ignorant of the niceties of civil conduct: he does not know how to pay his respects in saluting or bidding farewell, nor does he know how to make a courtly obeisance. "At once" might mean that he could not do both at the same time.

23 *His grave . . . acrosse.* He assumes the stereotypical posture of a melancholy man.

26 *borish.* Rustic, uncultured, coarse.

Commentary   233

36 *That . . . stirre.* The line is one syllable short and metrically defective.

49 *spawles.* Spits coarsely.

50 *asses jawbone.* Samson uses an ass's jawbone to slay his enemies the Philistines (Judges 15:15–17). It is difficult to see the connection with the hyperbolic description of Oldisworth's enemy's unmannerly elocution and delivery.

53 *schoole.* This is the reading of the manuscript. Is should read "schooles" to rhyme with "fooles".

57 *had (as.* This is the reading of the manuscript. There is no justification for the opening parenthesis.

69 *Elves.* Possibly, social inferiors or dependents.

69–70 *putt . . . themselves.* The enemy plays practical jokes on his dependents in order not to be thought inferior to everyone else.

[AP 6]

2 *gulph.* Gulf, chasm or abyss.

12 *wolfe . . . Constellation.* The southern constellation, Lupus.

14 *Dogge starres.* Sirius, the Dog Star, is the brightest star in the constellation Canis Major.

[AP 7]

Title See the headnote to [114].

2 *lamentable.* To be lamented, grieved for.

8 *If second you.* In the literature of friendship, the friend is regarded as a "second self." The reading of the manuscript is difficult; it should perhaps read "of second you."

14 *sawe dimme.* Folger MS. V.a.170 is written in an unusually clear hand, but the scribe's intention in the second of these two words is uncertain: "d" [three minims] "i" [three minims] "e" [he often mislocates the dot of the "i," but in this instance his "i" is clearly separated]. The word should have two syllables and rhyme with "him." OED, "dim." C , cites two instances (Gower, 1394; and Shelley, 1821) of the word used as an adverb. The sense of lines 14 and 15 is that Overbury took a dim view of self-interested behavior.

16–17 *that . . . Countesse.* Overbury initially connived at Robert Carr, then Viscount Rochester's intrigue with Frances Howard, Countess of Essex, but after her divorce he actively discouraged their plans for marriage. To forestall any interference, he was committed to the Tower, where, three months and eighteen days later (14 September 1613), he died after prolonged poisoning instigated by Frances Howard, who was by then married to Robert Carr, Earl of Somerset (and so still a Countess). The Countess of Somerset died on 13 August 1632, and might still have been alive when the poem was written.

18 *well place his Counties.* The sense seems to be that Overbury was not profligate, but judicious and circumspect, but I have no explanation for the phrasing used.

25 *favorit,* The lack of the second line of the couplet, and the punctuation of **F** indicate that the poem is incomplete.

First Line Index

A viscount, proude of his late-purchas'd Coate   44
And dost thou live? Wee stand amaz'd, to reade   17
And why to mee doe You stand bare   16
Appeare | My deare   154
As those, which for a While in Heav'n have been   140
As we walkt *Westminster,* a barge we spy'd   104
Aske mee noe more the Cause why Oxford-Winde   120
Asoone as I was dead, the World beganne   81
Bacon, thou hardly wilt believe that Wee   67
Behold him here to dust and ashes turn'd   110
Ben Johnson's wombe was great; and Wee   146
[*blank page*]   172
Blest creature, laugh at my Mistake. When I   116
But all this While I feare a spice of Pride   33
Cambridge, though in thy Praise wee dare not write   136
Come, come: thy Stay, mee thinks, is such a thing   134
Come Vertue, Honour, Wealth and Pleasure   53
Cosin, whilst You were one of London-people   58
Count me (vice-chanc'llour *Duppa*) or a traitour   21
Crown'd with May-flowrs, by night ther came to mee   93
Dearest: I call you so, because I spend   145
Die Johnson: crosse not our Religion so   7
Divinest: wee confesse, when wee did viewe   160
Doe, shew thy Art. But yet half way upp flie   179
England, I cast thee off: thou shalt not bee   82
Ere since the Deluge (when a spreading rheume   92
Faire Madam: since the World begunne   57
Friend: thinke not Time, or Winde, or Place,   12
From heav'n, noe doubt, wee are descended all   133
From thee I nothing heare; yet I can tell   166
God, ô our god, wee praise thy name   174
Goe, gett thee back to heav'n, thou sacred Fire   177
Have you seene fairies dance the Ring? or clowns   55
Hee could have pickt noe fitter time to die   91
Here joyn'd you see white Snow, and purple Fire   119
How haps it that the Spring so long does stay?   159

236 *First Line Index*

How often, in our selves, wee see reflections 87
How wise, how good, how faire art Thou, my dear! 122
Husband, I would not have thee to conceive 34
If, as | This way you passe 149
If both my Eies doe full of water stand 150
If ever any Angels die 73
If Oxford bee the kingdome's Eie 32
In seeing You, Sir, I have seene the Court 118
In vaine men came to see *Tharuleot* runne 115
It was the time that every Bird and Beast 69
Know you mine hostesse? shee's the Queen of slutts 51
Lean, slender, gracil, wither'd, lank, and thinne 167
Lett us alone, yee mortals, and permitt 168
Loe, laughing as I was at Play 73
Look what a litle shredd of earth it is 137
Madam: they say, when-ere 125
Madam, when I beganne to honour You 158
Madam, you are so happy, that you vexe 101
Marke this same Smith, how with his Bellowes hee 152
My censure, and my Verdict, which you crave 85
My dearest, if thou wilt agree 47
My mates, I give you here to understand 153
My rebell Eares, I wondred what they meant 20
Nay, Madam, you may very well bee seene 88
Never, till now, I thought that unreadd Bookes 14
Not that I am a King's house, or that I 68
Now | Thou | My deare | Art here 86
Now a Botch take thee, *Tom*: where hast thou beene 95
Now wee perceive why mortals have two Eies 123
Now will wee never wonder, though wee meete 65
O glorious Eie, thou miracle of Sight 75
O strange! Till I came hither 42
O thou All, conforme my Minde 171
Oft in my Sleep I think thee (dearest) neare mee 157
Poets, 'tis false: yee say that Niobĕ 84
Prethee away, Love: what a foole thou arte 190
Rejoyce yee that are borne anewe 185
Scorn, scorn to grovle on the earth, my Soule 176
Sir, all the Wishes, which an humble Friend 112
Sir, had you sent mee Gold alone 25
Sir you are one of those, who dare commend 192
Sirs, all the World confesse, yee love your wives 135
So joyes a rising Saint, when Angels tell 19
So proud, and yet so sluttish? Fie for shame 45
So yong? so small? and yet so good a Poĕt? 143

First Line Index

Stand still, bright Shadow; pompous Type, stand still   29
Stand still, who-ere thou art, and lett thine Eies   66
Still art thou sick, dear Youth? 'Tis my great griefe   117
Straight, straight I will goe back to heav'n. But here   178
Swain dy'd that day as Christ dy'd. O that *Swain*   142
Sweetest, if you believe your Glasse, and mee   49
That youth, whom you see walke before   109
The angels doe so wish for thee   121
The common Rodes about the realme are worse   138
The sand here never runs, nor thwarts your Will   40
The show is done: and now the Throngs debate   76
The sphears were once harmonious Sphears   98
The widow, which thou marry'dst, being dead   111
The wolf pursude am ewe; a Dogge, the wolfe   191
This knight was never married in his life   173
Thou best of good things, thou of badd things worst   132
Thou worst of all good fencers, Wilt tho feele   187
Though both thy Tongue and Eies bidd mee refraine   90
Thought wee that all the World was false, but You   113
'Tis true, Stone-temples can noe more containe   131
Treason, my liege. Your keeper, Coventree   183
Wake, wake deare creature. Does it not suffice   123
Wee know not (dearest) in what part   139
Wee know thee not, nor have wee ever seene   35
Wee would (blest Youth) that thou shouldst never goe   141
Welcome, thou totall summe of earthly Blisse   46
Were he but one brave person, and noe more   126
Were I in heav'n, Hall, or were I with Thee   169
Were it (Sir) any other time, You should   156
What did your Highnesse meane, to tarry forth   163
What good so-ere GOD gives mee, still the DEVÎLL   102
What meane my Armes? what would they have?   103
What meant our English grandsires to contrive   74
When I approacht that happy place   127
When I behold how numberlesse, how holy   41
Whether or noe the King to Scotland goes   161
Who can denye, the world is at his prime   186
Who would not now bee of his leggs bereaven?   80
Why dost thou weepe, blest babe? Thy happy Birth   99
Wonder not, if a black wench I desire   72
World, thou once fled'st; and I did follow thee   94
Yee fooles, which meerly judge by outward Show   27
Yee maides of honour, goe and tell the Queene   165
You doe well, Fairest, that although so many   147
You wonder why of late the Spheares   98

TITLE INDEX

Amorouse Dreames   157

At the Command of his reverend diocesan Godfry Goodman Bishop of Glocester.
    A translation of the *Te deum laudamus* after the tune of the 100 Psalme   174

Censure upon *Aristophanes* his States-women, A   76

Country-gentleman's Wooing, The   47

Divine Rapture, A   176

Eglogue betweene a Carter and a sheaphard, made on Master *Michaël Oldisworth's*
    Comming into the country, An   95

Epitaph on a discontented man, An   94

Epitaph on litle Thomas Bacon, who dyed sodainly, An   73

Epitaph on litle Thomas Bacon, who dyed sodainly, An. Another   73

Epitaph on Master Little of Abingdon, An   110

Epitaph on *Thomas Hulbert* Cloathyer of Cosham, An   66

For a discontented Scholar of Oxford, 1632, these following verses were written while the
    King was at Woodstock   118

For a Gentleman. On the embracing of his Friend   168

For a Gentleman. To yong Master *Henry Gresley*   169

For a Lover. To his absent Mistris   166

For a Lover, standing by a Smith's shoppe: An Ode   152

For a Lover, whose Mistris concealed her selfe from him   154

For an Innes of courts man. To his Mistris   145

Hampton-court here speaketh   68

His Farewell to *Poëtrie*   177

His Reply to *Poëtrie*   179

His rewarding a Musician   93

Hymne to God, An   171

Immoderate Love, An   117

In defence of a Girle, that went holding downe her head   27

ITER AUSTRALE, 1632. Or, A journey southwards   104

Letter to Ben. Johnson. 1629, A   7

Lover's fancie, A   122

Nobleman's wooing, The   46

Ode, An ("Husband, I would not have thee to conceive")   34

Ode, An ("Prethee away, Love: what a foole thou arte")   190

Ode, An ("Though both thy Tongue and Eies bidd mee refraine")   90

Ode, An ("What meane my Armes? what would they have?")   103

Ode, of 12 kindes of Verses, An   86
Of Nobility   133
On a Bagge of Perfume given him by a Friend   120
On a Lover   109
On a Moore   72
On a packet of Letters, drowned in their comming from his Friend beyond sea   92
On a painted Houre-glasse   40
On a paire of handsome children   186
On a Race   115
On a Seale of gold and pearles sent. . .by Master Michael Oldisworth   25
On Abraham Cowley the yong poët laureat   146
On Alexander Bainham Esquier, who was killed at the Siege of *Mastrich*. 1632   91
On an Arbour made by Master Richard Bacon, on the sea-shoar opposite to the ile
    of Wight   127
On an envious man   102
On an Ewe that was drowned   191
On an uggly Wench   51
On Complements   16
On Heraldry   44
On his Majesty's being in Scotland   163
On his Majesty's coming from Scotland   165
On his Majesty's going to Scotland. 1633   161
On his Majesty's Recovery from the small pocks. 1632   21
On his seeing the Study of Master Michael Oldisworth   14
On London Waies. 1632   138
On Master Swaine, who deceased upon good Friday   142
On Mistris Katharine Bacon   65
On Mistris Summer, who dyed in child-bedd   123
On mortalls   87
On my loosing my way   55
On Shottover   32
On Sir B.R.   81
On Sir *Thomas Overbury* and his poëme   173
On the birth of James duke of Yorke   99
On the Christmas at Cosham in Wilt-shire   140
On the Commencement at Cambridge. 1632   136
On the death of a Cripple   80
On the death of both Mistris Summer and her Childe   123
On the death of his deare friend Master Richard Bacon   172
On the death of Sir Rowland Cotton   126
On the picture of Beauty   119
On the picture of the Virgin feeding her babe   185
On the statue of Niobe well carved   84
On the transparencie of Master Tooker's house at Strettam   149
On treacherousnesse   74

Title Index   241

Paradoxe, A. To one whom hee both extremly loved, and extremly hated   132
Poëtry's Answer   178
Satyre, A. On occasion of Master his departure out of England   150
Sonnet, played by a Musician at my Entertaining of Master *Michael Oldisworth*, A   53
STATES-WOMEN // A show taken out of *Aristophanes*   75
To a Curtezan   167
To a friend of Sir Thomas Overburyes   192
To a gentle-woman that delighted too much in her garden   137
To a Lady, looking our of a window   125
To a Lady, on her walking abroad   57
To a Lady, that sung and played on the Lute   98
To a Separatist, that spoiled mens tombes, and built his house with tomb-stones   33
To a yong Lady, that hadd the greene Sickness   88
To all his Acquaintance   153
To an acquaintance   121
To an over-modest Ladie   158
To B.R. a Dissembler   113
To Citizens   135
To his aunt, the lady Litcott of Molesey   101
To his cosin *Michaël Oldisworth*, February 15 1631   69
To his Cosin, Mistris Dorothie Litcott   49
To his Enemie   187
To his Friend beyond sea ("And dost thou live?. . .)   17
To his Friend beyond sea ("Friend: thinke not Time. . .")   12
To his Friend beyond sea, March 26. 1633   159
To his friend beyond sea ("Wee know not (dearest) in what part")   139
To his Friend beyond see ("Come, come: they Stay, mee thinks, is such a thing")   134
To his Friend beyong sea ("Bacon, thou hardly wilt believe that Wee")   67
To his litle Brother Giles Oldisworth   143
To his musicall Valentine Mistris Anne Henshaw   98
To Master M.B. the whilst his picture was drawing   141
To Master Michaël Oldisworth comming to Oxford, 1633. March 30   156
To Mistris E.W.   45
To Mistris Katharine Bacon   147
To Mistris Thorold of Arborvill   116
To one of my acquaintance   111
To Sir Edward Hungerford of Cosham   41
To Sir *Giles Fetiplace*, high Sheriffe of *Glocester-shire*. 1633   112
To the builders or Repairers of Paul's Church in London   131
To the faire Mistris Burch, at his first sight of her   160
To the lady *Hungerford* of Cosham, December 28 1632   42
To the right honorable his Patron   20
To the right honorable, the lord Haies, earle of Carlile, &c   19
To the sacred Majestie of his dread soveraigne King Charles   183
To the University of Cambridge. 1631   35

To the Witts of Oxford, Cambridge, and London   82

To the worshipfull, his honoured Cosin, Mistris *Susan Oldsiworth*: upon her Removall
   from *London* to *Thisselworth*   58

To the worshipfull, Mistris Strange of Summerford, a Poëtesse   85

Wordes of a Lover, speaking to the reflection of his Mistresses face in a Looking
   glasse, The   29

General Index
to the Introduction and Commentary

Abingdon, 219
Aelred of Rivaulx, *De Spirituali Amicitia*, 229
Africans, 208, 218
Amazons, 210
Ambrose, St., 211
Amsterdam, 231
angels (coinage), 228
Anne, Queen, 229
Anselment, Raymond, xvii n9
Arborfield, Berkshire, xxi, 217, 220
Archy, royal jester, *see* Armstrong, Archibald
Ariadne, 214
Arion, 214
Aristophanes, *Ecclesiazusai*, xx, xxix, 209, 219
Armstrong, Archibald, 203
Articles, Thirty-Nine, 231
Ascupart, 218–19
Ashmole, Elias, 221
Astraea, 230
Aubrey, John, *Brief Lives*, 208
Augustan Peace, 206
Axe Yard, Westminster, 208
B., Mistris K., 203. *See* Bacon, Katharine
Backhouse, Samuel, 217
Backhouse, Sir John, 217–219
Backhouse, William, 218
Bacon, family of, xx, 218 [*see also* Burch (Bacon), Mistris]
Bacon, Francis, Viscount St. Albans, 201
Bacon, Katharine, 203, 207, 225, 227

Bacon, Matthew, xix and n19, xxxv, 195, 221, 224, 228; "A letter to Master Clement Harby at Rome," xxxv
Bacon, Richard, of St. Dunstan's-in-the-West, Fleet Street, xix
Bacon, Richard, xix, xx, xxi, xxii, xxxv, xxxix, 195, 206, 207, 214, 218, 221, 222, 223, 224, 226, 227
Bacon, Thomas, 209
Bald, R. C., 197
Balliol College, Oxford, xxv
Baptism, 231
Barcheston, xxiii, 193
Barker, Edmund Henry, xlii
Barksdale, Clement, "The Defence. To Master Francis Powell of Christ Church," xxxiv
Bates, Catherine, 196
Batsford, xxiii, 193
Baynham, Alexander, 214
Baynham, Joseph, 214
Baynham (Oldisworth), Elizabeth, 214
Beal, Peter, xxiv and n40, xxix, xxx n54, xxxiii n66, xliii, 202
beatus ille motif, 215
Bellarmine, Roberto, xxi, 217
Bennett, J.A.W., 204, 216
Bevis of Hampton, Sir, 218
Bible, Genesis 2:23, 205; Genesis 37:3 and ff., 203; Genesis 11:7–9, 222; 1 Samuel 2:8, 200; Judges 15:15–17, 233;

1 Kings 8:27, 223; Psalm 75:5, 199; Ezekiel 34, 226; Matthew 17:1–3, 232; Matthew 18:20, 229; Matthew 23:27, 200; Mark 9:2–13, 232; Luke 1:52, 200; Luke 9:29–36, 232; Luke 22:38, 231; John 8:56, 232; Ephesians 5:23, 211; 1 Corinthians 11:1–12, 211; 1 Corinthians 13.11, xv; 1 Corinthians 13:12, 200, 232; 2 Corinthians 12:2–4, 224; Colossians 3:5, 200; Revelation 16:2, 231

Bliss, Philip, xviii n11, xlii

Bodleian Library, xv, xxiv n39, xxxi, xxxiii, xli–xlii, xliii

Bourton-on-the-Hill, xvi, xxi, xxii, 193, 225

Brentford, 205

Britanniae natalis, xxv

British Library, xxx n55, xxxi, xliii, 195

Brown, Cedric C., 212

Browne, Robert, 200

Browne, Thomas, xxviii

Brownists, 200

Brumble, H.D., 210, 212, 214, 226, 230

Burch (Bacon), Mistris, 227. *See* Bacon, Katharine

Burch, Squire, 218

Butter, Nathaniel, 212

Calais, 197

Caley, Earle R., 213

Calfe, Peter, xxx n55

Calhoun, Thomas O., xviii

Cambridge, University of, xxi, xxvii, 195, 200, 224

Camden, William, *Britannia*, 209

Canis Major, constellation of, 233

Carew, Thomas, xxiv, xxv, xxx, xxxii; "In answere of an Elegiacall Letter upom the death of the King of Sweden," 212; "A New-Years Sacrifice," 202; "A New-years's Gift: To the King," 202; "To the New Year: For the Countess of Carlisle," 202

Carey, Lucius, Viscount Falkland, xxxv n70

Carlisle, Earl of, *see* Hay, James

Carr, Robert, Earl of Somerset, 229, 234

Carthage, 210

Cartwright, William, xx, xxv, xxvi and n48, xxviii, 198

Catullus, 219

Cavendish, William, Earl of Newcastle, xxx, xxxi, xxxv, 194

Chamberlain, *see* Chamberlayne

Chamberlayne, Mary, *see* Oldisworth (Chamberlayne), Mary

Chamberlayne, Thomas, xxii

Chandler, Master, 199

Chares of Lindus, 195

Charles I, xxv, xxxi, xxxvi, xxxix, 193, 197, 198, 199, 200, 203, 212, 215, 218, 227–28; smallpox, xxxvi, xl, 198

Charles II, xxv

Charles V, Holy Roman Emperor, 219

Cheapside, 231

Chilling Farm, xx, 218

Chillings, 218, 223

Christ Church, Oxford, xvii, xix, xx, xxi, xxiii, xxiv, xxv, xxvii, xxviii, xxix, xxx, xxxi, xxxii, xliii, 198, 220, 224

Christ's Hospital, Abingdon, 219

Clapinson, Mary, xlii

Cobham, Claude Delaval, 219

coins (gold and silver), 228 [*see also* angels, crowns, nobles, ryals, and farthing tokens]

Colbeck, Radford & Co., xlii

Coln Rogers, xvi, 193, 195, 206, 213, 225

Common Prayer, Book of, 200

Conway, Edward, Viscount Conway, 202

Copley, Frank O., 219

Corbett, Richard, xx, xxiv, xxv, xxviii, xxix, xxx, xxxi, xlii, 198, 204, 212, 216; "Iter Boreale," xxxiv, 204, 216

Corpus Christi College, Oxford, xxiv n39, xxx n55, 198

Corsham, Wiltshire, 201–2, 207, 224

Coscus, 216

Cotton, Sir Roland, 222

Court, the, xxxii

Coventry, Thomas, Lord, 231

Cowley, Abraham, xviii, 225

General Index 245

Craig, D. Hugh, 194
Crane, Gregory, 206
crowns (coinage), 228
Crum, Margaret, 208
Davenant, William, 208
de Bruyn, Frans, xxxiv n68
de Ricci, Seymour, xliii
Delphi, 229
Di Cesare, Mario A., xxiv n39
Dick, Oliver Lawson, 208
Dido, 210
Dixon, ___, xlii
Dobell, Bertram, xlii, xliii, 194, 202
Dog Star, *see* Sirius
Doncaster, Viscount, *see* Hay, James
Donne, John, *the younger*, xxviii
Donne, John, xxiv, xxviii, xxx, xxxii, 197,
    217; "The Anagram," 204; "The
    Comparison," 204; "The Flea," xxx-
    iv, 199; "To Sir Henry Wotton ("Sir,
    more than kisses, letters mingle
    souls"), xxxix; *Paradoxes and Prob-
    lems*, 211
Douay, English College, xix, 195
Dryden, John, *The Hind and the Panther*, 221
Dugdale, Sir William, 223
Dunlap, Rhodes, 212
Duppa, Brian, xx, xxviii, xxix, xxx, xlii,
    198, 209
Duppa (Killingtree), Jane, xx, xl, 198, 210
Dutch, 213
Dyde, William, *The History of the Antiqui-
    ties of Tewkesbury*, xxii, 199
Earle, John, *Micro-cosmographie*, 215
Edinburgh, 227
Emmanuel College, Cambridge, 205
engraving, 231
Ennius, Quintus, *Annales*, 201
Epicedium Cantabrigiense, xxvii
Eucharist, 231
Europa, 210
Ezell, Margaret, xxiv
farthing tokens, 214
Fell, Samuel, xxviii
Fellows, Jennifer, 218

Felltham, Owen, 222
Fetiplace, Sir Giles, 220
Folger, Henry Clay xliii
Folger Shakespeare Library xxxi, xxxiii,
    xlii–xliii, 199
Forset, Edward, 227
Fowler, Alastair, xxxiv n68, 194
Fraistat, Neil, xxxiv n68
Frederick Henry, Prince of Orange, 214
Frederick V, Elector Palatine, 214
Gloucester, Bishop of, 230
Gloucestershire, xxxii
Goldsmith's Row, 231
Goodman, Godfrey, xxi, xl, 230
Goodmen, Cardell, xxiv and n39
Goodwin, R., xxxv
Goodwin, William, xxviii
Gouws, John, xxxi n65, xxxvii n73,
    xxxix n74, xlii, 193, 195, 213, 230
Great Seal, Keeper of, 231
greensickness, 213
Gresham College, 205
Greville, Fulke, Lord Brooke, 213
Grisley, Henry, 229
Grisley, John, 229
Guerim, 215
Gustavus Adolphus, xxxi, 211–13
Gutch, John, 225
Guy, Earl of Southampton, 218
Habib, Imtiaz, 208, 218
Habsburgs, 213
Hammond, Paul, 195
Hampton Court, xxxviii, 207
Hannibal, 210
Harby, Clement, xxxv, 195
Hart, Clive, 211
Hay, James, Earl of Carlisle, Viscount Don-
    caster, xxxvi, 197–98
Hemmings, William, xxviii
Henrietta Maria, xxvi, 197
Henry, Prince of Wales, xxvii, 222
Henshaw, Flora (Flower), 218
Henshaw, Mistris Anne, 215
Heralds' office, 231

Herbert, George, xxiv n39, xxxvi, xxxviii, xxxix

Herbert of Cherbury, Edward, Lord, "The Green-Sickness Beauty," 213

Herbert, Philip, Earl of Pembroke and Montgomery, xxxv, 196

Herbert, William, Earl of Pembroke, xxxv, 196, 221

Herford, C.H., 194, 216

Herrick, Robert, xxx, 202; "Discontents in Devon," 215; "To the most accomplisht gentleman Master Michael Oldisworth," 196

Heylyn, Peter, *Microcosmos*, 213

Heyward, Thomas, ΓΥΝΑΙΚΕΙΟΝ, 210

Hobbs, Mary, xvii n9, xxx n54

Hobbs, Mary, xxiv and n40, xxix

Holdenried, Anke, 210–11

Holdsworth, Richard, 205

Horace, 217

Horace, 217; *Odes* 3.10 and 3.26, 219; *Satires*, 216

Hornblower, Simon, 210

Howard, Frances, Countess of Essex, 229, 234

Hulbert, Thomas, 207

Hungerford (Haliday, Hollidaie), Lady Margaret, 201, 202

Hungerford, Jane, *see* Strange (Hungerford), Jane

Hungerford, Sir Edward, xxxiii, 201, 207, 213, 224

Huntington, Henry E., Library, xxxi, xliii

Inns of Court, xxxii

Isleworth, Middlesex, 203, 205, 217

James, Duke of York, 215

James I, 197, 203, 215, 218, 229

Jealous Lovers, The, xix

Jones, Inigo, 223

Jonson, Ben, xxiv, xxviii, xxix, xxx, xxxi, xxxiii, xxxiv, xlii, 194, 195, 197, 216, 217; *Epigrams*, xxxiv; *Every Man out of his Humour*, 205; *The Forest* xxxiv; "Ode to Himself," 194;

The New Inn 194; *The Staple of News*, 212; "To Penshurst," 223

Jonsonius Virbius, xx, 198

journey poems, 216

Justa Funebria Ptolemaei Oxoniensis. . ., xxv

King, Henry, xxviii, xxx, xxxix n74, "Upon the Death of. . .Dr. Donne Deane of Paules," 208

Killingtree, Jane, *see* Duppe (Killingtree), Jane

King, John, xxviii, xlii

Knowles, Richard, 208

Latham, Robert, 219

Laud, William, xvii, xxxii, 198, 200, 223, 227, 230

Leiden, 231

Lincoln Collge, Oxford, xxxi

Little, Francis, 219–20

Lluelyn, Martin, xxv

Lobel, Mary D., 200

Lockey, Thomas, xxv, xxvi and n48, 198

London, 223, 227

Lord's Supper, the, 231

Love, Harold, xxiv and n40

Lupus, constellation of, 233

Lutzen, xxxi, 211

Lyra, constellation of, 214

Lytcott, Dorothy, 203–4

Lytcott (Overbury), Lady Mary, 203, 216

Lytcott, Sir John, 203, 217–18

Maastricht, siege of, 214

Maclean, Sir John, 214

Maecenas, Caius, 217

Magdalen College, Oxford, 198

Malay, Jessica L., 211

Malden, H.E., 216

Mann, John, xli

Mann, Margaret, *see* Oldisworth (Mann), Margaret

Manne, Thomas, xxviii, xxx n55

Marlowe, Christopher, "Come live with me and be my love," 203

Marotti, Arthur F., xxiv n40

Mars, 226

Matthews, William, 219

General Index   247

Maule, Jeremy, xx
May, Steven W., 202
Mayne, Jasper, xxv, xxvi and n48, xxviii,
    xxx, xlii, 198
McCauley, Janie Caves, 202
Men-miracles, xxv
Mennes, Sir John, xxiii and n38, xxv, xxxi,
    xxxii, xxxiii, 194
Migne, J.-P., 229
Milton, John, "Lycidas," 208, 226
Molsey, Surrey, 216
monarchal theory, 227–28
Morley, George, xxviii, xxx and n55, xlii
Mottershed, Thomas, xxviii
Mulsack, 206
Munby, A. N. L., xlii
Munk, William, 224
Musarum Deliciae, xxiii
Musarum Oxoniensium pro rege, xix, xxv,
    xxvi n48, 198
Nelson, Alan H., xix, 201
Nethercot, A.H.. 194
New Argument Against Women, A, 211
Newcastle, Earl of, *see* Cavendish, William
Nieuwpoort, xix, 195
Niobe, 212
nobles (coinage), 228
North, Dudley, Lord, "An Incentive to
    our Poets upon the Death of the . . .
    King of Swedeland," 214; *A Forest of
    Varieties*, 214; "A Forest Promiscu-
    ous . . .," 215
Offley, John, 203–4
Old Change, 231
Oldisworth, armorial bearings, 231
Oldisworth, Arnold, 214
Oldisworth (Chamberlayne), Mary, xxii,
    xxiii, xxxvii, xli, 193, 199
Oldisworth, Francis, xxii, 193
Oldisworth, Giles, xxii, xxiii, xxxiv, 225;
    "Sketlius," xxxiv
Oldisworth, Joseph, 213
Oldisworth (Mann), Margaret, xxii, xxiii,
    xli, 193

Oldisworth, Maria, *see* Tucker (Oldis-
    worth), Maria
Oldisworth, Merial, xvi
Oldisworth, Michael, xxxv, xxxvi and n71,
    xxxvii, 196, 197, 204, 205, 207–8,
    214, 215, 217, 221, 227, 230
Oldisworth, Nicholas, xvi–xxiii, 193, 212;
    dedicatory epistle, 214; "A Booke
    Touching Sir Thomas Overbury",
    xvi; *A Recollection of Certain Scat-
    tered Poems*, xv, xxix, xxxvii, xli–
    xlii, 212; *The Chronicle of Europe*,
    xxxiv; and friendship, xxxix and
    n74, xl; and private life, xxxix–xl;
    and women, xxxviii–xl
Oldisworth, Nicholas, poems referred to in
    the General Introduction:
    "Amorouse Dreames," xxxviii
    "Another. An epitaph on little Thomas
        Bacon, who dyed sodainly", xxxiii
    "At the Command of his reverend dioc-
        esan Godfry Goodman Bishop of
        Glocester. A translation of the *Te
        deum laudamus* after the tune of
        the 100 Psalme," xxxvi, xl
    "Country-gentleman's Wooing, The,"
        xxxviii
    "Divine Rapture, A," xxxvi
    "Epitaph on little Thomas Bacon, who
        dyed sodainly, An," xxxiii
    "Epitaph on little Thomas Bacon, who
        dyed sodainly, An. Another,"
        xxxiii
    "Epitaph on Master Little of Abingdon,
        An," xxxiii
    "Epitaph on *Thomas Hulbert* Cloathyer
        of Cosham, An," xxxiii
    "For a Gentleman. On the embracing of
        his Friend," xxxvi, xxxviii
    "For a Gentleman. To yong Master *Hen-
        ry Gresley*," xxxvi, xxxviii
    "For a Lover. To his absent Mistris,"
        xxxvi
    "For a Lover. To his absent Mistris,"
        xxxviii

"For a Lover, whose Mistris concealed her selfe from him," xxxiv, xxxviii
"For an Innes of courts man. To his Mistris," xxxviii
"Hampton-court here speaketh," xxxiii, xxxviii
"His Farewell to *Poëtrie*," xxxvi
"His Reply to *Poëtrie*," xxxvi
"In defence of a Girle, that went holding downe her head," xxxiii, xxxviii
"ITER AUSTRALE, 1632. Or, A journey southwards," xxviii, xxxiv
"Letter to Ben Jonson," xxix, xxxiii, xxxv
"Lover's fancie, A," xxxviii
"Nobleman's wooing, The," xxxviii
"Ode, An," ("Husband, I would not have thee to conceive"), xxxviii
"Ode, An," ("What meane my Armes? what would they have?"), xxxviii
"On a Moore," xxxiii
"On a painted Houre-glasse," xxxiii
"On Abraham Cowley the yong poët laureat," xxxiii
"On an Arbour made by Master Richard Bacon, on the sea-shoar opposite to the ile of Wight," xxxiii
"On an uggly Wench," xxxiii, xxxviii
"On Complements," xxxvi
"On Heraldry," xxxiii
"On his Majesty's Recovery from the small pocks. 1632," xxxvi, xl
"On his seeing the Study of Master Michael Oldisworth," xxxvi
"On Mistris Katharine Bacon," xxxiii
"On Mistris Summer, who dyed in child-bedd," xxxviii
"On Shottover," xxxiii
"On Sir *Thomas Overbury* and his poëme," xxxvi
"On the death of both Mistris Summer and her Childe," xxxviii
"On the death of his deare friend Master Richard Bacon," xxxvi

"On treacherousnesse," xxxiii
"Poëtry's Answer," xxxvi
"Sonnet, played by a Musician at my Entertaining of Master *Michael Oldisworth*, A," xxxiii
"To a Curtezan," xxxvi, xxxviii
"To a gentle-woman that delighted too much in her garden," xxxiii
"To a Lady, looking our of a window," xxxiv
"To a Lady, on her walking abroad," xxxiv
"To a Separatist, that spoiled mens tombes, and built his house with tombstones," xxxiii
"To a yong Lady, that hadd the greene Sickness," xxxviii
"To his Cosin, Mistris Dorothie Litcott," xxxiii
"To his Friend beyond sea" ("And dost thou live?. . .), xxxvi
"To his litle Brother Giles Oldisworth," xxxiii
"To Master Michaël Oldisworth comming to Oxford, 1633. March 30," xxxiii
"To Mistris E.W.," xxxviii
"To Mistris Katharine Bacon," xxxviii
"To Sir Edward Hungerford of Cosham," xxxiii
"To Sir *Giles Fetiplace*, high Sheriffe of *Glocester-shire.* 1633," xxxviii
"To the builders or Repairers of Paul's Church in London," xxxiii
"To the right honorable his Patron," xxxvi
"To the right honorable, the lord Haies, earle of Carlile, &c," xxxvi
"To the Witts of Oxford, Cambridge, and London," xxxi
"To the worshipfull, Mistris Strange of Summerford, a Poëtesse," xxxiii
"Wordes of a Lover, speaking to the reflection of his Mistresses face in a Looking glasse, The," xxxiii

General Index

Oldisworth (Poyntz), Susan, xvii, 196, 217
Oldisworth, Robert, xvi, xxii
Oldisworth, Robin, 225
Oldisworth (Sherwood), Mary, xxii, xxiii, 193
Oldisworth (Strange), Margaret, 213
Oman, Charles, 228
Osbaldeston, Lambert, xvii–xix, xxix, 198, 205, 206, 225
Osborne, Harold, 215
Overbury family, 208
Overbury, Mary, *see* Lytcott, Lady Mary
Overbury, Merial, *see* Oldisworth, Merial
Overbury, Sir Giles, 205, 216
Overbury, Sir Nicholas, xvi, xxi, 203
Overbury, Sir Thomas, xvi, xxxvi n72, 196, 225, 229; "A Wife," 225, 229
Ovid, *Amores* 1.6, 219; *Metamorphoses*, 212
Oxford, Univeristy of, xxiv, xxv, xxvi, xxix, xxxi, 198, 225, 227, 229
Padua, xix, xxxv, 224
Pamela, 218
panther breath, 221
paraclausithyron, 219
Peacham, Henry, *The Compleat Gentleman*, 211
Peters, Helen, 211
Peck, C. Wilson, 215
Pepys, Samuel, 219
Petrarch (Francesco Petrarca), 203, 204
Philip IV, of Spain, 198
Philistines, 233
Phillipps, Sir Thomas, xlii
Philoclea, 218
Pliny, *Naturalis Historia*, 195, 213, 221
Poetical Blossoms, xix, 225
Portland, Lord, *see* Weston, Richard
Poynyz, Susan, *see* Oldisworth (Poyntz), Susan
Prideaux, Peter, xxv
Propertius, 217, 219
proverbs, *see* Tilley, Morris Palmer *and* Smith, William George
Punic Wars, 210
Puritans, 231
Pythian Oracle, 229

R., B., 220
R., Sir B., 211
Rance, Adrian B., 218
Randolph, Robert, xxviii
Randolph, Thomas, xix, xxx, 222
Ravis, Thomas, xxviii
Raylor, Timothy, xxiii, xxxii and nn63–64
Raynham, Lieutenant, 214
Reynolds, Susan, 205
Ré, Ile de, 197
Rhodes, Colossus of, 195
Richards, John F. C., 213
Ringler, William A., Jr., 202
Roberts, R. J. (Julian), xxiv n39
Rogers, T.D., xlii
Rolls, Albert, 227
Roman Catholicism, xxi, xxii, 217
Roman Catholics, 201, 226, 227, 230
Rome, 210
Rosenbach Museum and Library, xxxi, xliii
Røstvig, Maren-Sofie, 215
ryals (coinage), 228
Ryan, William Granger, 205
sacraments, 231 (*see also* Baptism, Eucharist, and Lord's Supper)
Samson, 233
Saville, Sir Henry, xxv
Scotland, 227
seal, 231
Separatists, xxxiii, 200
Severn Stoke, Worcestershire, 229
Shakespeare, William, xxx; *As You Like It*, 206; *Sonnets*, xxxix; Sonnet 129, 204
Sharpe, Kevin, *The Personal Rules of Charles I*, xxvi
Sherwood, John, xxii
Sherwood, Mary, *see* Oldisworth (Sherwood), Mary
Shipston-on-Stour, xxii
Shotover and Stowood, Royal Forest of, 200
Shotover Hill, Oxford, xxxiii, 200
Shrewsbury, 229
sibylls, 210
Sidney, Sir Philip, *The Countess of Pembroke's Arcadia*, 218

silva tradition, xxxiv–xxxvii
Simpson, Percy and Evelyn, 194, 216
Sirius, 233
slaves, 218
Smith, G.C. Moore, 213
Smith, James, xxiii and n38, xxv, xxxi,
    xxxii, xxxiii, 194
Smith, Rowland, 207
Smith, William George, 232
Solis Britannia Perigaeum, xxv, 227
Somerford, Wiltshire, 213
Southampton, xx, 218–19
Spawforth, Antony, 210
St. John's College, Cambridge, 222
St. Martin-in-the-Fields, 60, 226
St. Mary-le-Bow, church of, 206
St. Paul's Cathedral, 222, 223
Strange, Mistris, 213; *see* Strange (Hunger-
    ford), Jane
Strange (Hungerford), Jane, 213
Strange, Robert, 213
Streatham, 226
Strode, William, xxiv, xxviii, xxix, xxx
    and n55, xlii, 202, 222; "On a
    gentlewoman walking in the snow,"
    202, 204; "To a Friend" ("Like to
    the hand which hath been used to
    play"), xxxix
    strong lines, 217
Stuart dynasty, 227
Suckling, Sir John, "The Deformed Mis-
    tress," 204
Summer, Mistris, 222
surrogate poems, xxxviii
Sutherland, C.H.V., 228
Swaine, Richard, 225
Swallowfield, 217, 218
Swedish Intelligencer: The Third Part, xxxi, 212
Swiss, 213
Syon House, 205
Tahah, 215
Taylor, Jeremy, *Holy Living*, xxxix
Teirsesias, 229
Terrent, Jeremial, xxv, xxviii, 198
Tewkesbury Abbey, xxii, 193, 199

Tewkesbury, xxiii
Tharuleot, 220
Theocritus, *Idyll* 1, 206
Theophrastus, *On Stones*, 213
Thomas, Keith, 209
Thompson, ___, xlii
Thorold, Frances, 220–21
Thorold, Mistris, 220–21, 224
Thorold, William, 220–21
Tibullus, 219
Tilley, Morris Palmer, 211
Titchfield, xx, 214
Tom Thumb, 205
Tooker, Robert, *see* Tucker, Robert
Tothill Fields, London, 206
Townley, Zouch, xxviii
Townshend, Aurelian, "Elegy on the death
    of the King of Sweden," 212
Trevor-Roper, H.R., 204, 216
Trinity College, Cambridge, xix, xxvii,
    xxviii, 225, 230
Trinity College, Oxford, 203
Tucker (Oldisworth), Maria, 226
Tucker, Robert, 226
Ultima Linea Savillii, xxv
Uxbridge, Treaty of, xxiii, 194
ventriloquist poems, xxxviii–xxxix
Venus, 226
Vesta, 210
Vestal virgins, 210
Villiers, George, Duke of Buckingham, 197
Vincent, Thomas, *Paria*, xix, 201
Virgil, 217
Virgo (constellation of), 230
Vitis Carolinae Gemma Altera, xxvi and
    n48, 216
Voces Votivae, xxvii and n51
Voragine, Jacobus de, *The Golden Legend*, 205
Vulcan, 226
W., Mistress E., 203
Warmestry, Gervase, xxviii
Warsash, xx, 218
Weaver, Thomas, xxviii
Webster, Richard, xxii n32
Welsford, Enid, 203

General Index 251

West, Richard, xxviii
Westminster Abbey, xxx nn54–55, 198
Westminster School, xvii, xix, xx, xxvii, xxviii, xxxi, xxxii, 194, 195, 198, 205, 206, 220, 225, 230
Weston, Richard, Lord Portland, 231
William, Page, 218
Williams, John, Bishop of Lincoln, Dean of Westminster, xvii, xxxii
Williamson, George, 217
Willington, Warwickshire, xxii, 193
Wilson, Edward, xxv

Wilson, F.P., 232
Wilson, John, xvii
Wilson, W.J., xliii
Wimborne, Dorset, 225
Wit and Drollery, xxiii
Wit Restor'd, xxiii, xxxi, xxxiii, 194
Wood, Anthony, xviii, 225
Woodstock Palace, 221
Worcester Cathedral, 229
Wotton, Sir Henry, xxx
Wriothesley, Thomas, Earl of Southampton, 218

RENAISSANCE ENGLISH TEXT SOCIETY

Officers and Council

President, Arthur F. Kinney, University of Massachusetts at Amherst
Vice-President, A. R. Braunmuller, University of California, Los Angeles
Secretary, Carolyn Kent, New York, N.Y.
Treasurer, Robert E. Bjork, Arizona Center for Medieval and Renaissance Studies
Membership Secretary, William Gentrup, Arizona Center for Medieval and Renaissance Studies
Past President, W. Speed Hill, Lehman College and The Graduate Center, City University of New York
Past Publisher, Mario A. Di Cesare, Fairview, North Carolina

Robert C. Evans, Auburn University at Montgomery
Margaret Ezell, Texas A&M University
Susan Felch, Calvin College
Roy Catesby Flannagan, University of South Carolina, Beaufort
David Freeman, Memorial University, Newfoundland
Elizabeth Hageman, University of New Hampshire
Margaret Hannay, Siena College
John King, Ohio State University
Ian Lancashire, University of Toronto
Leah Marcus, Vanderbilt University
Arthur F. Marotti, Wayne State University
Steven May, Georgetown College
G. W. Pigman III, California Institute of Technology
Nigel S. Smith, Princeton University
George Walton Williams, Duke University

Liaisons

Thomas L. Berger, St. Lawrence University, The Malone Society
Mary L. Robertson, Huntington Library
Heather Wolfe, Folger Shakespeare Library

254   RENAISSANCE ENGLISH TEXT SOCIETY

International Advisory Council

Peter Beal, Sotheby's, London
Lukas Erne, University of Geneva
M. T. Jones-Davies, University of Paris-Sorbonne
Harold Love, Monash University
Sergio Rossi, University of Milan
Helen Wilcox, University of Groningen

Editorial Committee for *Nicholas Oldisworth's Manuscript (Bodleian MS. Don.c.24)*:
    Arthur F. Marotti, chair
    Margaret P. Hannay
    Elizabeth H. Hageman

The Renaissance English Text Society was established to publish literary texts, chiefly nondramatic, of the period 1475–1660. Dues are $35.00 per annum ($25.00, graduate students; life membership is available at $500.00). Members receive the text published for each year of membership. The Society sponsors panels at such annual meetings as those of the Modern Language Association, the Renaissance Society of America, and the Medieval Congress at Kalamazoo.

General inquiries and proposals for editions should be addressed to the president, Arthur Kinney, Massachusetts Center for Renaissance Studies, PO Box 2300, Amherst, Mass., 01004, USA. Inquiries about membership should be addressed to William Gentrup, Membership Secretary, Arizona Center for Medieval and Renaissance Studies, Arizona State University, Box 874402, Tempe, Ariz., 85287–4402.

Copies of volumes x–xii may be purchased from Associated University Presses, 440 Forsgate Drive, Cranbury, N.J., 08512. Members may order copies of earlier volumes still in print or of later volumes from xiii, at special member prices, from the Treasurer.

FIRST SERIES

VOL. I. *Merie Tales of the Mad Men of Gotam* by A. B., edited by Stanley J. Kahrl, and The History of Tom Thumbe by R. I., edited by Curt F. Buhler, 1965. (o.p.)

VOL. II. *Thomas Watson's Latin Amyntas*, edited by Walter F. Staton, Jr., and Abraham Fraunce's translation The Lamentations of Amyntas, edited by Franklin M. Dickey, 1967.

SECOND SERIES

VOL. III. *The dyaloge called Funus, A Translation of Erasmus's Colloquy (1534)*, and *A very pleasaunt & fruitful Diologe called The Epicure, Gerrard's Translation of Erasmus's Colloquy (1545)*, edited by Robert R. Allen, 1969.

RENAISSANCE ENGLISH TEXT SOCIETY   255

VOL. IV. *Leicester's Ghost* by Thomas Rogers, edited by Franklin B. Williams, Jr.,
1972.

THIRD SERIES

VOLS. V–VI. *A Collection of Emblemes, Ancient and Moderne*, by George Wither, with
an introduction by Rosemary Freeman and bibliographical notes by Charles
S. Hensley, 1975. (o.p.)

FOURTH SERIES

VOLS. VII–VIII. *Tom a' Lincolne* by R. I., edited by Richard S. M. Hirsch, 1978.

FIFTH SERIES

VOL. IX. *Metrical Visions* by George Cavendish, edited by A. S. G. Edwards, 1980.

SIXTH SERIES

VOL. X. *Two Early Renaissance Bird Poems*, edited by Malcolm Andrew, 1984.

VOL. XI. *Argalus and Parthenia by Francis Quarles*, edited by David Freeman, 1986.

VOL. XII. Cicero's *De Officiis*, trans. Nicholas Grimald, edited by Gerald
O'Gorman, 1987.

VOL. XIII. *The Silkewormes and their Flies* by Thomas Moffet (1599), edited with in-
troduction and commentary by Victor Houliston, 1988.

SEVENTH SERIES

VOL. XIV. John Bale, *The Vocacyon of Johan Bale*, edited by Peter Happé and John N.
King, 1989.

VOL. XV. *The Nondramatic Works of John Ford*, edited by L. E. Stock, Gilles D. Mon-
sarrat, Judith M. Kennedy, and Dennis Danielson, with the assistance of
Marta Straznicky, 1990.

SPECIAL PUBLICATION. *New Ways of Looking at Old Texts: Papers of the Renaissance
English Text Society, 1985–1991*, edited by W. Speed Hill, 1993. (Sent gratis to
all 1991 members.)

VOL. XVI. *George Herbert, The Temple: A Diplomatic Edition of the Bodleian Manu-
script (Tanner 307)*, edited by Mario A. Di Cesare, 1991.

VOL. XVII. Lady Mary Wroth, *The First Part of the Countess of Montgomery's Urania*,
edited by Josephine Roberts, 1992.

VOL. XVIII. Richard Beacon, *Solon His Follie*, edited by Clare Carroll and Vincent
Carey, 1993.

VOL. XIX. An Collins, *Divine Songs and Meditacions*, edited by Sidney Gottlieb,
1994.

VOL. XX. *The Southwell-Sibthorpe Commonplace Book: Folger MS V.b.198*, edited by
Sr. Jean Klene, 1995.

SPECIAL PUBLICATION. *New Ways of Looking at Old Texts II: Papers of the Renaissance English Text Society, 1992–1996*, edited by W. Speed Hill, 1998. (Sent gratis to all 1996 members.)

VOL. XXI. *The Collected Works of Anne Vaughan Lock*, edited by Susan M. Felch,1996.

VOL. XXII. Thomas May, *The Reigne of King Henry the Second Written in Seauen Books*, edited by Götz Schmitz, 1997.

VOL. XXIII. *The Poems of Sir Walter Ralegh: A Historical Edition*, edited by Michael Rudick, 1998.

VOL. XXIV. Lady Mary Wroth, *The Second Part of the Countess of Montgomery's Urania*, edited by Josephine Roberts; completed by Suzanne Gossett and Janel Mueller, 1999.

VOL. XXV. *The Verse Miscellany of Constance Aston Fowler: A Diplomatic Edition*, by Deborah Aldrich-Watson, 2000.

VOL. XXVI. *An Edition of Luke Shepherd's Satires*, by Janice Devereux, 2001.

VOL. XXVII. *Philip Stubbes: The Anatomie of Abuses*, edited by Margaret Jane Kidnie, 2002.

VOL. XXVIII. *Cousins in Love: The Letters of Lydia DuGard, 1665–1672, with a new edition of* The Marriages of Cousin Germans *by Samuel DuGard*, edited by Nancy Taylor, 2003.

VOL. XXIX. *The Commonplace Book of Sir John Strangways (1645–1666)*, edited by Thomas G. Olsen, 2004.

SPECIAL PUBLICATION. *New Ways of Looking at Old Texts, III: Papers of the Renaissance English Text Society, 1997–2001*, edited by W. Speed Hill, 2004. (Sent gratis to all 2001 members.)

VOL. XXX. *The Poems of Robert Parry*, edited by G. Blakemore Evans, 2005.

VOL. XXXI. *William Baspoole's 'The Pilgrime'*, edited by Kathryn Walls, 2006.

VOL. XXXII. *Richard Tottel's 'Songes and Sonettes': The Elizabethan Version*, edited by Paul A. Marquis, 2007.

VOL. XXXIII. *Cælivs Secvndus Curio: his historie of the warr of Malta: Translated by Thomas Mainwaringe (1579)*, edited by Helen Vella Bonavita, 2008.

SPECIAL PUBLICATION. *New Ways of Looking at Old Texts, IV: Papers of the Renaissance English Text Society, 2002–2006*, edited by Michael Denbo, 2008. (Sent gratis to all 2006 members.)

VOL. XXXIV. *Nicholas Oldisworth's Manuscript (Bodleian MS. Don.c.24)*, edited by John Gouws, 2009.